ANOTHER CITY

Books by Patrice Chaplin

A Lonely Diet
Harriet Hunter
Cry Wolf
By Flower and Dean Street
Having It Away
The Siesta
The Unforgotten
Albany Park
Don Salino's Wife
Another City

Patrice Chaplin

ANOTHER CITY

A Sequel to *Albany Park*

A Memoir

THE ATLANTIC MONTHLY PRESS
NEW YORK

♦

Excerpt from "Burnt Norton" in *Four Quartets,* copyright 1943 by T.S.
Eliot, renewed 1971 by Esme Valerie Eliot, reprinted by permission of
Harcourt Brace Jovanovich, Inc.

First published in Great Britain in 1987 by William Heinemann Ltd
First published in the United States of America in 1988

Published simultaneously in Canada
Printed in the United States of America

Library of Congress Cataloging-in-Publication Data

Chaplin, Patrice.
    Another city : a sequel to Albany Park : a memoir / Patrice
Chaplin.

    ISBN 0-87113-256-7
    1. Chaplin, Patrice—Biography.   2. Novelists, English—20th
century—Biography.   I. Title.
PR6053.H348Z465   1988   823'.914—dc19   88-10319

The Atlantic Monthly Press
19 Union Square West
New York, NY 10003

FIRST PRINTING

ANOTHER CITY

Chapter One

I'd always believed fate was kind. I thought it came along with God and the inevitable. It was bigger than me so it had to be on my side – kind. It didn't occur to me that in some cases it should be fought to the death. José came along, one of fate's little gifts, and for years it pleased me to say, 'Well, he was fated. He was meant. There was nothing I could do about it.'

The second time I saw him was at the end of a long day. Fate could be said to have had a hand in it. Beryl and I, making a return to Europe because Albany Park, however hard we tried, had nothing going for it, not for us, had made a circuitous and penniless journey to Paris by way of Jersey and Alderney where we'd been hotel cleaners. Paris gave us the same welcome as before. We could enjoy the sights but didn't expect to survive. Little things like food and sleep and money were impossible to come by. There was plenty of crime and intrigue among the ragged splendour of the Pigalle streets and it was there that my dreams of Hollywood began again. You had to think of something crouched up in a black duffel coat on the Métro steps waiting for daylight. We got out of Paris eventually because three guys going to Spain wanted our company. At first it seemed they just wanted token girls along for the ride. As we got near the border it seemed we were their cover. At the border it turned out they were arms dealers involved in the Algerian war and we were their couriers. I assume that because they gave us their briefcases to take through customs. This discovery led to quite a lot of violence. Then a shot was fired. Beryl and I happened to be putting on make-up in the lavatory at the time. This wasn't unusual. We did that constantly. We left the scene by the lavatory window and ran across a mountainous area. We ran for hours. And then towards evening a car picked us up and the driver was going to Gerona. Where else? And the first person I saw was José.

The sky was violet and flashing with huge flat stars. Dogs loped in front of the fires being lit at the edge of the old quarter and the music started. The church bells chimed as though for a celebration and all the lights of the town came on, hundreds of yellow eyes. It was a true welcome. As I stood on the bank of the modern sector I must have known I was approaching a definitive territory. Once over there I would not be the same again. It had the look of a fairy-story kingdom. I crossed the iron-canopied bridge and I began to feel strong and clear and the exhaustion of the day had no place. The atmosphere was something I would never forget and have never again experienced. I wasn't aware of Beryl. I felt my body change, become weightless. I was without needs or fears. And then I knew this was where I should be. I'd just been born in another place. It was to get to this unheard of city I'd agitated and strained at the leash of Albany Park. It hadn't worked the first visit. It took the second to captivate me and once it happened I had no desire to move again.

I got a part in the small film being shot in the old quarter and the Spanish were ecstatic. I didn't realise then they could be ecstatic about anything. Not only was I photogenic, I was a star. Champagne was poured, a banquet prepared. To get his attention I asked José if he thought I was a star.

'Undoubtedly.'

And I thought of all the heroines of my childhood. Bacall, Grable, Lana Turner, Ava Gardner. Did they get there so easily?

I didn't realise José lived at the Hotel Residencia until one night he collected money from a group of locals for the dance beginning downstairs. Earl Bostic on a 78 played 'Smoke Gets in Your Eyes'.

'Do you sleep here?' I asked him.

José pointed straight up.

'Heaven?' I asked.

He laughed. 'It could be. Depends who I'm with.'

He kept calling me Patrice and after a while I accepted it. Looking back, it was a baptism.

The hotel had a deliberate simplicity and a regional style, Catalan, which was forbidden in those days. It had a feeling of being cared for and shown to advantage. It had an identity and that had been provided by José Tarres. This man brought out the essence of the place he was in. His profession as I understood it was interior decorator. He also wrote poetry. It was the first place I'd been in that had harmony. Just walking in there made me joyous.

Then a woman appeared, a cold cosmetic beauty. She was the epitome of the bourgeoisie. She was the co- owner of the hotel and José's mother. She had his eyes without the glow. She wanted us, the interplanetary creatures, out and she got what she wanted. She went to the newspapers and they got up a protest. Our clothes were made by the devil. We were beggars. Our morals brought plague and killed off sheep. That sort of thing. The press coverage coincided with the police chief and the mayor both fancying Beryl – so did the trainer of the football team. Their wives got involved. A letter was delivered to the hotel. Its message – 'On your bike, English'.

We were escorted by the civil police to the frontier and then, penniless, had to hitch across France. Perpignan was dreadful. I remember that. I was seared with unhappiness. We couldn't get a lift so had to sleep in the crowded Perpignan youth hostel. A solid depression had set in. The early moon and the Mediterranean smell made it worse. Gerona was just down the road, part of the smell, sharing that particular phase of the moon. The town had been the revelation of my life and yet I'd been put out like a disgraced dog.

The next day the wind and our luck changed. The first car we waved stopped and we started for Carcassonne. The pain started as well. I'd lost something and my life would always be in mourning, the punishment for letting joy slip so easily away. The driver put on the car radio and The Platters sang, 'Only You'. I wanted to stop the pain so I said, 'Stop.' He thought I meant the car. I got out. Then Beryl got out. We weren't friends any more. It was terrible.

'I have to go back to him, Beryl.'

She asked the driver to get my rucksack and without another word she got back into the car and it drove off. I'd been her friend for eleven years. It took José to break that. She went north. I went south and we never saw each other again. The lifts were fast, one after another speeding me back to Gerona. Of course, now I was going in the right direction everything was lucky.

José was waiting for me on the stairs of the hotel. He laughed. 'I knew you'd come back. I've got a room ready for you.' I told him I'd longed for him and had to come back.

'But of course. I was calling to you, Patrice.'

Chapter Two

I first saw Nina in the doorway of the Residencia Internacional hotel just before it went broke. She was standing very close to José, as close as she could in public seeing she was the daughter of a respectable French Catholic industrialist. José was whatever he was passing himself off as in those days. It was the early 1970s and it was during one of my optimistic visits to Gerona, when he and I were going to be married after my divorce and live together with my children on the Atlantic coast. And I'd write a book and he'd write poetry and then we'd move on to Istanbul which he said was our true home. Nina stood, the toes of her schoolgirl shoes almost touching his, the jut of her heavy breasts nuzzling his shirt like two unloved beasts straining over a hedge for attention. Her eyes clung to his. Their breath mingled as they spoke. It was a secret conversation, and his eyes responded to hers with interest and something else. I thought it might be sorrow. He was still absolutely beautiful. I got out of the taxi and he stepped away from her but her body still strained towards his. She was young, greedy, sexually untouched. She wore no make-up. The only thing about the sight of

5

them together that cheered me up was the fact that she was not beautiful.

We were introduced and she spoke perfect Spanish with a husky voice. I found out she was French and lived with her family on the Costa Brava. She did something artistic. I dismissed her. Over the years so many young students had been drawn to him. But there was something familiar about this girl. The way she made him a gift of her body; her youth was total. Many years before I'd done the same. Later José described this French girl as a sculptress, very talented, promising. He was simply showing her the province. It would add something to her work. That explained his involvement in her life.

He was no longer a political activist. That died with the death of the Separatist hero Quico Sabater. And then the province was granted independence anyway. Later Franco died. José's energy was now directed to the cultural life of the town. He arranged the fiestas, brought back the local customs that Franco had suppressed. He defended the Catalans' traditional style. He wasn't fighting Madrid as much as Carnaby Street, because everyone wanted the mod Anglo-Saxon styles. Gerona was becoming like anywhere else.

During this visit, I stayed in the Hotel Centro, part of a seventeenth-century rundown palace at the edge of the old town. He was no more available to me than he had been in the 1950s and 1960s. The town took all his attention and I'd wait behind the white lace curtains, and the cathedral clock would divide the hours into quarters. The torment of waiting would be quite gone when he walked in. The moment he came through the door it was as though something lovely had entered the room. He brought a glow and I saw he was a lovely man. After we'd made love I'd agree with his plans, pretend to believe in them, knowing the only way we'd really be together would be to get out. For that we needed money.

We did make a winter journey to the south, getting a slow train at Alicante at midnight. We'd spent the evening making love and my legs were trembling from exhaustion but I couldn't stop wanting him. There was a small country station full of blossom and we got off to wait for the night train to Malaga. The station was deserted. Gas-lamps blown by the wind cast huge shadows along the stone wall. There were peeling advertisements, years old. The air was warm and scented orange blossom and mimosa grew on the platform. The station was hardly used anymore. Men playing cards in the bar spoke roughly. The wind was loud and the trees were swished together sweeping furious against the scudding sky. We felt we were in another time. There was a presence, a suggestion of something in the wind. We were linked up with the past.

I jumped up and hung from a low branch full of blossom. Happiness made me do things I wouldn't normally think of. José held my legs, kised my stomach, lifted me down. He picked a spray of blossom, presented it to me formally. Solitary bells were jangled by the wind. There was a presence on that station which filled me with longing, with yearning for things I half understood, half believed could exist. José was affected by it. His gestures were ritualised – the handing of the blossom, the way he kissed my hand. I led him into the bar. I had to move, to go inside because out there on the platform the feeling, the awareness it provoked was overwhelming. It was as though the sky was opened up and all the secrets, the mysteries, were about to be revealed. But I kept my head down humbly and escaped amongst the people in the bar. The glorious unknown daunted me as much as horror did.

Everyone in the bar had looked up as I came in. I was covered with white bloom.

'Like a bride,' said the man behind the bar. 'Radiant. And so young.'

They thought I was sixteen. I'd just passed my twenty-ninth birthday.

The spray of white blossom quivered on the wrought-iron marble-topped table. It held all newness and innocence. When José went to the counter a drunk Guardia Civil officer came across to the table and took the flower. I got up, went to his table and took it back. Everyone was silent. They thought I'd behaved dangerously. José laughed but not so anyone would notice. 'My God. You deprive a policeman of his pleasure. They put you in prison for that here.'

I would have died for that blossom.

The Malaga train was full. José lay on his bunk in the couchette compartment. I sat beside him and he lifted my sweater, kissed my breasts. 'You will have my baby. You see.' He pulled me on top of

7

him but the door slid open and a man with no luggage took the top bunk.

Train stations, meetings, journeys, waiting for the future. It was all future. But I decided then you never can live with what you love. Everyday life would blunt it, make it stale, and this intolerable death I could not allow. Perhaps that's why I always had to leave him – to keep the ecstasy alive. Then Nina the French sculptress offered him something very much of this day and age. Domesticity, a monied life. It would soothe his ageing.

In the mid-1970s José and I tried again to live together. Living together consisted of me living in one place with my two children while he moved freely about Spain doing secret and necessary things which I could not share. These were political – anti-Franco – I didn't trust his absences. Drink soothed the loneliness. My kids were having trouble with Spanish. That was no surprise. They had enough problems with English. The local Spanish kids would not accept them, these fair boys of seven and eight, any more than José's mother would accept me. I got a clear picture of what life with José would be during that short summer visit. I'd have endless babies and spend my days cleaning house – on my knees with the scrubbing brush and buckets of well-bleached cold water. And I'd buy food and cook it and he might or might not show up for the meals and the nights, but whatever he did I had to approve, remain calm and flourish in his care. I wouldn't have too much time for writing. It occurred to me that the desire to write might well fade as I heard no discernable words around me. And I wouldn't be able to go for stimulation to London friends because there wasn't that sort of money, not for travelling. José had a job, a position in the local government running the newly opened provincial art centre. Whatever was in the pay packet went home to mother in the Calle Forsa. I paid for the living expenses out of a modest book advance and the sale of two short stories in the *London Magazine*. Wine was cheap in Spain. With my sort of money a cockroach couldn't have got drunk in London. This attempt at being together was serious – it even made him thoughtful. How it turned out would affect the rest of my life. The truth of course was that we were changed people – I was no longer the fifteen-year-old travelling girl on the steps of the Residencia Internacional, ready for any experience, full of life, and he wasn't the divine Tarres, the poet bird who brightened lives and would give his own to free his town.

Quite quickly two things showed me that a domestic life with José Tarres would not work. I was looking for signs and got them immediately. He'd come back from an overnight business trip and entered the house whistling. All *joie de vivre* stopped when he saw the state of the place. Being alone had made me depressed. I had not cleaned up and last night's dishes were unwashed. He patted the boys heads lovingly but his eyes glared at a bluebottle settling in a smear of tomato sauce.

'Clean up. How can I come back to this?'

He ran a comb through his sun-soaked hair and muttered obscenities. 'A third-class whore would live better than this.'

'Whores get paid,' I reminded him.

He encouraged a broom into my hand. 'There's no money for anybody to get paid. No cleaning woman. No nothing. Start sweeping. I'll be back for lunch.'

'How was Tarragona?'

He hesitated. 'Tarragona?' His voice ghostly. He'd forgotten the lie of yesterday.

'You know. Tarragona. The place you were supposed to be doing business in last night.'

'It has stood for thousands of years. Why should a visit of mine bring any change?'

Sighing, he swept out of the house. Later I found a train ticket in his pocket. Port Bou – Gerona. You couldn't get further away from Tarragona than Port Bou.

The key to this temporary house had jammed in the door. I never could unlock it easily and José said that was significant – the fact I couldn't get into my house. No one else, he said, had ever had trouble. And he'd shake his head, Spanish-wise, and look like his mother. I could lock the door and unlock it but the key stayed where it was, a sort of invitation to burglars. José said there weren't any. Not in Gerona. Did I have to soil the town with London ideas?

The house with its patio garden was opposite his, properly known as 'the *barraca*': A country path ran between them. The

9

barraca, a one-room house like something from a fairy-tale, stood in several acres of countryside. He'd planted a garden, made a pond. Lights hung from his trees. One day when he finally had money the *barraca* would be enlarged, become his family home. It was implied that I and my children would be his family.

I washed the clothes and spread them over the trees and bushes. I'd supposed he'd gone into Gerona to the art centre. Exhibitions were constantly being hung and exchange schemes arranged with other provinces. Catalonia was now firmly established. He'd been instrumental in that and he felt the town owed him one. I swept and washed the floors, scrubbed the table, looked out of the window. Was I having an hallucination from the heat? He was sitting neatly, attractively, in the *barraca* garden. Beside him, the local beauty wearing a minuscule suntop talked exuberantly. I wiped the sweat off my face for a better look, and when my eyes cleared of house dust I could see the beauty was wearing a skilful brown make-up and plenty of jewels, all fake. Her hair was hennaed, unusual at that time, and she had the most marvellous breasts. Everyone said so. Her shoes were gold and suggested expensive sin. I called my elder boy Chris and asked how long José had been sitting in the *barraca* garden.

'Since he left here. He's not gone anywhere else.'

I threw down the broom and glared across the country path. He was leaning back to advantage. Her exuberant story brought her close and the much-admired breasts swayed playfully in the suntop. Her laugh released some of the sexual tension. Not only the bluebottles were having fun. I ran to the edge of my property and screeched with rage. The beauty jumped as though a dangerous bird was loose in the garden. Then she saw it was only a rival. José looked at me bleakly. I shouted expletives. I'd known him for over twenty years but that didn't mean I couldn't feel jealous. He sauntered to his side of the path. 'Are you stung? Have you an injury? Well obviously it's some emergency.' He turned and gave a carefree smile and assured the girl he'd be right back. Then he crossed to our mutual home.

He attacked immediately because he was in the wrong. 'But this place still isn't clean.'

I flung the broom into a corner. 'Get on with it yourself, José. I thought you were supposed to be in town killing yourself working. Isn't that what you do? Turn an honest buck so people paint the right kind of pictures?'

'Patrice, this house is not orderly.'

'Well it would take you to notice that. Get on with it. You do it.' I kicked the broom towards him. 'You just sit in the shade with Goldilocks while I'm in here slaving in this heat.'

'But that's what women do.' An insulting pause. 'In this country that is.'

'While you play with the tart across the way. I notice she's not sweeping.'

'She happens to be very sad.'

'She didn't look sad.'

'She was telling me her problems.'

'Not that I noticed.'

'Spanish women put a good face on it.'

His face clouded as he picked up the broom and tickled it into the corners.

'Put the table in the shade. We'll eat.' He didn't want me to leave. He still didn't want that.

We went to bed as we did every afternoon when he was in residence. That didn't change. I didn't trust him. Had I ever? Could I live stuck without choice in one place, waiting for a man I didn't trust?'

The second sign was the pyjamas. I'd put that out of my mind because I believed if life with José Tarres was going to happen little touches that didn't make sense, however unpleasant, should be blanked out. In the past there had been many things that didn't make sense around José. Prying always led to rows, never clarification. So when we moved into the house he said it had been empty for almost a year. He knew the owners slightly and they were happy to accept a small rent to have their property cared for. He'd got the brooms and buckets and bleach out while I stripped the double bed. I was surprised, in the tangle of sheets, to find a pair of men's pyjamas. The pyjamas belonged to him. At first he denied it. He'd never spent one minute in this house, let alone one night.

However, not only did I recognise their scent but they also had his name in. He frowned as though trying to remember.

'Maybe it is just possible I spent a night here.'

'But why? When you have your own room?'

The answer was obvious. His room was in his mother's apartment and he couldn't take women there at night. The girl who came to mind was, surprisingly, not the local beauty but the little adoring inexperienced French sculptress. I'd forgotten her name.

The two signs pointed to London. To stay in Gerona with the boys, to take them away from their English school and security was dangerous. Dangerous because I'd become entangled in a life I couldn't handle. Drink would be the lifeline. For a while. Then I'd be dead. I couldn't face the fact that José was not mine as I was his. Drink took care of that. He didn't seem to make choices and sacrifices unless you counted leaving beauty in the garden while he swept the floor. So I challenged him with the things that seemed wrong. For a while he stared at the floor and I thought he was going to ask me to marry him. He said, 'I'll get you a cleaning woman.'

'But I don't like being in this house alone.'

'But you have your children,' he assured me.

'Of course I have my children. I also have my thoughts. And you didn't go to Tarragona, my darling, but Port Bou. Perhaps the heat made you lose your sense of direction.'

'It's too hot in here. That's for sure.' He looked sulky.

'It will lose you a lot more if you're not careful.' Generous sweat ran under my arms. He was going to tell me to fuck off – off to England – English woman! I didn't think I could handle a farewell scene in temperatures approaching a hundred. But magic was a very hard thing to kill. What we'd once shared would go in its own time. He looked up, his eyes full of tears.

'Don't go.' Then he ran outside.

It was the atmosphere in the house when I was alone that told me to go. It assured me all was not well. And I'd see less of him and get even sadder. From the white walls flakes of plaster drifted gracefully on to the scarlet floor. When the wind blew it came out in clouds like confetti and the trees moaned outside – a wedding, a wedding. The used double bed advised me like a wise friend. This place is not for you. It looks bright but you'll get the dark side of the coin. Someone else gets his glitter. How right that house's voice was. Nina was already in his life. It was she who got the bright side of the coin.

Chapter Three

He'd wanted me to have his baby. When he found out I used contraceptives he was so outraged he dragged me from his bed on to the floor and slapped me. I fought back. The fight didn't get too colourful because it took place in his mother's apartment. She was out but she could come back. She always chose the worst moments for an arrival. As she'd cursed me when I'd gone off to Paris with him when I was fifteen, I should no longer exist. Spanish curses put out at that strength of hatred worked. I was therefore a phantom and she treated me like one. José said he'd been deceived. Each time we'd made love was nothing but an abortion, in his mind. He could never forgive me. I could see he did want a child. I had little common sense and no sense of consequences. I was the kind of person who got into a certain amount of trouble. Yet occasionally I could work up a stubborn conviction. It wasn't rational or considered but once there it would not go away. It would not let me have his baby. I'd already had two and I could imagine myself having another especially with a man I adored. And a child should certainly have put José and me more together. I'd known him since I was fifteen and I'd been in love with him ever since. Yet I still did not trust him. The

14

conviction didn't bother with words. It was like an umbrella, black and strong and it kept out the rain. You didn't have conversations with umbrellas. They just did their job. It was on my side. No baby. So I said I wanted security and I supposed that was to be found in marriage. He'd always promised we'd be together. 'When?' I'd always ask.

'When the time is right.'

This time he said, 'Marriage in Spain is not like it is in England. You can't just walk into a church.'

I said I was prepared to do it Spanish style. Then he said we had no money. I should wait until he was solid with the local Catalan government, when he would be earning real money, the money he deserved, then we could talk about it. I wanted to talk about it now.

Furious, he said, 'The swine at the town hall – they're to blame. So short-sighted. They try to pay me only when I'm actually hanging up the lights for the fiestas. No thought is given to the months of preparation and the ideas. I do the flower exhibition, the parades, the Christmas pageants, for nothing. They want to treat me like a temporary typist. Without me Madrid would have turned this place into a hamburger stand.'

'But the art centre pay you?'

His eyes flared. 'Enough for one tortilla a day. The whores do better. Even the dead ones. What thanks do I get?'

And I saw art, although flourishing in Gerona, had to do it alone. As far as the payroll at the town hall was concerned art looked better if it came out of a garret. The mayor had traditional views.

So I hadn't got José. I didn't think anyone else would either. I packed to leave. He promised I would not be able to get tickets. Fate would have that in hand. All planes would be full. There was no way fate would allow my two children, whom he loved, to be deprived of a proper life in Gerona.

When I came back from the travel agency he was hosing down his *barracca* garden. His shirt was off and his body silky skinned, brown, perfectly toned and he wasn't even aware of it. He had no vanity. Vivaldi from the portable record player made the garden rejoice – it rang forth from the trees. The birds joined in. And for a moment I remembered how he had once enchanted me, how in the old days he could brighten lives, give hope. Perhaps he still did. But not to me.

'I've got tickets. We go tomorrow.'

He shrugged. Fate, not me, had let him down.

'There was no problem. Plenty of seats,' I added.

'Then the children will be very upset. You will have that on your conscience too.'

I didn't know what the 'too' referred to. We were getting on so badly it could be a dozen small domesttic grievances. I saw the boys on the patio and called to them. We were going home. They gave a football supporter's cheer. José, angry, turned off the hose. I asked for a drink. The goodbye certainly needed that. Although I drank to excess he never seemed concerned. Once, during a particularly bad hangover, I told him I might be an alcoholic. I could have left out the 'might'.

'Of course not. You are a child at a children's party. You are greedy. You do everything to excess and make yourself sick. That's all.'

'So you don't think I'm hooked or anything?'

'Of course not. You're just thirsty.'

He should have known. His father had died of drink. He just never saw it in me.

As he didn't have anything except a purple liqueur in the *barracca* we walked down the tricky country path, pitted with narrow holes, to the nearest bar in San Daniel on the outskirts of the city. The draught beer took away the heat, the flies, the pain. I kicked off with, 'I don't think Gerona suits the boys either.'

'It would if I looked after them.'

'You heard the cheer, honey.'

'Only to please you. That's why they did it.'

'Well I sure need someone to please me.'

'You sure do, *chérie*,' he retorted quick, effortless. It was just playtime to him. He saved his real stuff, his spite, for the rivals in local government.

I looked down at my feet and noticed my toenails were jagged, the nail paint peeling. My legs weren't shaved and the hairs were bristly. And I'd always taken such care of my appearance. That worried me, the loss of pride in myself. Drink dealt with that too. After several beers I could have been Marilyn Monroe on an upday. I switched to wine, then we crossed to the workmen's tavern for lunch. I could be getting a drinker's face. Who would see it first? Me? The world? Him?

I tried to tell him again that I felt left out. He went places. I stayed at home. He went to art gallery openings. I drifted around cafés and bars. He went to important people's houses in the country. I made the best of it in the gardens by the cathedral.

'Patrice, you don't understand my situation. I am trying to keep the identity of this province. They call me the conscience of the artists. I have to be always at their side or who knows? They will become like the rest of Spain or worse, Europe.'

That sounded OK but I'd heard it before. I told him I got on with artists. Some of them had been my friends in the old days.

He agreed with that but he was trying to get promotion in the local government. That required a certain reticence. Did he mean he had to go everywhere alone? Did they only give work to hermits?

'That's one way of putting it,' he agreed.

Of course the places he went, Nina and her group went too. He could not be seen with me. Beautifully innocent I sat half pissed at that last lunch and believed he'd marry me. I said I'd stay on if he married me.

He couldn't have been sure of her, of how he felt about her, because he said, 'Stay the month, then we'll see.'

'What's all this about a month? What's a month got to do with it? We either marry or we don't. I'm not some hire-purchase fridge you've got on trial.'

He smiled attractively. 'A lot can happen in a month.' He jerked the plastic top off another bottle of wine.

'But we've known each other half our lives.'

'Oh more,' he said. 'Other lives.' The local fruity wine flowed into the glasses and he made me eat more beans and bacon fat. He still looked after me from time to time. 'You are my true child, my child wife,' he said. But he'd been at the wine too.

We went to bed in the afternoon as though nothing disagreeable had happened. He agreed, as a gesture to our possibly getting

17

married, not to go to the mayor's dinner that night. He'd come to me around nine.

After siesta I staggered with the kids into the town. Once he'd left the house a depression set in and it was essential to keep moving, to let in some new ideas, fresh sights. The kids were bored and the younger, Tim, hated heat. I had several draught beers to kill the beginning of the lunch hangover, and on impulse took a taxi to the sea. Every part of the journey, every tree, I'd known and loved because I'd been in love. It should all belong to me. Yet it didn't seem to want me, any of it.

José was forty-five and his life was not as he'd anticipated. His role in the town was superfluous. There was nothing to fight anymore, not politically. He had no wife, no children and still lived with his mother. I was somewhere in my early thirties. I'd lied so much about my age even I couldn't remember exactly when I was born. I should have been in Hollywood. I should have been a movie star. I should have been a lot of things. But one or two mishaps had got in the way.

I had two children, I was a writer, I had no money. I still had hope. And the other thing I kept not thinking about was the fact that I had a steady London friend. I'd left him somewhere between Bruges and Paris, we were having some kind of holiday, because I knew life was a wasted thing, a compromise, dull. It only became magnificent if José Tarres was part of it. So I'd slipped away with a drunk's cunning and brought my children to Gerona. The man may or may not have believed I was writing a book about the city. The trouble was when I was away from José I remembered him as he'd once been. That memory would not let me go. In reality he was colder, less caring, sometimes conceited. I put it down to his work crisis. When he got the position he so wanted, he'd be again the way he once was.

The seaside resort, Tossa de Mar, was transformed by the needs of tourism. The Spaniards complained but it had made them rich. I tried to tell Chris, my son, how I'd once stayed there with José, how it had been a gift from God. I didn't get beyond the year, the month. It belonged to another person.

The boys hadn't brought their bathing trunks so they couldn't swim. I didn't have enough money to buy them new ones. There wasn't enough for Spanish Tin Tin books either. Tim grizzled and kept to the shade. He thought he wanted a Coke, an ice-cream, a hamburger. What he really wanted was security. He eyed the Spanish children with suspicion. It was returned. A stone was thrown. Chris swaggered up to the Spanish group ready to defend his brother. That was when I knew Tim would never fit into a Spanish school. He had enough trouble in an English one.

Tim believed a bad experience need never be repeated, so he was unlike me from the start. When he'd finished his first day at his first school I'd asked how he'd got on 'OK. Not that bad. But I wouldn't like to go again.' He heard the word 'must'. It always had a dreadful effect on him.

Now I told him we must get the coach back to Gerona.

'Why? He kept scuffing his shoe on the cobbles wanting it to break.

'Because there's no money for a taxi.'

He dreaded the coach. It made him sick. 'Well let him find out once we're in Gerona. It'll be too late then,' he suggested helpfully.

'Who?'

'The taxi driver. Send him to José. Let him pay.' In certain moods Tim resembled his father. He had a hardness I used to suppose was logic.

'José hasn't any money, stupid,' said Chris. The he gave Tim a belt on the ear and we all got on the coach.

Of course in my youth I'd have taken a taxi as Tim suggested. I'd have relied on my charm, my entertainment, my looks and so make the driver forget anything as mundane as a fare.

If I married José the boys would have to go to a Spanish school. Or they could go to their father. He'd remarried and had other children and I was not absolutely convinced that he wanted Tim and Chris. I felt anyway that the responsibility for their being in the world at all was mine. If I had a child with José it could turn out I'd have not two but three to bring up alone. I wasn't a pessimist but it could turn out like that.

The coach stopped in the modern sector and I went into the nearest bar.

'You can't buy bathers,' said Tim. 'But you have enough money for beer.'

'You know what I think you should become?' I said smoothly. 'Bilingual.'

'What's that exactly?'

'You speak two languages fluently.'

The fluently gave Tim trouble.

'Never mind the fancy words,' said Chris. 'She means she wants you to go to a Spanish school, Dumbo. Then she can stay with José.'

'I'll run away.'

'They have high walls out here,' said Chris. His golden curls attracted the drinkers in the bar. He was known as Angel. I didn't know what they called me but I reckoned they had a name.

Chapter Four

At nine I fed the boys, the light was fading. No one passed on the country path, not in the evening. It was unlit and dangerous. The nearest neighbour was further down towards San Daniel. From the patio I could see into his garden. He had a large family and they kept themselves to themselves. At all hours the kids wore bleached white clothes. It was a sign of Godliness. My children did not resemble theirs.

Nine thirty and my fiancé had still not arrived. But this was not unusual. An artist had a crisis, the mayor invited him for a drink, friends arrived from Paris. These were the delays he told me about.

Chris said, 'I wish I could watch television.'

'You can't go to the bar. It's getting dark. The path's too steep.'

'Not Spanish. I want to understand something for a change.' He threw himself onto his bed, cross and sulky. So I got out the drawing books and the comics but Chris wouldn't even look at them. He was a co-operative child. He'd been described by his friends' mothers as a delight. He never asked for the big things like, I want my Dad. I want a normal person's house. I want big meals every day. He'd learned early not to rock the boat. Yet, insistently, he went on about television. He wanted to watch it now. His eyes streamed with tears.

'It's OK.' Tim was also exasperated. 'You'll see it tomorrow. We'll be in London then.'

'I don't feel as though I'm really here,' said Chris. 'Today I was at the sea, yet all I did was look at it. I couldn't go in it. And in this place – well I'm on the edge.'

I knew how he felt. Didn't I just! 'Do you miss London?' I asked.

'I wouldn't live anywhere else,' he said decisively and covered his head with a sheet.

Because of my inability to break with José they'd lost their father, a comfortable life, security. In exchange they had a gang of London friends, mostly from split homes, and this company of divided children was strong and supportive. Staying in Gerona would lose them that.

It was almost dark and I switched on the light outside the front door. Once again I tried to free the stuck key. I smeared olive oil on the lock, banged it with a spanner. The key, more stuck, useless, could still lock and unlock. I shut the door and put on a record. I could do some writing but too much drinking had gone on. Ten o'clock came and went. Churches all over the town joined in announcing the hour, condemning José, the wayward groom. 'It's not about the local beauty,' I said aloud. 'It's not even a ticket from Port Bou.' Of course women cleaned house. I didn't object to that. It was just that if I held the broom and swept the floor and gave up everything else I'd be in a very bad place and he wouldn't be there with me. I should go back to London, to my own sort.

At eleven I heard footsteps on the path. Then the key in the lock jiggled. That meant it wasn't José. He knew enough about the key not to bother with that. Swift, silent I slipped to the door and slid across the night-time bolt. The key jiggled some more but the intruder had no more luck than I did. There were bars on the lower front windows but not on the others. Feet hit the patio stones as I slammed shut the back door. A face I didn't recognise watched me from an unbarred window. Then he shook it, trying to prise the lock loose. His mode of entry into my life told me he was trouble. His face did the rest. So I woke the boys and we gathered in the hallway.

22

I turned out the lights and the boys' underpants gleamed in the darkness. I thought the nearest neighbour would be proud of them.

'The back window,' whispered Chris. 'He can always get in that. I do.'

'Then let's get the fuck out of here.' Fear had made me sober. 'Let's run together to the neighbour and let's all fucking scream.'

So Tim pulled back the night bolt and I pulled the door catch and nothing happened. The new friend had locked us in.

He made a noise jumping down from the patio. He was now amongst the easy windows. Tim and Chris had their heads together. They knew things instinctively – they'd seen it on television or it was in their blood – in the past I'd had my share of vacating an unfriendly scene. The way out was through the front door. Tim climbed up to the barred window. The bars were moderately wide and he was small and double-jointed. Like an eel he slithered between them and jumped down on to the path. He wanted to run for the neighbours but I was never absolutely sure of other people's reactions in adversity. I felt Chris and I should be part of the night too – running.

'Come on, Tim. Unlock it.' Chris was shaking.

'Turn it to the left. Left.' My mouth was dry.

A huge crash at the back and the new pal was in the house.

'Turn it left,' I hissed.

The front door clicked open. Tim always had trouble with left and right. We ran to the neighbours. I wore a daring sundress and nothing else. The kids had their underpants. We pressed the bell, banged, screamed. We shouted for God to help us. The only reaction the neighbour had was to turn out his lights. Higher up on the path, the intruder approached, wishing us harm. Without word, the three of us ran towards the village of San Daniel. We'd been in too many scrapes together – bailiff trouble, electricity cut-offs, low life violence in the car-park by the London flats – not to know when to get the fuck out.

San Daniel belonged in my worst nightmare. It was dark and closed. Even the tavern. It wasn't yet midnight so I had no answer for that. We kept running, past the Barrio Chino, the brothel area, and up towards the cathedral. We took the same route as many an invader had in the past. We arrived at Luis's bar where a crowd sat outside enjoying the night. Amongst them, José. Only as I stood in the light did I realise we wore no shoes. We were like beggars come up from the south, the fearless hungry ones that the rich Gerona inhabitants dreaded. I also realised that José was sitting with a girl, but before I could absorb any idea of who she was she'd slipped into the night.

José dismissed the intruder idea because it made him guilty for not being with us. The kids were given an ice-lolly each. Luis got real with me and started pouring the brandy.

'He wore a white shirt. Tall.' The trouble was he looked like anyone. 'Black trousers. The shirt might have been pink. It came out white in the light – '

'He had a flick knife,' said Chris. 'I didn't tell Mum.'

José turned on rather a lot of charm and chucked me under the chin. 'You English. You read too much Agatha Christie.' He laughed. It was meant to reassure the onlookers. Some of them were not reassured. A girl wearing trousers and a huge belt said we must spend the night with her. Luis, who owned the bar, took it seriously. 'I think I know who it might be. He is recently out of the hospital.'

'Is he dangerous?'

'Very.' Luis's eyes rolled behind the pebble glasses like fish in an aquarium. He adored a bit of scandal.

A group of men formed a well-dressed posse and set off along the side of the cathedral.

'Are they looking for the guy?' I asked.

'No,' said Luis. 'They are going to shut your front door.'

'It takes five men to do that?'

Luis shrugged. 'No one wants to go up there alone.'

I was amazed.

'Well it's near the closed quarter where the Jews lived. No one goes there.

José pulled me on to my feet as though inviting me for a dance. 'No more questions, English girl. You inflame Luis the *Loup*'s imagination. You always have.'

He made a charming exit, full of laughter, and we trooped off to the girl's apartment.

'I love it,' I said. 'I've been living up there mostly alone for nearly a month and five guys have to hold hands just to shut my door.'

'There's never been any trouble in Gerona,' said José swiftly. 'People don't even lock their doors.'

'They don't open them either. The neighbour down the lane sure didn't want to know.'

So José said his bell didn't work.

The girl made clean, deft sleeping arrangements for the boys and brought out a bottle of something strong and exotic.

José put the boys to bed and said a quick goodbye. No, he could not stay the night alas. He had a sick mother at home.

I followed him to the door. 'You didn't show up.'

'Patrice, I was on my way to you.'

'You were with a girl. I saw her outside Luis's place.'

'So I took a drink. It's a hot night.' He was now furious. 'Why did you make such a fuss? Now all the town knows.'

The intruder didn't exist as far as he was concerned. What he meant was that all the town knew he and I were together. The girl in the shadows had been Nina and she knew it too.

As I watched him from the balcony he had to turn in the direction of his mother's apartment. That fitted in with the story of her being sick. He whistled casually. He had so much life in him. Each day was a constant rebirth. Even though he didn't write a word, he was a poet. His love of life had fashioned him for that. I could still hear his footsteps echoing along the tenth-century streets. He was less mine now than the moment I first saw him on the steps of the Residencia Internacional Hotel.

The stars were huge, feathery and cold like snowflakes about to fall.

'He's gone,' I said to the girl.

Chapter Five

The day after the intruder's visit, I left for the airport. The relief was huge as I got into the taxi. I knew I'd have to see José to say goodbye. I thought I'd have to go to his mother's flat.

'But he's in there.' And Chris pointed to the nearest neighbours.

The driver pressed on the horn and José came out smiling. He was casual and friendly. How I longed for the day when he would be no longer beautiful. Behind him the neighbour and his wife were also smiling. The sun shone. Another God-given day. The bleached children stood around them like a Persil advertisement.

'Off to the beach?' José asked, full of confidence.

'The airport.'

Then he remembered. He said a quick goodbye to the neighbours and got into the taxi. The neighbours approached and wished me a good journey. No deafness today.

'So you see they like you,' said José and the taxi left the lonely path and turned down towards the modern sector.

'They only communicate between the hours of sunrise and sundown and only if you are there to see.'

'They're very friendly,' he said.

'Their mouths do the smiling but the eyes say fuck off.'

'They heard nothing. Absolutely nothing, Patrice.'

'So they're deaf.'

'You heard an animal, a rat perhaps.'

I looked at him hard. 'Oh I'm used to rats. I see enough.'

So we sat in silence. But I knew he knew there'd been an intruder. He also knew the smilers in the next house had heard plenty and done nothing. I asked about last night's reference to the closed quarter that made the Gerona inhabitants so wary. He couldn't sound scathing enough. 'Fairy-stories to scare the tourists.'

So the taxi driver threw in his share. 'She means the old Jewish quarter. It's been covered over for years. Orders of the church.'

So I asked why.

'That's where the torture, the Expulsion, happened. It carries a curse. That's why it's covered.' The driver said it simply, in the same tone as he asked for the fare.

At Gerona rail station we took the train for Barcelona to save money. José said goodbye, I let the kids do my share. I sat down and snapped fingers at the passing trolley. 'Beers four. And wine.' The waiter started to hand the beers to the kids and José. 'Mine!' I gathered them all into my lap.

'José's going, Mum,' said Tim. Leaving and arriving always frightened him.

'Yeah.' I wasn't looking out of any windows.

The train started and I got busy with the beer. The kids waved but José had gone. I'd done the parting scene too often with him to waste one tear. I slipped off my espadrilles and put my feet on the seat. The carriage door slid open and in came José.

'I'll come with you to the airport.' It was going to be hard to dismantle the love affair, even for him. Too many dreams had gone into it. Too much of the future had already been spoken for. 'We could go to Puerta de la Selva,' he suggested. 'We were happy there. We could take a fisherman's house for next to nothing.'

The next to nothing was always something and it always came from me. Next to nothing had put me into shit at the bank and when José was no longer residing in the seashore house I'd have to return to London and spend the rest of the year working double to clear the debt. 'Are we talking about now?' I asked.

'Of course not. Next time you come. Come out in the spring when the weather is cooler.' He'd lifted Tim on to his lap and optimism was returning. 'Give me his ticket otherwise they will charge me double for not having one.'

'What about him?'

'I'll say he's under age.' He took the ticket.

'Who was the girl? Last night. You know. Outside Luis's bar?'

'The wife of a friend,' he said promptly. 'She had something worrying her.'

'I know the feeling.'

'You must understand, Patrice. Spain is a very hard country. It is not England. I work myself to the point of collapse.'

'Not for me you don't.'

'Patrice, I get less money a month than you spend in bars. Or on this!' He pointed brutally at my dress. An unwise choice. It was already spotted with spilt beer. 'Or that.' He pointed to the small bottle of wine. 'I work like a dog for my country and don't have enough to keep my mother.' He lifted up his feet. The shoes were holed. He put them back on the floor. 'And now they are trying to take away even that. I should do the fiestas, the concerts, the exchange schemes – ' he counted his fingers savagely – 'for nothing.' His eyes glared, a yellow colour.

'But you're the director of the cultural scheme. Why don't you get director's pay?'

'Because they're short-sighted fools who only care for tourist cafeterias and hamburger stands. I rescue the past, so I'm a lunatic.'

The ticket collector chose that moment to enter the carriage. He wasn't happy that Tim didn't have a ticket. 'How can this child be under five?'

José shrugged. 'He's big. It's not my problem.'

'I don't believe you.' said the collector.

'They grow fast in England.'

So the collector asked for Tim's passport. So José told him about Spain, what was wrong with it. They were on the same side.

In Barcelona I had to have so many drinks there was no money for a taxi and we took the airport bus. The pain of leaving was still there. Of course he could still keep me with him. We could get married.

That made him sigh. 'Marriage in Spain is difficult. A lengthy business.' He had no money for that.

'Has she got money?'

'Who now?'

'The little French girl. I don't remember her name.'

'I wouldn't know.'

'I believe she has, because she's the daughter of the industralist who owns a factory on the Costa Brava.'

He put his hands over his eyes like an exhausted child.

'And I think she likes you.'

He shook his head, eyes still covered.

'I remembered seeing you with her just before the Residencia Internacional was closed down.'

'When that closed our world ended, Patrice. The innocent lovely world we knew.'

'Hasn't she tried to make you?'

'I don't know her.'

So I tried a lie. They sometimes worked on liars. 'I know for a fact you see her regularly.'

He was outraged. 'Oh come on, Patrice. Maybe she did want a little more from me. Maybe I saw her once, twice – '

'You slept with her. In our house.'

'Of course not. She is intact.'

'How do you know?'

Wild with fury he looked for a way off the speeding bus. No stops till the airport. The driver asked if he was sick. He agreed and the doors slid open. I got off behind him.

'What a reaction, José, seeing you don't even know her.'

He sat on the roadside, head in his hands. 'I have nothing to give her or anyone.' Tim was grizzling and José realised people on the bus could see the holes in his shoes. So he stood up and brushed down his shirt. That was the ending. We'd been together twenty years. No word was spoken but then none was when we first met.

'How could I go out with such a girl when I have no position.' He brushed his hands together, a final gesture.

'Is the job at the art centre coming to an end then?' He didn't answer. The passengers on the bus wanted action. Two of them would miss their flights. José didn't move. What were their travelling plans, so mundane, compared with our goodbye?

'If only we had money,' I said. 'It comes to that.'

His hand touched mine in sorrow. Then he was ready to get back on the bus.

I desperately wanted a drink. If only I could make the next book really work. If it could be filmed then there'd be real money.

'What if I got a filmscript, José? Would you come to Hollywood?'

We were off on dreams again so he felt safe. 'Of course.' He blew life into several plans for the future and that got us over the heartache.

At the airport the plane was delayed. He looked agitated and said he must make a phone call. I got settled in the bar and put down what it needed to get on the plane without him. A few drinks put me where I wanted to be – married to him and without the trouble. I was that sort of drunk. Like a genie coming out of the bottle granting three wishes, my bottles gave thirty. The only drawback, the genies in mine were pissed too.

José bought comics and chocolate for the boys then went back to the phone. Whoever he wanted he couldn't get. He was doing a lot of unnecessary smiling, so he was speaking to someone of importance. Lack of money obliged me to leave the bar. I was now so drunk I was anaesthetised. They could have taken out my kidneys and I wouldn't have noticed.

'You didn't get the police.' I could still speak. 'When the guy tried to break in.'

'There's no point getting police. Not in Spain. They see a tourist and they see a cause for crime. Blonde, English. You'd be to blame.'

'Luis said the guy could be dangerous.'

'I don't want a scandal.'

He went back to the phone and I followed him. I could always walk straight whatever the drink level. I never threw up. Drink was too precious to let go of. The bill came in with the hangover. I watched him slide some twenty-five peseta coins into the box. When he started to speak I kicked open the kiosk door. He tried to shut it but the call needed all his attention. He got two servants then a secretary then he asked for Mademoiselle Nina. His voice was a dove's wing. She wasn't available. She was out riding and doing what smart girls did. So he left a message. He had to, even though I was half in the kiosk. He was delayed but he'd call at the house by three thirty. I realised nothing bad had ever happened to Nina. Nothing had happened to her. I said I didn't want to discuss it with him. I just wanted money for drink. He said he had nothing. When I couldn't beg a hundred pesetas off the inmates of the airport lounge I went outside. Drink was the only solution. I tried the cab drivers. To beg successfully, as I well knew, you had to be beautiful and free and not giving a shit about the material world. I did not fit that description. Drunks got nothing. Chris came after me.

'José's upset. He really is, Mum.'

'Don't make me cry,' I said insolently. 'I'll ruin my make-up.'

'But you haven't got any on. You haven't even washed your face.'

I couldn't believe it. I felt my face as though it were a stranger's. How had I come to such a state? I crouched down in the road defeated. What I wanted had defeated me. I could never come back. The temperature soared. It was now over ninety. The plane was called and I started towards the International building. I hadn't seen a band of alcoholics, squalid and unwashed, over in the long grass. They shouted at me and waved their one bottle. One, a tall lanky guy with red hair lurched after me. 'You're a drunk,' he jeered. I refused to look at him, at any of them. The departure door seemed a long way off and I was shaking and all of a sudden chilled. He followed, also shakily. 'You're a drunk! Drunk!' He said it with the conviction of a producer discovering a star.

'I'd worry about your own problems, arsehole,' I retorted. Every eye in the place was now on me. Still, strangers saw the most pertinent things. It took a stranger to tell you the truth about your life.

José brought the kids to the passport control, the final frontier where we could quarrel. I'd drunk so much I was a physical danger. If someone as much as struck a match near me I'd have gone up. But

I was holding it together because I had to get on that plane. I would also have to go back to the past and find the ways of surviving. I'd had answers then. He was saying something suitable. I needn't have left, that sort of thing. At the same time he was nudging me towards the last barrier.

'Well, it leaves you free to run around with the French – what's her name?'

'I am simply arranging an exhibition of her work. Nothing more.'

'Let's hope you get paid for it. It's all give in our relationship.'

'I agree,' he said, sarcastic.

'No, I give. I hate doing it. You didn't even give Chris a present on his birthday. I bought the cake, the meal, the champagne, and your sister came with her kids and your brother's kids and not one of you gave him a present.'

'In Spain we do not give presents on birthdays but on Saints' Days. It was not his Saint's Day.'

I couldn't tell if that was a lie or not.

'You got it wrong, that's all.'

So cultural differences were really to blame. Chris hadn't cried because he didn't cry. He could hardly fail to notice that they all arrived, these people who never got dirty, and he blew out his eight candles and there was nothing for him.

As I went through the barrier José jumped forward and grabbed my hand. The police stirred.

I said, 'We will see each other again, José.'

'Of course.'

'Even though we've quarrelled?'

'Twenty bad minutes. So what? We've known each other twenty years. It would take more than a quarrel to divide us.'

On the morning I had bought my ticket and decided to leave Gerona, José had been fired from his position as cultural director of the city. In the evening, as the intruder tried to break into my house, José became officially engaged to Nina.

Money might have saved our love. I did get rich in the end but nothing comes at the right time.

Chapter Six

I knew I had to be in a state of grace before I could reach Hollywood. I had to be the way I was when the dreams began. Aged four, in Albany Park, I knew I'd be a filmstar. After the kind of childhood provided by Hitler and my mother, I suppose filmstar was an occupation that made sense. A neighbour had given me my first filmstar annual. It may have been American or even pre-war, and I stared at the filmstars' faces for hours, entranced by their glamour, until they became real for me, part of my thinking. For a while Albany Park was quite deserted of children because of the evacuation. What I didn't have I invented. The filmstars became my world. I imagined Hollywood as an orange place, always sunny and safe. It didn't have doodlebugs droning nearer and nearer like interplanetary insects. They always came from the same direction, very fast, behind the living room wall in the bungalow, and the pictures and china shook and shuddered. And there'd be a high shriek and the sky was full of murder and my mother would say, 'Another one down.' Or, 'Sidcup's been hit.' Or, 'That was near.' And then we'd be in the Morrison shelter in the bedroom or the Anderson shelter in the garden, and I'd be getting more than a touch of claustrophobia and out would come a jar of Vick to help me breathe. The sky in Albany Park wasn't safe. Shrapnel would explode out of a blaze of sunshine. At night it would be lit with flashes like distant storms and the rat-a- tat·of the anti-aircraft fire would start. The black-out curtains were snapped shut before light faded. They were full of dust and moths.

The gas-mask smelling of death terrified me more than any bomb. Breathing in that rubber smell was when I became a difficult child. The warning siren wasn't too good either, but I kept that to myself. Hollywood didn't have shivery names like Molotov, Hitler and prisoner of war. It wasn't ruled by a sick and sometimes tyrannical mother who kept threatening to 'end it'. It seemed odd in retrospect that Hitler managed to wipe out millions who wanted life, yet the one sad, death-seeking lady, actually living in his bombing zone, he never touched.

Burbank studios, home of the stars, was the true air-raid shelter. I'd seen several films when my Dad was on leave. I couldn't understand what these huge, beautifully dressed people in the shimmering white and black world were talking about, but if this was life, I wanted part of it. I did drawings of them when I got home, using wax coloured crayons. I thought their world lacked colour. I created houses and families for them. I was in there somewhere.

My mother said films weren't the real world. It was something you paid for in a picture palace and it took your mind off things. My mother said they were a long way away, these beautiful people, nothing to do with my life.

Quite often she was a long way away too, in hospitals or in a solid depression. I could do nothing for her. I could see people could be changed by sickness and I, in turn, wanted to change it back, get rid of it for her. I learned early, wanting something didn't mean you got it. She stayed sick.

When it got really bad and even Doctor Abrahamson, with his huge bottles of cherry-red or thick white medicine, couldn't make an improvement, I became something to be moved on. But where? No one was ever sure. 'What do we do with Patricia till her Dad gets here?' Once again he was recalled on emergency leave. 'Where can she stay?' And my legs would tingle with fright like the first time

I saw a cockroach, and I'd go into the garden and look at the sky. That was always dangerous, jammed and muddly with hundreds of barrage balloons.

I knew the relatives and neighbours couldn't take me in. In retaliation I felt they could have fared a lot better if they'd been more Hollywood, if they'd had long, black, silky lashes and crimson mouths. I couldn't think how you could get to that age and not wear silk dress-suits with the belt tugged tight and hats with black spotted veils. Hollywood people were always wanted.

When the war ended things still weren't good on the home scene. There was a violence, more of a private kind. Father was off the sea and back on land. In retrospect I think it was a downhill move, an evolutionary mistake on a par with the human species coming out of the slime on to the land, growing legs, then crazily dropping back into the slime again. So he threw in his share of depression and I decided to go to Hollywood. I was seven then, but it was a real commitment. It just happened to take rather a long time to fulfil, something like thirty years.

At junior school I started collecting filmstars. I'd write away for a shiny signed photograph and later when I got pocket money I'd buy *Pictureshow* and *Picturegoer*, at 3d. and 4d. I'd feel actual heartache when I saw pictures of Cornel Wilde. The beauty I found in his face made me restless with an emotion I suppose was lust. When I went to grammar school I was thinking straight, nice clear thoughts and all of them about escape. Hollywood was my way out of Albany Park. To get there I had to be glamorous and I spent the Saturday odd-job money at the toilet counter in Woolworth's. My accomplice Beryl and I made lists of ways to grow older. Grooming was vital. As Hedy Lamarr said in *Picturegoer*, there's no good putting a lot of make-up on top of a flawed face. It doesn't fool anyone. You had to have a good wash with Cuticura soap then smear on an oatmeal face-mask. Then you snapped shut the pores with icy water and dabbed on some Pond's vanishing cream and let the world enjoy your natural look, she said. It was OK for Hedy Lamarr. Not quite such beautiful people had to put rather a lot of everything over rather a lot of flaws, just to get out the door. Being unbeautiful was not a confident business. And the American make-up was taking over from the English rose look. Pancake and panstick from Max Factor revolutionised Albany Park.

The Odeon Sidcup was my fix, especially if a Hollywood movie was playing. The escape was immediate. *Gentlemen Prefer Blondes* cheered me up so much I didn't really notice the state of things in the bungalow. Then my mother was taken away, all flat in an ambulance, and I could have been very sad but luckily *On Moonlight Bay* was showing next and Beryl and I saw it eleven times, for free. We'd get in by the exit door. I was jerked back to reality by my Dad coming into the cinema with a torch and dragging me out into the hideous glare of Albany Park to get on with life – for Godsake! So Hollywood was never just a career move, a stab at the bigtime or an adventure. And it was right I had to give up drink and out-of-date thinking, then go. I had to wait that long. It was inconceivable I could go there on a low. As I never expected to see José again I took the TWA flight to LA in 1977 quite free of all that dark love.

It was a couple of years since I'd last seen him at the airport in Barcelona. On impulse, when I was feeling particularly up I did try and phone him. As he didn't have a phone at his mother's I had to rely on Luis at the Arc bar. José was no longer the director of the art centre. He was building a studio for a sculptress. Diffidently I asked if he was married.

'Of course not,' said Luis. 'How can that one be married? He belongs to Gerona. Not a woman.'

Then two friends of mine, a painter and his girlfriend, went to Catalonia because I said you could be reborn there. I told them to look for José. After some weeks the painter rang me and sounded soothing and careful, like a doctor dealing with a very sick patient who might not make it to the end of the conversation. So I asked what was wrong and he said, 'Have you heard from José? I thought he should tell you himself.'

But José never delivered bad news so I had to reach him. At first he tried to deny the marriage but then he realised I wasn't standing in front of him but miles away at the end of a phone.

'Well you did it,' he said. 'Married. I'm only doing what you did.'

My heart broke – cracked like the trunk of a tree.

To comfort me he said things didn't have to change between us. As we never saw each other there wasn't anything to change. 'Don't take this too seriously, Patrice. She is a nice girl, *très gentille*.'

I asked him to see me, just for one night. He did hesitate – he was taking the bridegroom business seriously. I waited, my heart in pieces. Then he agreed to meet me. 'We're old friends, no? She'll have to understand that.' He was trying to make it open and honest, all friends together. When he arranged to meet me in the old Hotel España, Barcelona, I knew he wasn't going to tell Nina. Before I hung up he said, 'I cannot go on being alone. Why should I? She is a girl very proper, respected.' He used adjectives that never applied to me.

'Why marry her?' Even my voice was breaking.

'It's foo far advanced to stop now.'

As I'd spent joyous nights with him in the old hotel off the Ramblas, it seemed an ironic choice.

I told the man I was with in London that I was taking the boys on a sudden trip to Paris to see their father. He knew it sounded all wrong. He knew all about infidelity. His eyes narrowed and I could be losing him too if I wasn't careful. I did take the boys to Paris and delivered them to Michael who was living in Belleville. That was the truthful part.

Then I walked around Paris. It was August, empty. It occurred to me that I could be past my best. Here I was waiting for the big moment, the big stuff. Had I passed it? What was so special about me? Here I was a woman getting on chasing a sixteen-year-old's dream. I took the night train from the Gare Austerlitz to Barcelona. Every rocking kilometre assured me it was a wrong move. Insecurity, a rat at my throat, stopped me sleeping. I wasn't going to anything. I was just kicking away the only safety I had. The London guy did not hand out second chances. I just wished I loved him enough to obliterate José Tarres. Nearer to Spain the dream got unreal and I saw that seeing José was a sacrifice. He'd filled me with light and ecstasy once. Then my mind fixed on 'The Wedding'. It would be serious and he would make it beautiful. He'd choose a simple old church in a nearby village and fill it with flowers. He'd engage a pipe and drum band to play sadanas. All the friends would be there and afterwards there'd be a banquet in the *restaurant typique* in the hills. Nina would wear white and say 'I will' and mean it. They'd exchange rings.

In the morning, shattered, I stood in the corridor and watched Gerona slide by. One of my couchette companions stood beside me. She was middle-aged, elegant, tough, and knew all about looking after herself. She was alone, unfed by any affection. I thought that was a bad place to be. I admired her rings. One, an amber stone, I actually wanted to take between my teeth and bite. It made me hunger for jewels and stones. They didn't change or let you down. After a while I guessed the need for men changed to a need for gems. At least they provided a well-heeled old age. She said she'd bought the rings herself, for investment, and talked about each one as though they were her children. Looking into her scrupulously cared for face – it got the best, she told me that – I could see what I might become, if I was careful enough. But the best way to deal with ageing was identity. Have a strong enough identity that people respond to and who cares how old you get to look?

I got off at Barcelona and immediately phoned my London lover. He let me say how great Paris was, how I was staying an extra day or two because something had come up, a French film – Michael's sister came into it. He let me lie for several minutes at great expense, then he said, 'How's Barcelona?' So I thought he'd heard the odd Spanish *Ola* and *Buenas dias*, and said we'd got a crossed line.

'José's rung,' he said simply. 'He can't meet you tonight at the Hotel España. His fiancée is in town.'

I thought I'd have a heart attack.

'I told José I might not be able to reach you so he then said he'd do his best to be at the hotel. OK?' And the line went dead.

I went into a bar intending to order a substantial brandy. It said a lot for my doctor who'd got me off drink that a request for mineral water came out instead. Then I had a Coca-Cola and another mineral water. It was the day I should have fallen off the wagon. But I went back to the phone and my London lover said he was pissed off. No, he never actually came out with what he felt. That was one of our problems, just one of them. But the message was be back here tonight or don't be back. I said I was desperate. He said, 'No. You just got found out.' And he disconnected himself from my life.

So I sat on the ground on the station near the beggars and gypsies, just like the old days. Nothing changes. I had money but I was still on the floor when it came down to it. So I tried to reach José through his sister in Gerona. She was outraged. How could I be in Spain when he was marrying the next week? So I told her he'd arranged to meet me that night and I'd be there at the hotel off the Ramblas. So get the message to him. And her outrage exceeded my knowledge of Spanish. I recognised the words 'rutting pig'. That was for him. I think I was the 'hungry whore'. I certainly wasn't the 'young angel'. That would be the rich Nina.

So I took a taxi to the Hotel España intending to rest and get over all these shocks. I was going to see him again because he was my destiny, as he'd always said. I might lose the man in London and José had an angry sister. That was the bill. I could think straight but my body was shaky.

At the hotel I ran into a problem. There were no vacancies. No, José Tarres from Gerona had not booked a room. They kind of knew who he was. I asked to speak to the owner. What good would that do? He couldn't build an extra room. So I went to find another hotel. They were all full around the Ramblas. Then I got a touch of the Paris beggar horrors. Was I so incredible, suddenly, that I didn't need a roof over my head?

I took a taxi to the airport to book a night plane to London. No night planes. Not after nine o'clock. And I had to check in at eight. So I made a tentative booking then went back on the airport bus to Barcelona town, and walked around and around the same streets and kept checking the hotel for a message from José or a room vacancy.

It was one of the worst, the very worst, days I'd ever spent but I did use it later in my novel, *The Siesta*, which was filmed so I did get something out of it.

Everywhere I went a man, young and meek, kept crossing in front of me, brandishing a Bible, quoting paragraphs and texts which all assured me I was damned. So I started to run and thought I'd surely die. I thought the price for wanting a small-town Spaniard

39

was too high. I thought I'd definitely had it that day. But I didn't touch alcohol. That was the miracle. I didn't go back on.

At seven o'clock the hotel said my friend had not arrived, he hadn't telephoned, there were no rooms. I rang his sister. She said I was destroying his life. She also said she hadn't seen him. She heaped disgraces on me. I hung up in the middle. At least she was better than her mother. She didn't use curses.

I walked or rather drifted around the streets for another half an hour. Every part of my body was ill and I was in there suffering with it. I spent my last money on a cab to the airport.

I had to pay the expensive fare Barcelona to London because I was only going one way. I could have lived a month on that. Before I got the plane I rang the hotel one last time.

At Heathrow something died in me or was already dead, so I didn't care much about anything. I hadn't eaten for over twenty-four hours. I didn't even want a cab. I could have ridden on a log in a sewer. Dazed, dead, I got the tube and travelled back into my London lover's life. He was still in residence and opened the door prepared to have a real go, until he saw my face. I said, 'Don't say anything or I'll kill myself.' And I shut myself away in my room and phoned the Hotel España.

José Tarres had arrived at 9.00 p.m. and had gone to and fro looking for me for an hour and a half. Then he'd waited in the foyer and was now searching for me in other hotels. That night in Barcelona nearly cost him his marriage because his sister, in her outrage, told the bride. But the bride wanted what she thought she'd got anyway so let that one pass. Of course she'd never got him.

Chapter Seven

I was unattached and ready for anything when I took the plane to Los Angeles. My career wasn't in bad shape either. I was now with Duckworth who'd published three of my books to good reviews. Another earlier one was attracting movie interest. I felt sure I'd sell it well in Hollywood. It was the story of a vanished filmstar, and I believed absolutely that Lauren Bacall, one of my all time favourites, would go for it. No one else shared that belief.

I arrived at Los Angeles airport alone and that felt right. I was stripped of the years of struggling. The old dreams were out-of-date luggage. As I stood in the tropical sunshine I felt that whatever I had on board, as they say, this town would do justice to.

My visit had three purposes. First, to sell the filmstar book. Second, to engage a finance man, a tycoon, to come in on a Harlequin Mills and Boon formula romance, and third to see my old friend, the film director J.

One way I'd made money in the previous months was as a reader for Harlequin Mills and Boon in their film department. Roughly twenty-four books were published a month and my job, for which I was paid £15 a book, was to read them and locate one suitable for

41

film. The £15 wasn't enough. There was something about formula books that drove me insane. Even when I was broke. I heard you got upwards of £25,000 for knocking out one of these love stories but I didn't even try.

When the company knew I was going to LA on my own ticket they slipped the deal to me with a bonus if I was successful. I knew they thought my name might open the tycoon's door. He didn't have to know I was only married into that family. I'd met J when I was a student at RADA. He lived in Beverly Hills above the smogline and had worked with the legends – Monroe, Gable, Elizabeth Taylor. J was considered to be something of a Hollywood legend himself and there was nothing about the place and its history he didn't know.

When I passed through immigration control it was 1.00 a.m. London time. The flight had taken over eleven hours. It had taken me over twenty-five years.

J was leaning nonchalantly by the arrivals gate. So, less nonchalantly, was the Mills and Boon American film representative, carrying a bunch of flowers and the news that I was to meet the Tycoon straight away. J didn't like that idea. He'd only just about heard of Mills and Boon and he hadn't driven all the way from Mulholland Drive to the airport to have someone else give me my first sight of Hollywood. He thanked the guy for the flowers, stuck them into my hand, said I'd call later and shut me into his car.

Now that was potentially a very bad move for me. Mills and Boon might still be at the stage in their film development where they had to wait for things to happen but the tycoon sure wasn't. Also he was not what anyone imagined. The word tycoon covered a lot of ground.

As J drove along the freeway and up to Sunset then into the hills to Coldwater Canyon, he pointed out the houses of stars long gone, the scenes of drama, excess, glory. It had everything, Hollywood. It was the springboard where superlife got off.

J lived in what had been Valentino's guest house. The main house was higher up the steep track and was owned by an estate agent. It was isolated in the hills but you could always hear the swish of traffic along Coldwater Canyon. To get into Valentino's grounds you used an electric device which J called the key, that opened the electrically operated gates, then swung them shut. J didn't mind isolation. He loved nature, flowers, insects, wild animals, climate. It's when it got to people it got tricky. He'd just finished two epic movies, back to back, and was preparing another.

He'd left Europe two years before because Hollywood was where they made films. Hollywood was easy as long as you lived there. Getting work was ninety per cent dependent on their liking you, and they had to see you to do that. He made some English tea and insisted I stay awake. It was now 3.30 a.m. London time.

'You have to break it in and switch to LA time otherwise you'll be all over the place.'

'Break what in?'

'Your body.'

J and I got on because he put up with me. My drinking days while he was in London had been a sweat for him but he wasn't exactly slow to open a bottle himself. However, his behaviour did not change in the course of the session as mine did. Probably because he was not an alcoholic. We had a successful erotic affair that did not depend on love. We weren't possessive with each other. Perhaps that's why it worked. He never discussed José Tarres. The Spanish incident was just something I had done and did not talk about. It was hormonal. I didn't question his many other sexual affairs.

J was sometimes abrasive, especially about my appearance. He liked things to be at their best and he had a good sense of 'best'. In that way he was good for me.

Since I'd started writing, clothes were something I put on. As an object I ceased to matter. All energy went to my head and travelled on to the paper like a beam of light. It didn't mean what came out was any good, just that there was energy to do it. Clothes, as long as they felt easy and didn't need attention, got me to the shops, doing things for the kids, doing my exercises. They kept me humble and out of trouble. It was only when I went out, it all came on, the glamour. People were often surprised, even alarmed by meeting me in public and finding me at home. A psychiatrist once told me it was because I was depressed. My clothes were flags of sadness. I have to say I wore more eye make-up as a beggar in Paris than I did standing

43

at the sink washing up. But for Hollywood it all came out, the filmstar trouseau. J watched with suspicion as I began hanging up the dresses. Then for once he didn't shut his eyes in horror.

We knew each other very well. I wasn't in love with him and he was relieved. So many women had been. His life was always harmonious and ordered. The bedroom was for sleep, sex and watching television, the mainroom for playing backgammon and working. Everything else happened around the pool.

The pool was turquoise and leaves of many colours floated on the water. It gave light to the house in all weathers. It had an hypnotic effect, suggested all sorts of moods and appetites. I thought it was a sinister pool and David Hockney, who lived down the road, should have captured it, subdued it on canvas. He'd have got its moods. It needed an artist to understand it. What it got was the Hollywood élite swimming about, messing it up. To J it was something to get cool in. To me, the first time I saw it, it was a pale, beautiful slow-moving eye looking up at the sky.

After tea J said I should take a shower and change my dress and we'd go out to dinner. He pointed through the trees to where Charlton Heston lived, Jean Simmons, Marlon Brando, Jack Nicholson. All that kept me awake. It wasn't a coming home, like the first time I'd stepped into Gerona. But it wouldn't hurt me either. And all the memories, the whispers, glimpses of Harlow, Gable, Harry Cohn, Valentino, James Dean, they were all around, the fabulous ones. There wasn't a breeze in the weather sense, but their presence set going a change of air, a definite chill. These people and events wanted to be recalled. They were glad I was there and my visit was a sort of homage to them who'd seen me through many a bad year.

I watched the sun glow over Burbank Studios in the valley. It had the same reddish glare as the bombs falling on Albany Park as the fires were dying.

Chapter Eight

We went to dinner at the Beverly Hills Hotel and I noticed he got the best table. I also noticed he stuck a bill into the *maître d*'s hand which is no doubt why he got the table. *Maître d*'s all over the world knew a J when they saw one. It was all established, the introductory tip, the prominent table, the service, then the usual tip, then any other little favour should J want it. That night I was the favour. It wasn't just the tip. J had class, breeding, he looked right, mixed with the right set. He enhanced any dining room and gave waiters confidence. It was the right place for my filmland début. Every star throughout history had graced the Beverly Hills Hotel.

Afterwards he showed me Hollywood. It gave him pleasure because his home town was something, a shrine possibly, that I'd been inching towards as long as he'd known me.

Hamburger Hamlet in Beverly Hills became one of my favourite places. The regular people, agents, directors, actors, the occasional star, typists and legends, went there because the food was good and the atmosphere was easy, yet stable. No one crossed the room to sit in your lap. Mervyn LeRoy came across to say hello to J, that first night, and he told me some of the stories of old Hollywood. It was as though I'd read the menu in Albany Park, as a child in the solitude and the war, and put in my order and thirty years later the banquet was served. Of course the name Chaplin didn't do any harm. Charlie had been the superstar. I put the town's acceptance of me down to knowing J, loving the place, having work to offer and my name.

From Hamburger Hamlet J could whizz back up into the hills and be home in minutes. This was something to be proud of, apparently. Seeing the amount he drank I had to agree with him. He was still neat at the wheel and his thinking never went either.

Wild animals scattered as the car doors opened. If J was alone they stayed. We looked over LA at the lights spread below, the freeways, Century City, Santa Monica pier. J could simply stand by his pool and see the lot. Of course the higher you lived the higher status you had. Sometimes it must have seemed that Hollywood was his. Yet his dreams, whatever they were, had never been fulfilled. He was too critical to be a happy man. Watching him I thought of Jay in *The Great Gatsby*. J had known Fitzgerald, but then J did seem to have known most people. Apart from the Hollywood connection he had the right kind of relatives on the East coast.

'Do you still have dreams?' I asked.

'I never remember if I do.'

'I mean the other sort.'

'Same answer.'

I thought I should at least call the Mills and Boon representative but J wouldn't hear of that. 'Honey, no one gets off a transatlantic flight and goes straight to a meeting. I've never heard of such a thing.'

We played backgammon until he thought it was the right time for me to go to sleep. It was eleven thirty LA time. I'd given up trying to work out London time. My time, whatever clocks I chose to be on, should not be spent in Beverly Hills, however, but down in the suite in West Hollywood booked for me by the Tycoon. We were supposed to be doing a film deal. He liked things straight. Business was not negotiable. It always came first. But I was part of J's Hollywood and selling romantic novels could wait until I'd been to sleep.

I woke up four hours after I'd gone to bed and wanted lunch. My body had gone completely mad and was demanding things with the shrillness of a baby. It had to be a big meal, not some two-bit breakfast and my mind was racing because it was the middle of my day and I should be doing things. The only drawback, it was night where I was. I've heard many ways of settling jetlag. Give in to your body and do what it wants. Break it in and make it do what you want. Take sleeping pills and force an eight-hour respite and so get on local clock time. Never do deals when you're jetlagged. You're not sharp. The travellers' old wives' tales didn't mean too much up in J's place with the kitchen unfamiliar, J wanting sleep, and big night-time animals squinting through the trellised kitchen window.

I had to agree with the advice about not making deals. I certainly wasn't sharp. When I finally got to the West Hollywood suite at noon there was a pile of messages at reception. For a moment I thought I must be popular. They were all from Mr Romance of Mills and Boon who was in an increasingly fearful state. Tycoon, who normally went to bed at 9.00 p.m., had waited up till after 11.00 to meet me. Putting out his schedule wasn't a good idea. In other words, I'd better get my arse across town and apologise. Everything was arse. Kick arse, shift arse, get your arse, arsehole. But J took me to lunch at Hamburger Hamlet where I fell asleep because I was approaching my normal bedtime. I saw Natalie Wood and Dean Martin amongst the throngs of agents and starlets. Everyone ate there at some time except the money guys. I don't suppose they'd heard of it.

In the afternoon we sat by his pool and played more backgammon. J was a champion player, so any winning I did was down to the law of averages. I'd get one game in twenty. It infuriated me because generally I made the same classic moves as he did. He didn't help my mood. Remarks like, 'I wouldn't take that move, honey. Not if I was you. No one would,' made me angry. I'd take the move. I'd accept the double and be more in the shit. I asked why he won. Our styles weren't so different. The answer was simple. 'I'd never throw the dice you do.' So it was down to luck like most things.

J had his no-go areas. It seemed to displease him if I talked about my career. He didn't like that word. It was OK for me to write 'little' books – he emphasised the 'little' – but start talking about actually writing a screenplay – that was his territory and he was too impatient with the lunacy of the idea even to discuss it. As for the filmstar book it was a nice 'little' book but not for Hollywood. His friend Betty Bacall wouldn't touch it.

Now I'd started being published by Duckworth the 'little' was not necessarily the insult he intended, because my novels were rarely more than 130 pages long. Their slimness terrified the Americans and it wasn't until they became celluloid that they could be taken seriously. For an American publisher, holding one of those slim novels was like picking up a famine victim.

The eager hungry child that had still not altogether gone from my personality suited J the best. In the days when I'd been broke he liked the sight of me going barefoot, my black jeans done up with a safety pin, my hair all around my face. I still carried hints of my Parisian hardships. I hated to be without food and I dreaded underground stations. Although I had phobias I also had a certain glamour in his eyes. For all his successes he could never have found Genet in a drawing room. I quite effortlessly found him in the street. So if I was eager to absorb Hollywood – fine. As a companion I was OK too. But if I wanted action, like who should I go to for an agent – he had the best – his green eyes would harden, even his tan would go a bit funny. He was never lost for a reply, however overwrought I made him feel.

'Don't you think it's time you grew up, honey?' – the last thing he wanted. 'That sort of thing is for professionals.' Meaning people like himself. Except the sentence of disapproval would be more biting and eloquent than that. Actually he did me a lot of good. His very disdain whipped and lashed me along Sunset Strip to the agents, the film lawyers. But I didn't have really to try because in that place, unlike any other, things came to me.

Apart from the fact I did love the town it was also all available. I could just walk into a drugstore or foyer and see Steve McQueen or Hal Ashby or Warren Beatty or Joseph Cotton. And I got invited to parties, filmsets, and my days would begin to look like a page from *Tatler*. I was at a time on my writing road when I felt I was on an up, so I was confident and had something to sell. The good reviews I'd had didn't do me any harm either.

I didn't feel alone in that town. I enjoyed the differences in the areas, especially Venice, arty and old fashioned, full of reckless energy. You felt anything could happen. Then Boys Town, West Hollywood, where everything happened. The atmosphere in each quarter was distinctive. You couldn't have all those charismatic people living there for so many years, leaving no trace. They'd lived at the very edges of excitement, lust, daring – they'd done everything that could be done, then died. Nothing said to me by the existing tenants of Hollywood could dull my view. I felt loyal to what Hollywood had been and I paid homage in the way it wanted most, by enjoying it. There were so many so-called sophisticated people griping because there weren't any art galleries or culture and it wasn't Paris. Why didn't they shove off and live in Paris? Because they wouldn't have got the same money. But it was changing. I'd have liked it in the 1940s and 50s. What I got were memories – shadows of a more romantic time, but I was used to those.

Chapter Nine

The hotel suite was in Le Parc, West Hollywood, a sedate outfit popular with the English. It had recently opened and was considered fantastic value at $56 a night. I loved hotel life because it was temporary. It could also be luxurious, sudden swoops into grand luxury were fine. It wasn't as though I had the responsibility of wealth, and I could go back to my stark life in the Victorian dusty London house, the poorness of which made me work hard. I had to write my way out of it. So reduced circumstances turned me into a writer. I'd never have bothered with a word of it if I'd had money.

Mr Romance was palpitating by my door as I crept along the expensive pale green carpet.

'I've been waiting,' said Mr Romance. 'Like all day.' It was early evening for him. I was still spinning with a mixture of fatigue and novelty. Flowers, lots of them, were propped awkwardly in identical white vases. I thought they were compliments of the management. They were compliments of Tycoon, but he was no longer feeling complimentary.

Mr Romance chastened me with a soft New Jersey accent as I washed my face. No one ever kept Tycoon waiting. Everyone was now on the line. The office in London, in New York and he, Colin (Romance) Diamond from Manhattan. His reserved manner at the airport had made him faceless. Now with his job threatened he looked suave and dark like a 1930s bandleader. I noticed later he could change physically several times a day. It could have been an asset but unfortunately he had no control over it. Anyway, trying to please with a bunch of flowers in his hand certainly didn't suit him. Anger brought out his features.

I was to accompany him immediately to the penthouse office in Ocean Park. Was the romance story fresh in my head? Could I pitch it? In America they did things when they said. Now was a serious word.

I phoned J and said I had to go to a meeting. Meetings were things he went to, not female writers of little books from quaint England.

'Tell him you'd like to see him in a few days. There's no hurry, I promise you that. Nothing will come of it.'

'But I should have gone straight from the airport yesterday.'

'Who is this person exactly? Only you could find him.'

I said his name.

'Never heard of him.' J was used to hearing Sam Spiegel, Billy Wilder. 'Put him on the line.'

'But he's in Ocean Park.'

'Put the one you've actually got with you on the line, honey.' The 'honey' was a little tricky, his tone more glacial than the stiffest air-conditioning. I handed the phone to Mr Romance who introduced himself properly this time and mentioned the magical bucks made by romance books and how Tycoon wanted in. He made it all sound sensible but it wasn't old Hollywood, proper Hollywood. It wasn't Swifty Lazar or Elizabeth, so J stayed aloof. The phone was handed back to me and my instructions were to get into a taxi and meet J at Hamburger Hamlet. From there we'd go to dinner. He reminded me there was a lot of fancy in Hollywood, unstable deals, improbable talk. 'I've told your friend you're busy this evening. Wear a pretty dress. No one wears blue jeans anymore. Not in this town.' He hung up.

To keep it sweet I decided to slip down to Ocean Park with Mr Romance to be introduced to Tycoon then take a taxi back up to

Beverly Hills for the meeting with J. But I hadn't allowed for the huge distances between one sector and another. From West Hollywood to Ocean Park was like crossing an entire city. J would already be on to his second whiskey sour in Hamburger Hamlet. But I felt free with Mr Romance. He wasn't putting anything on me. Out of the shadow of a Hollywood front-runner like J I was able to remember what I wanted.

The new friend said he'd help me find an agent. No sweat. A writer of hardback books was class in a community comprised of transitory ideas never more than a hundred pages long, beautifully turned out on electric typewriters which made words gleam. A script could kick off for the day at 6.00 a.m. between soft new blue covers like baby blankets. By 6.00 p.m. it would be raped, half destroyed and replaced by something younger and different altogether. A hardback book was a piece of history in comparison.

I asked what Tycoon did.

'This and that. Money.'

So I asked what Mr Romance did. This and that as well. He didn't include the money. In New York he acted as an agent.

I asked why the Tycoon wanted to see me.

'He likes your judgement.'

'Is he already in films?'

'Just do your bit. Pitch it to him.'

When we got to Ocean Park a guard at the entrance gate asked for a pass. We waited while he phoned reception. There were three or four apartment blocks facing over the harbour. This complex was occupied by those who loved boats and the rest who liked leisure. Everything was on hand. You ate in a choice of restaurants or had meals delivered to your apartment. Piped music took the fear out of the corridors and elevators. It was helped by an efficient and obvious security system. Some people felt too rich. There was a health club, a beauty salon, several bars and boutiques. I got the drift of most of it. Divorcees of a certain age on effective alimony and hormone replacement therapy, and wealthy men from out of town wanting company. They all looked the same. I thought they were all ugly but that could be just my taste. The complex occasionally housed a movie director's ex-wife or a filmstar's widow but mostly it was a certain kind of wealth wanting company, a veneer of respectability, and those who liked boats.

We were escorted from the reception to the top floor by a security man exuding goodwill. He went with the piped music. But when we got to Tycoon's patch he was replaced by serious guards. One said, 'I have to check your bag, lady. Nothing personal.' He looked me over for whatever it was that threatened the rich.

A camera? A gun? Not today. So we were let through and a polite secretary took over. Mr Romance had a clean bill anyway.

'Robert Hartman has been just dying to meet you, ma'am,' the secretary trilled as we walked along an outside covered passageway circling the building. The view was sensational. I realised I was looking out at the Pacific Ocean. It was the first time I'd seen it, except in films.

At the penthouse door the secretary said goodbye. She didn't sit in on meetings, she said. Mr Romance tensed as though meeting royalty. I reminded him I had to be at Hamburger Hamlet in twenty minutes.

'Just play this as it comes, please.'

An electric buzzer released the doorlock and we stepped inside. The walls were circular glass and gave uninterrupted views over Hollywood and the ocean. The penthouse continued on the floor above. There was a lot of space. And then I saw him. Life did have some surprises. I remembered Mr Romance saying he wanted to meet me because he liked my judgement. What did he know about that?

He sat alone which surprised me. I'd imagined he'd have his people with him. He was listening to Verdi which was turned off in honour of our arrival. He was tanned, his eyes were very dark. He was agile and I saw what the writers of romance books were trying to get at. He had a panther's style, a natural physical pride. Predatory, very still. He had all the charm he needed. His attractiveness was so immediate, almost an embarrassment, I couldn't look him in the eyes.

Mr Romance and I got settled in chairs and the drinks came out. He didn't understand why I didn't drink wine. It was a very good bottle, he said, opened especially for me. I felt cold. Did he know I'd drunk? Had I met him on some drunken excursion in Europe? I couldn't quite see him in my part of London.

'It's Spanish. But very good.'

Mr Romance explained that I had been held up, due to jetlag. It was my first visit. I read for Mills and Boon's film department and I'd come up with an eminently suitable idea, and as Tycoon had expressed interest in film development, the company reckoned this was a good shot. He reminded Tycoon I was a literary writer, well respected in England. Mr Romance had changed. The dance leader Brylcreem-slick look had quite gone. He was boyish and preppy from the right side of the tracks. It was a quick rehearsed speech. Then it was my turn. I had to pitch the story. That meant I had to tell it in an entertaining way bringing out the key points of finance and audience interest. Pitching a film story was no different from extricating myself from a dangerous situation. I'd been in plenty of those in my time. The Tycoon watched me. It was hard to say what he thought but he didn't look as though he was buying anything. At the end Mr Romance gave a swift review of my literary credits, embroidering a little. I thought he should become my agent.

The Tycoon sat quietly, not moving, which was more effective than a lot of words. We sat waiting, ill at ease. I hardly thought he'd been struck dumb by the emotion of the story. Then he asked if I'd like something else to drink. I was on Coca-Cola. I said I had an engagement in Beverly Hills.

'So what do you think of the proposal?' Mr Romance cut in.

The Tycoon took my glass and refilled it. 'Have dinner with me.'

Mr Romance broke into a sweat. Everything in him pleaded with me not to refuse. Even the crocodile on the pocket of his T-shirt seemed to come alive with anxiety.

'But I already have a dinner fixed.'

'You can call him and unfix it,' said the Tycoon. He pushed a phone towards me. I explained that my friend was already at the meeting place so he told me that made it easier. 'Lift the receiver, give the name of the bar, you'll be put through.' I hesitated. Mr Romance was poised to throw in his nickle'sworth. He was going to tell me not to forget I was in LA on business but he was too nervous to make one move. Swiftly the tycoon lifted the receiver to my ear. He was attractive, but I thought that was a little pushy. I could make my own cancellations. But I smelt money. I smelt it deep in my nostrils, in my lungs. It was stuck in my sinuses. More than money. Power. Tycoon was catlike. He was sad and alien, missing something, like a bereaved panther. My own schemes had found a place here in the penthouse. I thought the 'little' book could perhaps have its day and find its way into the hands of Lauren Bacall.

J was irritated at being paged at Hamburger Hamlet. As I wasn't meeting him he was swift to tell me he'd be going on to a party. He made it sound glamorous and enviable. He wouldn't be home until 1 maybe 2.00 a.m. so I'd have to wait if I needed a bed at his place.

The Tycoon laughed, a slow laugh. Humour was something he kept to himself. 'What a lot of punishment. Denied a Bel Air party. Poor Cinderella. Well, we'll have to see what the fairy godmother can do.'

I noticed the wedding ring. It looked lonely. His hands were something to watch. They were beautiful and very alive.

He let Mr Romance loose for the night. He didn't want to go. He even suggested staying to drive me back to the hotel. Finally he said, 'What about the story line, Mr Hartman? Does it work for you? What should I say to London? We could bring it in in under a million five. Below the line that is.'

'Good.'

The secretary was at the glass door ready to escort Colin into the ordinary world. When he'd gone we both said what a sweet guy he was.

I was surprised when he went into the adjoining kitchen and made dinner himself. It was composed of strictly organic produce he had grown on one of his farms in – it sounded like Mexico. He spoke Spanish far more fluently than I ever had. He waited for me to join in.

'But I thought you'd enjoy speaking Spanish.' He made the meal swiftly without fuss.

'Why should I?'

'I thought you'd lived there. I'm sure someone told me.'

We ate at a glass circular table in the kitchen.

'Are you Spanish then?' I asked.

'No.'

'But you're not Anglo-Saxon exactly.'

'My family come from Italy. I'm second generation.'

I didn't know what to say to him. I felt it all came down to asking questions but that was too intrusive. My anecdotes would not exactly fit the occasion. He wouldn't understand the people I came across. He wasn't like anyone I'd ever met. Then I saw that silence didn't bother him and I supposed he spent a great deal of his time alone. As tycoons were usually interested in money, they could never talk enough about that, I decided that was a safe subject. I was about to say, 'How's the German mark doing?' but the phone rang, a musical sound, and lights flicked on a panel in the wall. He reached across and pressed a switch which meant he could hold a conversation without lifting a phone to his ear. The caller spoke a mixture of Italian and American, and Paris came into it. There seemed to be an argument about how much a French politican should be paid. It didn't sound like Mr Romance country.

When the call was over Tycoon made coffee. The music was on again. Lights flicked on the communication panel. Answering services took care of all that. I was desperately tired, felt unreal and told him about my filmstar book, my head lolling on my arm. It must have been the worst LA pitch he'd ever heard. Then he surprised me. He said he'd read one of my novels, one published by the *London Magazine* in England. It was my first book and had done all right as far as critical response went but I wouldn't have thought it was the sort of thing that reached his world. So I gave him the filmstar book I just happened to have in my bag. He promised to read it. I liked the way he held it. The way he touched things. Some people, what they did you never even noticed. You'd just about see them stab someone. He made me feel alive. I said I didn't think he fitted in with Ocean Park's clientele.

'Why not?'

'They're all ugs.' I'd used my son's Kentish Town slang, I was so tired.

'Are they? I never see them.'

'What else do you know about me? You seem to think I lived in Spain.'

He gave a secret bitter smile, then gestured upstairs. 'You go to bed. You're tired.'

I said I'd prefer to go back to the hotel.

'And then you'll hang around for J to leave a party. You'll hang around a long time. Come on.' And he took my arm and led me up the circular stairs to a guest bedroom with adjoining bathroom. He pointed out the heated towels, the new toothbrush, the steam cabinet, the sunlamp. I thought he could snap the long brown fingers and the girls would come jumping. I wondered where his wife was.

He said, 'I have things to do, so goodnight.'

I wondered what his wife was like then fell asleep.

The smell of cooking woke me. The phones were going musically. Robert Hartman called, 'Your breakfast is ready. Come and get it.'

It was only when I was downstairs dazed with sleep at the table that I discovered it was only 6.00 a.m. I thought some ghastly mistake had been made. 'Did you know it's only 6.00 a.m.?' I said.

He put in front of me a huge plateful of waffles, bacon, egg, vegetable. 'I've had mine. I get up before five because of the phone calls. There's fruit juice and fresh coffee.'

I knew people did business early in LA. He meant worldwide. Businessmen in his line seemed to peak at 5.00 a.m. LA time. He'd already done his regulation thirty minutes workout. He now went for his regulation ten-mile run along the beach while I put myself together. Then I looked at his other rooms. Telex machines, clocks showing the time across the world, recording machines and mechanical filing systems. I wanted to look at the piles of documents and letters, but that felt wrong. It was a hostile territory, this money world. There were no photographs, no sign of a personal life.

I could hear him running back along the passageway. At the door he checked the metre strapped to his ankle and scribbled the distance and time on a sheet of paper. 'I thought you'd be sunning yourself, Patricia.'

'Why do you call me Patricia?'

'It suits you better, that's all. I liked your book very much.' His voice was caressing, almost seductive. 'But you haven't done it yet, written the real story.' He pointed at my chest. 'Inside you.' And then he reminded me of José Tarres. He had the same trick of making unexceptional moments magical.

He took a shower and told me the things wrong with the book. I got ready to leave. I'd never been up at 6.00 a.m. in my life, except during a family disaster or after a party in my youth. I felt doubly disorientated, the jetlag, the exceptional early rising. How would I fill the rest of the day? It was far too early to call J.

'Do you always get up so early? I was almost angry.

'But of course. Don't you?'

'Not exactly. I mean it's only a quarter past seven.'

'So?' He dried himself with the door part open. His body was all he wanted it to be. The running, the exercising, the good food, the sun. It hadn't gone to waste. I put him around mid-forties but he was probably older.

'Well, it makes the rest of the day kind of hard to get through. How do you fill all those hours until bedtime?'

He let that one go. Of course he made money. Jetlag had made me querulous. 'Do all your associates have to get up at 5.00 a.m.?'

'But of course they get up. I'd never do business with a man who didn't answer his phone by 6.00 a.m. I wouldn't trust a man who didn't answer his phone by 6.30.'

I thought of the men I'd known. José, Michael. Were they untrustworthy? Was early morning rising a moral advantage?

'If they get up early they have a positive desire to do business. I only like a positive attitude.'

As he'd read my book, one and a half hours cover to cover for a fast reader, I supposed he was some kind of insomniac.

'But what about your wife?'

'She's not here.' He poured coffee and handed it to me. He refilled his cup. His silences were his defence. You didn't break into one of those with questions. So the absent wife stayed where she was. It was odd, I felt so intruded upon, being woken early. So many men had done more outrageous things. It wasn't as though I'd been perversely treated. Simply woken from sleep and given a huge breakfast. Was it because he hadn't consulted me? His time was my time.

'I'm glad you liked the book,' I said, trying to sound polite.

'Oh, you're good.'

'I mean the romance one. I think it will make a – '

'Let me talk to your people. I'll deal with that.'

He swept up a phone and asked the desk to call a taxi. Then he pressed a buzzer and the secretary appeared at the glass door. So I was out. Seven forty-five. I was deeply glad I wasn't still drinking. I'd have definitely come unstuck in a hundred mixed ways.

'I suppose the book, your book, is based on your own experience?'

I picked up my bag, found my jacket. 'Not at all.'

'But you have been to Spain obviously.'

I nodded.

'Spain is important to you.'

'It was. Yes.'

He came up to me, his eyes were flecked with little yellow lights. 'You put it in the past.'

'Do you know it?' I could be evasive too.

A gesture took care of that. He wasn't going to recount every holiday he'd spent there. 'I expect it's changed. You were there young.'

'How do you know?'

He pointed to the book. The look he was giving me made my heart flutter. Another hour with him would turn me into a Mills and Boon heroine. Behind the glass door the secretary waited patiently. She was dressed smartly as though in uniform. I wanted to see him again. Why play evasive games? Because he was evasive did I have to be?

'I first knew it in the mid-1950s. That was a lovely time. I lived in Gerona.'

'Gerona.' He made it sound good.

'Do you know it?'

'I've passed through.'

The phones were busy. Blue, red, green buttons on alert. He released the glass door and said the taxi fare was taken care of. The secretary led me along the passageway. I hoped he'd stop me and say we'd see each other again. Almost around the circular building, out of sight, then he called, Patricia. We turned back promptly. He came towards us.

'You know Gerona, the old city. In amongst there are hidden remains. There's a covered secret part isn't there?'

I said I didn't know it.

'Oh yes. The church had it covered over in the fifteenth century. Mystical practices were carried on there.'

I couldn't think what part he meant. I knew it, every stone, every arch. Then I recalled vaguely the intruder and the five local men holding hands to close my front door.

Robert Hartman described a road I recognised as the Calle Forsa where José lived, but I couldn't think of anything hidden there.

'But I haven't seen it, this covered area.'

'Well that's the point. It's covered so you don't see it.' He went back inside.

So a complete stranger was telling me things I didn't know about the city I loved most in the world. So I asked the secretary if he was reliable. The question shocked her. It was like asking if he was really rich. She said nothing about his character or his missing wife, or his business, though I did try and pry. The staff came with smart outfits and discretion. Then the tough guys took over. No, I hadn't stolen the jade ornaments. Then the polite security guard led me along the halls of piped music, passed the pampered people to the taxi.

'It's like seeing God, getting to him,' said the doorman.

I was all of a sudden depressed. I could see going back through the different grades of guards to his quarters was unlikely. I'd been given no phone number or invitation. He hadn't even accepted the Mr Romance proposition. No, I had not pleased him. I'd been put out like a cat that hadn't made it as a pet. It made me angry. I'd been put out of Gerona a couple of times and now here by a man who allowed himself moments of resembling my ex-lover. Then I remembered I existed too. Not just these clever charismatic men. I had my writing, my acceptances. I'd conquered the drink problem, brought up two kids, survived Albany Park. My English voice rose two notches up the social scale and I asked the doorman who owned the complex. I intended coming back and needed to meet him.

The doorman seemed confused.

'Who owns all this? Where will I find him?' I spoke like a querulous deb from the country to the doorman of Fortnum and Mason's. 'I'd like to see him.'

'But you've just seen him, lady. Robert Hartman owns this and this and that.' He pointed to the other blocks and the harbour. 'In fact, most of Ocean Park.'

Chapter Ten

I arrived as the sun was setting at J's house. I was wearing a fairly good yellow dress, tortuously high-heeled shoes and a full make-up. I didn't look as though I was getting married exactly, but I was looking as good as it got for me at thirty-six. J was not ready for our special 'welcome, meet Hollywood drink' in the Beverly Hills Polo Lounge. That was the place where everyone hung out, if they could afford it. It was the status lounge. Deals were done, films were cast, rumours born. J was lying on a sunbed with his first whiskey of the day. His eyes were bitter.

'Did you enjoy your party?'

'What party?' he sighed.

'The one you went to.'

'I went to one at noon. Then I went to The Dome for lunch with my producer. Last night I went to a party for Brooke Hayward. She's had the biggest paperback advance recorded and it's her first book.'

OK. I got the drift of the atmosphere. As though lancing a boil I brought it all out with one painful statement. 'I stayed the night down there because he has a spare room. It was a long way to come back.'

J rattled his glass and the ice-cubes caught the last of the sun. They were good-sized cubes, gleaming and cold, but they were nothing compared with his eyes.

'Who is this person exactly?'

'The same as he was yesterday. I think he's in oil.'

J gave a dismissive cough. I realised I didn't know much about my previous night's host. 'He owns the complex down at Ocean Park.'

'Never heard of him,' said J promptly.

'He's into films. Definitely, and they want him to buy a romance which – '

'Who are these people?'

'I told you. I've been reading for Mills and Boon. They want to tie up a film deal. I've selected a possible book and as I was coming here anyway – '

'He's never backed a film, honey.' He took a long drag of the new cigarette. The 'honey' was getting a bit tired.

'Well, he's in films,' I said stubbornly.

'Not to my knowledge.'

He dived into the pool and everything was disturbed. The perfect mirror of the water, the animals, the birds. The trees swung. It had a sinister feeling like a Polanski film.

He was dressed casually and I hoped I wasn't too overdressed for the Polo Lounge. His phone kept going and was picked up by an answering service.

'There's a lot of – ' He hesitated. 'Punters in this town.' He didn't like that word but had to use it. They never reached his part of Hollywood. 'They come thinking the streets are paved with gold.'

'Perhaps they are.'

J shook his head. 'Not any more.'

'Anyway, this one brings his own. Gold.'

Scripts, dozens of them, were piled by the window. An elegant tea service was laid out on a dining table.

'It's up to you what you do of course. You'd be better advised to have a holiday. All this running around. Well, you'll just exhaust yourself. Why don't you have a swim?'

'But I'll ruin my make- up.'

I was surprised to see him pick up his backgammon board.

'Where are you taking that?'

'We're going to have a few games with Bunny. He's not a bad player. You might even win. I can't give you dinner, alas. I'm dining with friends.'

'But I thought I was going to the Polo Lounge.' My disappointment made me sound like a child.

'Not in that dress you're not.'

I looked down, couldn't see much wrong.

'It's creased. It's a nice little dress but not for the Polo Lounge.'

We got into the Daimler and the electronic key swung shut the gates. So I was being paid back. A mispent night and I missed out on Hollywood. I'd come out as his guest. That's how he saw it. I tried to explain again about my writing ambitions. They only made him laugh.

'Darling, so many people come out here with some kind of dream or half- thought-out idea.'

'But I've got books.'

'Not suitable for film. They're fine as books, incidentally.'

'Why aren't they suitable?'

'They're English. What cinemagoer in Texas is going to understand about Hampstead Heath or Jack the Ripper?'

So I gave up but I knew he wasn't right. He was right for the majority but not for me. Life didn't work like that. If you passionately wanted something enough and fought for it, not only could you get it – getting it could be good. If you had your own voice and used it, eventually someone listened.

He described my backgammon partner as a middle-aged cynic who'd directed thirty near-B movies, one or two of which had made it. His place was lower down than J's, just above the strip, and cosy and lived in. He was sharp, streetwise, witty, and meeting him I thought his films should have been better. But he turned out a particular sort of picture that grossed a particular amount. It meant he was never out of work. For some reason he needed to feel safe. He didn't take chances and the talent stayed inside him.

I played six games and lost five. I started losing the moment J said I couldn't possibly lose to Bunny. No one could. J did something horrible to my luck. At the end I brought out my money to pay my debts. J was watching TV.

'Oh no,' Bunny moaned when he saw my purse. 'Please don't pay me.'

'But I must. I lost.'

'For Crissake put that thing away. If you pay me the miserable thirty bucks it'll put ideas in his head and I might have to pay him. D'you know how much I owe him? Over $6,000.'

I slid the purse back into my bag.

'How d'you get on with a crusty bachelor like him?'

J was pretending not to hear.

'Oh we know each other,' I said casually.

'If he gets difficult you can always come and stay with me.' Words spoken in jest. But I thought how likely it was that I would come speeding down the winding road to this man looking for warmth, approval, even for an agent.

J pointed the Daimler towards Hamburger Hamlet. 'So how are you going to spend your evening?'

'I'll go to the hotel, I suppose.'

'I can't drive you there, alas. I haven't time. You can ring for a cab at the hamburger place.'

He let me out on the corner by the medical building. He was still very angry. I considered explaining more about the Tycoon but there was nothing to say. For a moment I did not want to be alone. The evening stretching away into the night. Not in Hollywood, not in my dream town. I think he saw the panic and that satisfied him so he handed me an electronic key. 'Now that opens the gate. Don't forget to close it. You can go back there and stay the night if you want. Don't lose it.'

And he spun the Daimler round and swooshed off for a front-runners' evening.

My throat felt tight and a black depression began to close in. I felt conspicuous as I approached the hamburger counter. Awkward in my movements, I kept bumping into people. They could see I was alone. And I was lonely. In my eyes my yellow dress had become my calling card, a low common one. I just wasn't good enough to go where he went. Yet how could I be good or amount to anything if

65

I didn't get an opportunity, and he had the monopoly on those? I drank a coffee and mineral water and called a cab. But when I came to pay for the drinks the purse was not in my bag. I thought it might have been dropped on the floor at my backgammon partner's house. His protestations had confused me. But then I saw the electric key was also gone. So I asked if they'd put the drinks on J's tab. He didn't have a tab. It was that kind of evening. Then the cab arrived. Cheeks blazing I asked the cab driver for a $5 loan so I could settle my bill. He was an immigrant and didn't speak a word of English. He did however know 'poor' when he saw it and drove off cursing in Spanish.

The terrace of Hamburger Hamlet had never had it so good. Poverty was unknown in Hollywood. It was like being at the movies for them. So the manager got involved. Yes, he knew J. No problem. J was a gentleman. The drinks were on the house.

Humbled, I walked along the strip to West Hollywood. No one walked in LA. You had a car. If you didn't, it meant you were poor, crazy, hopeless and shouldn't be there.

As I turned by The Source, a vegetarian restaurant, I saw Shelley Winters surrounded by people at one of the tables. Just seeing her cheered me up.

When I got to the hotel Mr Romance phoned and came right over so the evening wasn't going to be the sort J thought I should have. He wanted to know every nuance of 'the deal' evening. I threw the yellow dress into the rubbish. I hated it so much I tried to burn it. I went through my bag but only the purse and J's key had been lifted. I put on some trousers and a sweater and we went to Barney's Beanery, which James Dean had immortalised in the 1950s. It wasn't J's style. The music was too loud, the tables were too close and he couldn't get aloof with a female friend. Eating wasn't J's thing. He liked drinking but he did that anywhere. He'd take a couple of mouthfuls of food then fork the rest around on his plate. He said it came from his childhood. But then he'd had trouble with his mother as well. Mr Romance, far more easy going, ordered chilli beans and fresh apple juice and buckwheat cakes. He was intrigued by the disgraced dress. What adventure had I had in it?

The wrong sort.

Then he asked me about the Tycoon evening. What I described didn't amount to a deal. 'You've got to get in there again,' he said.

'Why me? Why am I so important, by the way?' I was beginning to see things from J's point of view. 'How can my talking about a book influence a man like that?'

'Because you turn him on.'

'Do I?'

'Well, you could. And he did ask for you.'

'Me?' I stopped eating the chilli beans and wanted some background. I never questioned lucky breaks but I was at an age when I could use a little perspective. 'So I wasn't just offered this by Mills and Boon, London?'

'They knew you were coming out. He'd been approached anyway about backing some movies because he wants in. He loves films. He's seen everything. The old ones, the silents. He's a real film buff. But before he'd talk to us he checked us out. When he heard your name he asked about you. We said you were coming to LA. So he said let her pitch it. So it's like you came at the time when he wanted to see you. D'you know what I mean?'

I did. But all that sort of thing belonged to José and Gerona.

'So he reacted to my name?'

'Well, it is Chaplin. Maybe he wants to get a little close to the family for some reason.'

Was that it? I could just see him getting a little close to the family. I could just see Oona going for that one.

'But you said something about he respected my judgement. Last night, you said it.'

'Look, you were a reader. You were already coming to LA. Simple. He respects you because he knows you write hardback books.' That concluded that, as far as he was concerned. So I asked how Tycoon made his money and Mr Romance said investments. Then I asked about Tycoon's wife.

'She died. Cancer. Years ago. She was a brilliant pianist. He never married again.'

I said I was sorry. Had the marriage been happy?

Colin didn't know. 'He tried everything to save her. Even took her to Lourdes in France. They had a son, Jamie. He was brilliant

67

too. Science. He was tipped to become very big in the space programme. He was only twenty-five or twenty-six. One night in New York he went into his apartment and shot himself through the head. Robert Hartman hasn't been lucky in his private life exactly.'

'Why did the son kill himself?'

'It was a couple of years ago. The hush on that was so big you could hear it.'

'How old is he?'

'Older than he looks.'

'Does he have lots of women?'

'Not that I know of. But he'd be discreet. I don't know anything about him but – well, there's no happiness for anyone there.'

So then I asked if he was straight. I meant legal.

'Look, I hear he has Robert Redford sitting in his kitchen. He finances hospitals. He's near the President. It's just he was Italian.'

'Is he good or bad?'

I'd asked the same question about José. Colin didn't know. He said good, because then I'd stay with the action. I thought selling this English romance book was not the real action.

'So he saw my name on the employees' list?'

'Why be so suspicious? You've heard of coincidence surely. He just reacted to the fact you were coming out here. Like pleased. But no big deal. If you hadn't been here I'd have pitched it.'

Chapter Eleven

I didn't do anything as structured as sightseeing. I just stood by Swabs drugstore or the Beverly Hills Hotel and took it from there. To sightsee would be greedy and impertinent. I had to treat this city as a lover would. I'd let the doors open and go through each one as they came. If they didn't open I'd go home. It was amazing how many people I met without introduction. It all seemed familiar and they'd say, 'I know your face don't I?' Or, 'I'd love to see your book. Send it to my agent.' But that was their way, welcoming. Apparently, and I didn't know this at the time, Hollywood did give you a big wide welcome and your phone rang and you went places because they were anxious to look you over. For three weeks to three months that happened. Then they lost interest and switched on to the next arrival and you were left to get on with it. If you survived it meant you had legs and you got respect. And then your phone started some serious ringing. To get to that stage could take three years.

I loved waking up back at the hotel with the sun streaming in, always reliable, filling the room. And I could hear birds and the cars, regular as the sea. And I'd have breakfast on the terrace – orange juice, waffles, maple syrup, bacon, hash brown, and lots of coffee. Then I'd have Californian fresh fruit salad and carrot cake. I did my exercises in the sun. Taking care of my body was a pleasure. I looked forward to a beauty realisable in Hollywood. I read a T.S. Eliot poem, 'Burnt Norton', especially the passage,

> What might have been and what has been
> Point to one end which is always present.
> Footfalls echo in the memory
> Down the passage which we did not take
> Towards the door we never opened
> Into the rose-garden.

It reminded me of Tycoon.

I was grateful because I knew this was a reliable time, secure. It was paid for by Tycoon and I didn't once think of José Tarres.

Colin Diamond and I got on well enough. We had similar surface pleasures, sitting by the pool seeing the ones who'd made it, listening in on conversations, improving our stamina, going for fast walks and workouts. We had ozone treatments and relaxation therapy. Also we giggled a lot. In fact there wasn't a lot to giggle about because Tycoon was away and hadn't exactly fallen in love with the chosen book. Well, if he had he was keeping it to himself like his sex life. Colin blamed me for the lack of enthusiasm. If I'd gone to the meeting straight away as arranged it would bave been taken on. Tycoon wouldn't let a thing as blatant as my rudeness go unpunished.

For a few days Colin kept me company. And then he decided I could write and that's when we really got close. Of course *Harriet Hunter* should be a film. He gave it to a Hollywood agent immediately. Twenty people would want to option it, said Colin. Acceptance would be no problem. He quoted the minimum price. Even I could live on that for five years. But he was seeing the world as it should be.

My purse had been returned to Le Parc. But not the electric key. I thought that was odd because the purse contained only money, nothing with an address. But then this was Hollywood.

When J found out I'd lost the electronic key to Casa Valentino the shit hit the fan. The pool glinted cruel and pale, reflecting his mood.

'You can't just lose a key, Patrice,' he said.

'Why not?'

'Because you of all people don't lose things. I'll have to have the electric system redone.' He sighed, glad he wasn't married to me.

'I'll pay for it.'

'It's not the money. It's such a bore.' Had he not warned me that my idiosyncratic habits would bring me trouble? Why was my handbag always open? Bags were meant to be fastened. Wearing trousers done up with a safety pin was trouble too.

I reminded him that that was years ago. He still saw me that way and the style would cause trouble. And no one in Hollywood wore blue jeans. That was definitely a thing of the past.

'But I don't wear them.'

'You look as though you might.'

'I do happen to like them, so I will wear them.' I tried to sound as though I still had an identity.

'Not with me you won't.'

And I was glad I wasn't married to him.

So we quarrelled, then went to bed. It worked because neither of us put anything on it that wasn't there. It was honest.

Afterwards there was tea and backgammon to fill the hollow of not loving each other. I told him his lost key wasn't a problem. After all, it didn't have a name or address on it. I was about to score on logic. He said, 'But they knew where to return your purse. There's something funny about that robbery. I'll just have to have the whole thing rewired but don't you worry about it.' Effortlessly he won the game, then peered into the bushes around the pool to see if the coyotes had arrived. Most people shot them. He gave them food.

We got on well but never talked about it. It was just that I wasn't going to get what he had. He already knew it. I was getting to know it.

His answering service would be crammed with messages. Sam Spiegel, the William Morris Agency, people in Washington, an ambassador or two. For him. He wanted me on the outside. The little matchgirl in the snow looking through the opulent restaurant

71

window where he sat eating the fat of the land. Did it increase his pleasure? The waif audience? Then he'd come out into the snow and give the underprivileged the fuck of her life. But matchgirls had their day. What would happen if I got on the inside?

I got Mr Romance.

Colin had a sense of balance. He could adjust to trouble and he wasn't overtly ambitious. He knew about my connection with J and wanted to meet him but sensed the unlikelihood of that and didn't ask. The Mills and Boon office was pushing for a deal and pissed off with me, but Colin kept that to himself and I was grateful. Like the rest of the movie colony, he was fuelled by enthusiasm so his response to my filmstar book had been over the top. There weren't twenty bids for the option nor was there any agent. But the companion to a declining moviestar had read it and wanted to meet me. Colin said this was a good connection. I was to meet her at the Actors' Studio during a professionals' class, 'moderated', as they called it, by Shelley Winters.

It was a lovely morning, the air and light made the buildings luminous. For a while they looked as though they were made of crystal, then the sun heated up the dust and the petrol fumes took over. I felt free. Like a butterfly risen from the grub stage, and I could have enjoyed anything. The only slight shadow was it reminded me of an earlier time when I was a kid and mad about José. I'd had one or two glorious days with him and I didn't want to think about it ever again. They'd make everything else just a rehearsal, second best.

The Actors' Studio – it had a temporary feel like a lot of LA buildings – was packed. An actress and actor were doing a scene from Strindberg's *Miss Julie*. I remembered it from RADA and could never get it right. Neither could this actress. Shelley Winters saw the scene, then took it apart. She took its head off the way the actor in the scene took the head off the bird. She stripped it to the bone and beyond. The actress wasn't feeling anything, certainly not hot sex and power and then suffering. Shelley Winters took everything apart, scene, script, Strindberg. She had a way of making something universal. She gave out a strength that stirred everybody and the whole theatre was chilled with excitement. She gave a magnificent performance. Afterwards, there was a total silence. It could have been huge applause, it was the same response. Then the actress burst into tears. The man next to me shouted kindly, 'It's all right, honey. Just cry. We can take your tears.' Wouldn't I have loved to hear that up at J's. Shelley tried to get the girl to see the scene pulsing with sexual desire. She wanted to get the girl feeling the heavy longing in her groin, or wherever Americans felt it. The girl didn't feel it. Had she ever? Shelley wanted to know. More tears. The girl was too on the spot, so Shelley deftly turned the action round to herself, sharing her life, showing herself to disadvantage, making the audience laugh. She gave a performance I'd not seen her do on any screen – and she had three Oscars.

The audience came out into the sunshine, shattered. It had been a moving, a memorable morning. I located the ageing filmstar's companion and gave permission for the book to be considered for option. Then Shelley Winters came out surrounded by actors. The companion knew her and after a while I got introduced and became part of a large group that went to The Source for lunch. Shelley said she wasn't eating. She was on a diet and ordered a hot drink with lemon. She had a companion too, an Australian girl, Helen, who looked after the letters and walked the dog.

Shelley turned her attention to me and asked if I considered she'd been too hard on the actress. I didn't know. I did know the part was hell.

She espied a waitress, attractive, dark and raunchy. She called her over and said she was casting a play for New York in the fall. The girl gave her phone number with speed. Every waitress was a star except no one had discovered them. Just as every taxi driver was a screenwriter. Shelley turned back to me and asked how I liked Hollywood. I said it was wonderful and meant it.

'But it's all estate agents these days. But if you like the real Hollywood go down to Santa Monica, the Mirimar Hotel. That's where they went for weekends in the old days. That's if they didn't have houses on the beach. It's all airline pilots and hostesses now but occasionally you get the atmosphere.' She looked at me, studied me. 'You'll get it.' She suggested other locales still tinged with the past.

Shelley was powerful, many faceted, highly intelligent, spontaneous, wonderfully articulate, talented. And lonely.

I went up to J's and said promptly, 'I just saw Shelley Winters.' 'Yes,' said J. 'So did I. Last night at the Academy dinner.' Always one ahead.

Chapter Twelve

Six days after our original meeting Tycoon called Mr Romance. I was a golden colour and definitely high on Hollywood. I put on my best clothes, Polo Lounge good, and Mr Romance drove me to Ocean Park.

'I'm not coming in because I've got to close a deal with the Stones.' I thought he meant 'the Rolling Stones'. He meant the Stones who owned cinemas but he let me go on thinking it was the pop group. Actually he wasn't going anywhere but Tycoon wasn't feeling social. Just me was enough.

'Now go in there and get it,' said Colin. 'I don't want to put pressure on but everyday here loses me business in New York.'

'But I'm no saleswoman. And if it's the Chaplins he's after, forget it. I draw no water there.'

'Give him an idea or two. Juice it up a bit. And I'll close the deal when you come out.'

'And if he wants the deal left open?'

'Then pack for London. Expenses will be a thing of the past.'

I saw my lovely peaceful suite at Le Parc slipping away like an ocean liner out to sea, with a different set of passengers.

'Think positive.'

I remembered Tycoon called me Patricia. My name on company files was surely Patrice. It was my usual writer's name. Colin wasn't too interested in that. He made my name more usual. Where was the mystery? It could be worse. He could have called me Pat.

I went through the security performance. A different secretary took me to the penthouse door. Like the others, she stayed outside.

He was beautifully dressed in a black suit. He'd been East, which meant New York, on business. He poured me a Coke and asked what I'd been doing. I mentioned the book going to the agent.

'He's not bad,' he said thoughtfully.

He was in fact one of the top agents. 'But it didn't take.'

He lifted the phone. 'Let's try again.' He said the agency name and waited for it to connect. He asked for the reluctant agent then spoke another language. It turned out to be Yiddish. It was a short communication. When he hung up he said, 'You've got your agent back.'

So I thanked him.

He asked how my friend was, the one who treated me like Cinderella.

'He's doing *Quark*, isn't he?' he said.

So he had an ear to the ground. He'd be asking to meet him next.

'I'd like to meet him.'

The idea appalled me.

'So let's have lunch. Shall we go to the Polo Lounge?' His voice was very level. 'Tomorrow? Noon? I'll book the table.'

It was an ironic choice of lunch place and I didn't like it. J would like it less. Crumpled strays like me didn't get in there. Tycoon was watching me. He had all the charm in the world. But weren't these the dangerous ones? It's what went on under the charm you had to watch.

Delicately I put together a description of J's life, of how it was dictated by movie-making needs. It wasn't really his own. I described a life J would no doubt have been delighted to have.

'Oh really.' He smiled, amused. A childlike amusement. He was quite unique, the Tycoon. How was it no one in this city of beauties had captured him?

76

'I wouldn't have thought preparing a movie from a trash book like *Quark* would be so arduous.'

'Look, to be honest, I don't think I'm the best person to ask him. Ideas coming from me don't usually – well, prosper.'

'So he doesn't do what pleases you?'

'Exactly,' I said without thinking.

'Then he is hardly a good person for you.'

'No but he's what I've got.' Quick as a flash. I was proud of that.

'You don't have to spend the rest of your life surviving.'

So I asked what else could I do.

'Try living.'

I was suspicious of advice, especially from wealthy people. Surviving was the right thing for me and I didn't want anyone taking it away.

'Yet J must be very pleased to have you. After all he won't meet many like you.'

'How d'you mean?'

'Well you're experienced but still rather childish. Which can be fun. You're perceptive, witty, entertaining. I should think that's rare out here.'

He'd come too close.

His tone changed. 'Well, propose it,' he said practically. 'I think he'll come.'

To a different rendevouz possibly. To the Polo Lounge, never. We'd spent some part of every day scrapping about the subject. The Polo Lounge was synonymous with rejection, the unstable yellow dress, humiliation, for me. For J, it was the whip.

Tycoon took off his jacket and lay back on one of the sofas. And that's when I wanted to touch him, to hold him, caress him. So I said, 'Excuse me, Mr Hartman, but are you going to take on this book?'

'Which book?' Catlike, about to pounce.

'The romance book.'

'What about *your* book?'

He even sounded provocative. I thought I was being tested. 'I'm sure if it appealed to you that much I wouldn't have to try and sell it to you.'

'Exactly.' His eyes were on me now. They were black and

77

disquieting. They belonged to a cruel race, a desert people. Whatever J said, this man was no punter. The eyes showed high intelligence, quick thinking. They weren't showing passion because there was nothing to get passionate about. Unfortunately. The silences bothered me. Also I didn't know what was going to happen. I could be put out again or given a meal or a deal or I could end up in bed with him.

I tried to bring some control into what happened so asked about his work.

'Do you work continuously?'

He nodded.

'Are you very rich?''

'I make other people very rich.'

I was getting so reckless my next question was going to be, 'Do you want me?' I thought my mood was due to the high temperature outside and the chill of the air-conditioning inside. Or I was very affected by him. Emotional excitement was always registered in me by dramatic temperature change. It wasn't the ice of 'in love', more the shiver of sexual hunger. He leaned close and I thought he was going to touch me. And then José came back. I thought, what an unfortunate time for him to come so strongly into my mind. He felt so close he could have been in the room. José and I took each other high, higher – we got high in the same way. His ideas, my enthusiasm, his charm, my energy. We'd go by boat to Istanbul and live by our wits by the sea or we'd open a nightclub or make a film. And I'd believe him and go back to London and work like shit to get the money together and of course I never did, because money is a very hard thing to get together. No, the highs were better than that. When we met we were the only people in the world. He made me special. When he wasn't there I was a nothing, a worm crawling along the gutter, ignored. The memory of him forbade me to belong to anyone else in that way.

'I listen to a hundred ideas a day,' Tycoon was saying. 'If you have one that's viable I'll listen.'

'Why don't the secretaries come in here?'

'Because I dislike their perfume.'

He got up and walked around me, disturbingly close. I wasn't

78

wearing perfume. A touch of Howard Hughes perhaps? Or was he kidding?

'So you've been to Gerona too?' I said.

'Only in passing.'

'Which years?'

His journeys started back in the 1950s and could have coincided with mine.

'It must have made an impression on you. Have you been back?'

'I think you should have been an actress, Patricia. Your face. You're so photogenic.'

I thought that was a strange way to answer.

'It's too late now.'

He agreed with that. He said he had to work. As I left I saw files by the door, the names of companies on each. He said he'd see me at noon tomorrow in the Polo Lounge. I asked if he had a number where I could reach him. I had no confidence in this meeting. He felt in his pocket and chose a card. 'Rodeo Productions' and an address in Beverly Hills. Two phone numbers.

His eyes were depthless, almost hypnotic. I said goodbye. I wouldn't like to tangle with that, I said to myself. I'd never be the same again.

I went back to the hotel and reread the T.S. Eliot poem, about the rose-garden. But I kept seeing his eyes. And the poem reminded me of him.

Chapter Thirteen

At first J distrusted the invitation and blamed me for bringing it. He covered it with ridicule. Then he said, 'But at least you'll get to the Polo Lounge.'

'So you'll come?'

'You go.' He was waiting to have a new electronic system put in and was not in a good mood. Also the immigrant cleaner had broken a piece of the tea-set. Although no linguist, the girl understood enough American to get the hang of Mr J. Her instincts did the rest. She looked so fearful before she even touched a broomhandle, I was sure she prayed before cleaning up for him. He'd taught her that china was not something to dust or even touch. He'd mimed it for her, written notes, he'd even overseen her work. This china you do not touch! And like Eve in the garden she had to go for the forbidden. Curious, rebellious, she'd picked up a saucer, a cup cautiously, expecting some mystical change. Then she'd seen J's reflection in the pool. It seemed to be looking at her. In fact he was chastising the pool cleaner, another immigrant. The girl smashed the saucer.

J was very drawn to wildlife. A bat, a spider, a rat were beautiful creatures to him. He even protected scorpions and would have set up a fund for the continuation of their species. The pool cleaner could say yes and no. He didn't understand emotions, however. When J took him to the spider swinging theatrically in a huge web in the corner of the pool and shook him and made gestures – 'No touch. Leave alone – ' the cleaner had got it wrong. J did some work on a script then sauntered out for a swim. The pool had been drained, cleaned and refilled. The sky made it blue. The sides were clean, tiles gleaming. The spider had gone. So J took the man by his skinny arm and propelled him to the corner and pointed, 'No spider. No spider.'

The man seemed pleased. 'Spider all gone, sir.'

'But I wanted it left alone. I specifically asked you not to touch it.'

The man had understood that J was scared of spiders. J had warned him, spiders dangerous. So he, brave Vietnamese, had done away with J's childish fear. J fired him on the spot. Then he remembered he was a civilised, privileged human being and voted Left. Underprivileged people could be included in his passion for wildlife. He gave the man his job back and said next time forget the pool and clean the car. J hated cars. And now the girl had smashed the china. I stayed out of it.

I did say spiders were not attractive exactly. The look he gave me assured me he'd rather have one on the chair than me. I said I'd written about one in *Harriet Hunter*.

'No you haven't. You don't understand spiders. You write about them badly. No spider could behave as you describe in that book. You make it behave like one of your business contacts.' He loved that one. 'It'll be dining in the Polo Lounge next.'

So I said I'd observed a spider in an Oxford field behaving as I'd described. He replied he'd studied them for years. What did I know? I didn't have the patience or the attunement even to perceive a spider correctly. So I said he should maybe marry one and give me a break. The quarrel was not about spiders.

'Not only is my yellow dress a bow-wow not fit to exist in Hollywood but I don't even have the sense to appreciate spiders. I lose at backgammon and my business associates are a joke.'

'Never put yourself down, honey. Leave it to others.'

So I threw his one truly beloved possession into the pool. He watched the backgammon board flounder then start to drown. It was such a shocking event, neither of us could say a thing. Then he took off his clothes, dived in and saved it. The cold water revived his mood. He apologised. He said he'd behaved irrationally. Maybe my spider had behaved in an untypical way. Perhaps it was the effect of all that toxic spraying they did in the English countryside. Then he buried the broken china in the wastebin. Some days were not lucky for possessions. I was glad I didn't have any.

The next morning J prepared to work. The immigrant cleaners came and went, chattering continually. What they made of us I couldn't say. Safe behind their secret talk they could criticise, ridicule, gossip. They made me feel awkward because I wasn't doing anything, just sitting in the sun by the pool. Then one of the men gave me a huge wink. It was like an insect closing down, then opening its wing. J, never happy if his guests were pally with the help, came outside.

'Another lovely day. Up here. They've got smog.' He pointed to the coast and all the duds who thought it smart to live in Malibu and, more pertinently, Ocean Park. 'You can't breathe the air down there.'

'Well, if it wasn't for you I could be living down there.' The sky might be clear but the clouds were rolling in domestically.

'You could indeed. So what are you up to today?'

'I have to see an agent,' I said absentmindedly.

'Have to?' he didn't like the sound of that.

'About my book.'

J lit a cigarette. The paws were a bit shaky. I suspected a hangover. 'What book is this?''

'The one I wanted you to show to Lauren Bacall.'

He shook his head, looked wise. 'Betty wouldn't go for that. Anyway she's doing a stage show.'

I told him the agent's name and asked if he'd heard of him.

'I think I have. Yes, he's been mentioned.'

He was one of the top five but J wasn't telling me. Now his world and mine were drawing closer. He suggested driving down to Palm Springs. 'The air is good there. Or we could go to Mexico.' He pointed out I was the mother of two and my vacation couldn't go on for ever.

'But we are invited to the Polo Lounge for lunch. Shouldn't we do that first?'

'That's a little implausible. Who is this person exactly? A novelette printer?'

'You never see my friends. Oh no. You're a fucking snob. What do I have to do to please you? Get up a party of spiders?'

'You used to be fun. Perhaps the air here doesn't suit you. It doesn't everyone.'

I got edgy. Disapproval didn't suit me, not too much of it. I could see why his three marriages had gone down the plug.

'Why don't you have a drink? His voice was now silky.

'Oh that's a great thing to suggest to an alcoholic.'

'You were never an alcoholic, Patrice.' He shook his head sagely. 'I never believed that myself. I admire, of course, the way you gave up. But you take it too far as usual. You should drink something. A beer. Now a beer isn't a drink. It's not alcoholic.'

'What's the problem, babe? Having trouble drinking alone?'

He picked me up and swung me into the pool. The cleaners laughed and stamped their feet. When I got out of the water I could hear him inside typing. Beautiful stray birds visited the pool and preened themselves. I hung out my clothes to dry and the cleaners commented on my naked body. J's phone rang constantly. He blamed himself for the short bout of unpleasantness and wanted to make it up to me. At 11.30 he came to the poolside and said to get ready. 'We'll go and meet your friend. I've checked with a couple of people. They seem to know of him.'

He'd obviously heard how rich Robert Hartman was. Even someone in J's position couldn't snub the very rich.

He made some sneering remarks as he dressed. I could see he couldn't help it. 'I expect he'll be overdressed, don't you? So I'll keep it down. Let him have his fun. He'll order eggs benedict of course. Those types do.'

'So you've never met him, but you already dislike him.'

'Not at all. He'll turn out to be a hard boy from Chicago washing money in the film business. I bet you ten dollars he orders eggs benedict. He'll have checked it out. That's the thing you see for those who don't know. He'll overtip too. You'll see.'

'Well it sounds like your idea of a good time.'

'I must say you do bring me colour. I'd never meet these people but for you.'

He thought up some more predictions on the winding drive down to the Beverly Hills Hotel. The attendants stowed his car away as smooth as a hand into a glove. Just as smoothly J was bowed into the cool of the foyer.

Five people greeted him. Two were top agents, he said. I figured that was for my benefit. They were probably real-estate brokers but I didn't get to meet them.

'You should have worn your yellow dress. He might have liked that. It might have moved him.'

'D'you know something, sweetie, and I'll bet you ten bucks on this. If I was married to you I'd kill you.'

'That's no way to talk. Not when we're about to have lunch with a Chicago gangster.'

'Why do you say things like that? Do you get pleasure out of it?'

He shrugged, didn't like being challenged.

'How does it make you feel to insult me?'

'Darling, I'm trying to educate you. Now where's your friend from the East? I take it I won't get shot if we don't get on?'

'D'you want it this way or d'you want a big fight?'

He stopped, intrigued, because he liked a bit of brutal. It was there in my voice from the old bad days, when there wasn't too much money around and I was sleeping on the Métro steps in Pigalle.

'Or d'you want me playing the matchgirl? Or just doing nothing and sucking your cock? What?'

The waiters were getting an earful. I'd never seen so many gathered around us.

'Of course I might write a script and get an Oscar.'

His eyes flicked over me. Had the other wives been ambitious too? Had they used him? His eyes assured me a lot had gone wrong in the past.

'I want the best for you.' And he took my hand and squeezed it. 'Having you around is like having a puppy. I give it the best of care

84

and food and love and conditions, yet it lopes out to the alleyways and comes back with a dead rat.'

I had to laugh at that one.

The head waiter pushed through the eavesdroppers to say our host was already seated and waiting.

'You need a father for your children,' said J.

'Come and meet him.' I indicated the Polo Lounge.

J wouldn't let go of my hand. 'You never know when to stop, do you?' His eyes had settled down now. Like his pool they reflected the past. The three wives had been there, the stinging fights, the failure.

We were led to the best table where a huge Irishman with a badly set broken nose was already buttering a pile of teacakes. He stood up. Six foot four, a ruddy face, beaming smile. No roughneck this one. All of it to be taken seriously. J greeted him, not a sneer in sight.

'Delighted to have you at my table, Mr J, and little Miss Chaplin.'

The waiter was there quicker than he could spit and we got drinks ordered and the menu. I supposed this was a partner, even a bodyguard. J called him Mr Hartman and he didn't object. J was immensely pleased. He had proof now that my sense of perception was screwy. How could this type have Italian blood and look elegant?

When Irish started his order J nudged me. 'Waffles, bacon, two eggs over easy, hash and bring some more juice.'

So I ordered the eggs benedict.

J, amused, chose kedgeree.

Irish told J how much he admired his films. He asked about *Quark* and seemed to know as much as J did, like where the money was coming from and who would be the likely stars and what points J made in the film. Irish told J he was a legend. He also liked J's manners and style and said so. 'You can't beat a public school upbringing.' Then it was my turn so it was a short one. I was a talented writer, a good companion and it must be a privilege for J to know me. We got into the first course. J ordered another whiskey. Irish wasn't drinking. J asked about his life. Irish invested money for corporations and made a profit. When he ceased to make a profit he'd be on the breadline. That was a joke and we all laughed.

'Or potatoes, where I come from.' He had offices in every capital city in the free world and listed some of the companies he held stock in. He'd now got J's interest. 'We're one happy family,' he told J. 'We're in constant touch. That's the secret. No *longueurs* for them to make mistakes in.'

'But surely communication is difficult,' I cut in. 'They're all on different time, these cities. Or do you rely on a telex, Mr Hartman?' I was interested to see how he'd juggle that one.

'No, sir. I get up at 5.00 a.m. and run for ten miles. My business life starts at a quarter of six, never later. I never do business with a man who doesn't take calls by 6.00 a.m. If he's still asleep he's no good to me.'

He had all the same lines as Tycoon. If he was the real one, who was the Mediterranean guy cooking in the penthouse kitchen? J asked about Irish's advance in Hollywood. Irish quoted the films they were backing, the budgets, the stars they favoured, the audiences they'd pull and the profit at the end of the day. It was all worked out. Nothing arthouse about this lot. Had Irish kidnapped the real Tycoon? Did he want one day of glory? Didn't mental patients want to be doctors? Get the white coat on and impress the visitors. They always slipped up. Irish wasn't doing any of that. He called for the cheque and said he wanted to do business with J one of these days. He gave him a card. Rodeo Productions. J did not give him his phone number. Irish said he was privileged to meet him and we left.

Irish bowed low over my hand and told me again what a talented little lady I was. His car came first, a huge black job. The number plate, IRISH ONE, amused J. I waited until Irish got behind the wheel then ran forward and held on to the window.

'Who are you?'

He started the engine. 'Just a nice guy who likes you and your friend.'

'But you're not Robert Hartman.'

He chewed gum and that made him look brutal. 'In this town you can be anything you want, honey.' And he drove off fast.

J was talking to a group of English film people who had come over for the Oscars. Invitations for dinner and parties were flying in all directions. After J had filled his dancecard for the week we drove to a huge health store where he spent seventy- five bucks on health products – creams, vitamin pills, fruit juice, treatments – to placate me. I loved health stores. They promised me a better future.

Then we whizzed back up into the hills.

'He's nice, your friend. A lot of goodwill, all bogus. But he's keen.'

'He seemed to want to do business with you.'

'Well, we'll see. Let's see about that. Like I said, there's plenty of people in this town offering things they don't have to offer.'

I thought for once he might be right.

'But he didn't have eggs benedict.'

'No, he chose what he enjoys. I liked that about him. Your descriptions of people are terrible. No wonder your writing is – well, it stays in England.'

I let that one pass. He gave me the eggs benedict bet. Ten bucks. He could afford to pay his losses.

'D'you think you'll see him again?' I asked.

'Nope. He just wanted to look me over for some reason.'

I tried to phone Mr Romance. Then I tried the Rodeo Productions office on Rodeo Drive. Mr Hartman was not available. Would I leave a message. I didn't think they'd understand what I had to say.

Chapter Fourteen

Everyone's Hollywood is different. I sniffed out the old atmospheres. They hovered by drugstores, in hotel foyers, at intersections, in the big houses amongst the sunbright trees in Bel Air. The studios were sad places because it was all being dismantled. I couldn't bear to hear about the ludicrous auction sales of the props, costumes and personal belongings. But what was I going to do? Start a movie town museum? Shelley Winters had directed me to the Mirimar Hotel in Santa Monica. It was transformed by the demands of the 1970s. I couldn't blame the airline hostesses and pilots for staying there. But you could see the way it had been if you knew how to look.

Shelley had heard I played backgammon and wanted a game so I went to one of her houses in Beverly Hills.

Her companion Helen made tea and as I played backgammon with Shelley she told me some of her anecdotes. She told them precisely, with a merciless humour. She was a good mimic. Also she was real Hollywood. We got on but I knew it was just a momentary thing, a sudden friendship like a rather lovely house flower. It would do one season.

Shelley's backgammon was sometimes original, which helped her to win. I didn't mind because I was high on nostalgia. She was the umbilical cord to all that I'd dreamed of and obviously missed.

When she was tired of winning, she lifted down a huge pile of manuscript. 'My life story, the first part from forty-five to fifty-six. Could you edit it for me?'

The pile was nearly as tall as her and that was only the first years. I never turned down a job but on this occasion I really did think a professional was needed. She wanted it all in. Helen was supposed to help. I could see by Helen's drawn looks, that had been downhill. How did you try and take a piece of Shelley Winters' life away? She described herself as a Jewish mama. Before that she'd played hookers, before that victims. She'd given her Oscar for *The Diary of Anne Frank* to the town where Anne Frank had lived. She'd made the journey herself and placed it there. She'd do a lot for a cause if she believed in it. Which got us talking about Jewish subjects and I mentioned Gerona. She was surprised to hear that it had a Jewish past. So she got out some books and that's when I discovered Gerona had been the centre of Jewish mysticism, the cabbala, in the thirteenth century. The great cabbalist and scholar Nachmanides had lived there. The book gave other accounts of Gerona mystics and how the nucleus came to an end with the Expulsion in 1492. I got no clear idea what cabbala was. Shelley said it was mentioned in Lawrence Durrell's books. It was a secret society concerned with human elevation. Then we got on to less sacred subjects, her next film, my writing career. She'd heard good reports of my book about the vanished filmstar.

'You should have shown it to me first.'

Delicately I suggested she wasn't right for the part.

'I realise that but nor is she. I could have told you who is. Bankable is a horrible work but that's what you need.'

I asked if she knew Robert Hartman. He'd passed through Gerona too.

She wasn't sure of the name. So I said he wanted in in Hollywood.

'Oh there's so many of them from out of town. Who knows where they come from? Some of them own shoe shops and filling stations. Or they've got television studios or oil wells – so they say.

It's funny money, a lot of it. Who knows where it comes from? They know nothing about making movies. Gone are the days of Zanuck and Jack Warner and Louis Mayer.'

She was interested in me because she thought I might have something to offer and she'd like to see it first. I liked her because she filled me with Hollywood. As I left, she said, 'So you've stayed where they practised cabbala. That must have a strong atmosphere. I expect you came under its influence. No wonder you write books about the place.'

J said he'd known Shelley when she started. She'd made a film in Italy and was very glamorous and sexy and not eating much. That was the image. But when she returned to the States the real Shelley showed through. The Jewish mama who liked eating, got fat, not too much make-up. The glamour was something on the set.

'Well at least that won't happen with us,' I assured him. 'You've seen me at my worst.'

'No, you've done well. You've survived.' He stroked my hand, encouraging me. The jealous pool hissed and gurgled.

'Don't you get scared being up here alone?' I was thinking of the Manson murders.

It wasn't part of his make-up. Scared came in when someone tried to live with him. He said even the best host gets tired of his guests. He was far from being the best host or I the best guest, so I moved back to Le Parc. And yet we did like one another. But it was as though a tiger were dating a mouse.

The reluctant agent called me to come for a talk. It went wrong immediately. I was wearing delicate high-heeled shoes and a black imitation fur coat. I thought he was still sitting behind his desk. 'Don't bother. Don't get up,' I said. Then I realised he was up. His hand came out and shook mine. Then he climbed on to his seat and his little legs hung down. He was shorter than his main superstar client which was no doubt why he was his agent. It was a bad start. It got worse. He said the book was fine but didn't I know Billy Wilder was going to set up a movie about a filmstar, *Fedora*. If it rolled it would kill mine dead. He'd still show the book around. 'You know some big company.'

'Meaning?'

'Robert Hartman.'

'Is he in movies?'

'He's in everything.' He fingered the fabric of my coat and another mistake was on its way. 'You may come from a famous family but I know good fur when I see it. My wife's father is the top furrier in Manhattan. What I don't know about furs you could stick in a thimble. And I know right now I'm looking at one hell of a beaver lamb. Four thousand bucks minimum. Right?'

So I should have kept my mouth shut. So I said, 'Wrong. It actually cost £24. It's imitation fur. Acrylic.' I showed him the label. He didn't move. He looked as though he was holding on to quite a lot of aggression.

Then he said, 'When it rains I'd be careful. I bet it smells like skunk.'

I was no soothsayer but I didn't think a lot of work would come to me from that office.

Back at Le Parc, Colin was waiting with gloomy news. 'The deal's off. So you pack and I go back to New York.'

I told him about the switch in the Polo Lounge. He had no answer for that. The Mr Hartman he dealt with was the slim Mediterranean type who lived alone and cooked his own meals. So I asked why the deal was off and Colin didn't know. 'He just didn't go for it. Or something else came up. Who knows with these guys. We're out.'

'I suppose it's because I was discourteous the first day.'

'It doesn't matter. We got to be friends, so something came out of it.'

I told him about the agent, how he didn't want me, then Tycoon got busy on the phone so he did.

'There's no mystery about it. Robert Hartman put in their biggest star and his percent keeps the agency going so they owe Robert Hartman one. If you come to New York look me up.' He wrote his address and phone number and gave a bright smile. He believed in positive. It was his religion.

I started to pack then stood on the terrace and watched the lights come on and the cars streaming along The Strip. In LA I felt free because a lot of colour and light came in, new ideas and sensations. I had to make it work because this was what I'd left José Tarres for.

I could be sitting in a fisherman's house in Puerta de la Selva eating sardines and bread with José, instead of looking out at West Hollywood. I could be having his child instead of sleeping alone. It had to work. The phone rang and Helen, Shelley's assistant, was coming to pick me up right away. Shelley wanted dinner in Joe Allan's. I said I had things to do.

Helen said, 'Not tonight. Do them with us.'

Within five minutes they were there with the dog and we drove to the restaurant. The dog was let in because it belonged to Shelley Winters. The table was already lined with her friends and some studio executives. I thought it was some kind of occasion, except that I was sitting at the top of the table. Maybe it was because I was a stranger. Sheley entertained a dozen people effortlessly.

The restaurant was packed and Helen pointed out the celebrities. J wasn't among them because he was doing something important with Elizabeth or Warren. I told Helen I'd have to move from Le Parc. A deal had gone down. She was sure absolutely that Shelley would let me stay in her other house in the Canyons. She was sure too my book would be optioned by the declining filmstar, although unsuitable. 'She can't act,' she said. 'And she's getting to the age where it matters.'

Helen had no history. She just said she was Australian and worked for Shelley.

'But you know Colin Diamond, don't you?'

'He's a good friend.' She said nothing about herself.

I was fairly relaxed when out of the kitchen came a line of singing waiters. The one in the front carried a small cake with candles on. They sang 'Happy Birthday'. How sorry I felt for the recipient of that little ceremony. The whole restaurant joined in and the dog howled. The waiters came nearer, up to our table, up to me. The cake was put under my nose and the song came to an end with a crescendo of cheers. As I blew out the candles, my face scarlet, I remembered it was my birthday. I'd forgotten things like that. Shelley hadn't.

'You let it out the other day, saying your zodiac sign,' said Helen. 'Last day of Aries, Hitler's birthday. Shelley didn't want you to be alone in the hotel. And she lined up these guys' – she indicated the executives – 'because they could be helpful to you.'

I felt touched. I was nobody, a stranger. My name wasn't my own. She was going to get nothing out of it. But she took the time and cared enough to celebrate an anonymous person's birthday.

Chapter Fifteen

When I got back from the birthday dinner it was after 11.00 p.m. LA shut down early. I called my kids in London. They were getting up for school, or said they were, and sounded OK. Then Chris said, 'Mum, when are you coming home?' It was there, in his voice, the insecurity. I said I'd come straight back. Then the man I lived with came to the phone and said the kids were fine. No panic. But I knew panic when I heard it. It was in Chris's voice. I said I was coming home.

I'd been in Hollywood thirteen days and felt transformed. I'd have stayed on, something would have come up. I was sure of that. But I was Chris's security. That came first. Without me even having to think about it. So I packed my stuff and said I'd be leaving the next day. The receptionist said the bill was taken care of. However I had to settle my phone bill. Within five minutes Tycoon called. So they'd told him I was off.

'Were you going without saying goodbye?'

'You're hard to reach, Mr Hartman.' I would have left a note for him at the desk.

'Come and have a Coke. I'll send a car for you.'

It was 11.25. 'I thought you went to bed at nine?'

He laughed. 'Only when I don't want to see people.'

He was waiting by his security door. No guards tonight. He took me along the circular passageway to the penthouse and I said, 'Where do you really live?'

'Why?'

'I'm sure you don't live here.'

'On planes.' He gave a sensual shrug, the sort that would have a Mills and Boon heroine come over funny.

'The sky gypsy,' I said.

'Hardly. I always know where I'm going and what I'll find. But it would make a great romance title. You should sell it to them.'

He got inside and poured the Coke. 'So you're going home.'

'I have to. My children are just kids and I'm divorced. The usual story.'

'The romance book won't work. I've thought about it.'

'Perhaps I pitched it wrong.'

'It's nothing to do with you. You can't put that sort of thing up on the screen because it's fantasy. A woman reads the book and she has a fantasy. It's her own. Suits her tastes. The books sell because they arouse the woman who then gets off on her own stuff. Put it on the screen and it's flat. It's too obvious. And the men won't go for it. They don't read those books but they do take women to the cinema and pay for the tickets.'

'The books sell well,' I said, ridiculously loyal.

'Let them. Why lose money turning them into something they're not?'

I thought he had a point. And in fact not one of the titles ever was made for cinema.

He opened some wine and ate a cucumber sandwich. He indicated for me to sit beside him on the long black sofa. I felt nervous because I wanted him but I had to go home so I didn't want to get involved. 'I missed you the other day. The stand-in wasn't so much fun.'

Still eating, he switched on a video and there was J looking swell and swanky and me – well, you always hate the way you look unless

95

you're Sophia Loren – and then Irish eating as though it was his last chance. He had it all on tape.

'Why?'

'I wanted to see J, I told you.'

'Why?'

He had a symphony of shrugs. This one showed disinterest. 'He wouldn't like me either. I come from the wrong side of the tracks.'

So I wondered why he wanted to see J in the first place.

He finished the sandwich and wiped his mouth and hands on an Irish linen napkin. He chose a piece of fruit from the copper bowl. He was dressed in black, black jacket, high-neck sweater. 'I've always heard good things about him. I thought I'd respect him. I do, his work, usually.'

'But why send the other guy?'

'Because I knew he didn't like me.' He accentuated the 'knew'.

'He's never met you.'

He threw J's lost electronic key on to the low table. 'I'm into bugs as well.'

'Bugs? Insects you mean?' Not another spider lover.

'Surveillance, Patricia.' He spun the key on the table. He'd used that to shake down J's life. Through the key he'd somehow got linked with Casa Valentino. He'd heard everything, the lot. I wondered if he'd got visuals off the key. Frantically I tried to remember how often I'd gone to bed with J since the theft. And how I looked. If he had the Polo Lounge in full colour why not the house?

'I think meeting J on celluloid is better, don't you? That's how he'd like to be seen. It suits him best, I think.'

I was now, as the love victims in Mills and Boon land say, out of my depth, up the Suwanee. I thought Robert Hartman was unscrupulous. I knew this was very unusual but I could not show any emotion or anger.

'I know this is very simple-minded, but how did you get the key?'

'I had it removed from your handbag in the hamburger place. I was curious about J. I suppose if you reach a certain point you want to know about people.'

'You want to be accepted, you mean?'

96

'Not accepted. To know about people you've only heard about and suppose are admirable. But he's not very nice. Elitist.'

'Did you video his house?'

'No.' A silence.

'But you listened to the conversations?'

He gestured some sort of agreement and the wedding ring sparkled.

'Did the Polo Lounge video come off this?' I pointed to the key.

'No, of course not. My stand-in was wired up. We can do all sorts of extremely sensitive surveillance these days.'

There were one or two scenes at J's house I dreaded him having seen. But the worst was the way I looked first thing in the morning with no make-up.

'So that's why you picked me. Because I'm J's mistress?'

'Are you?' His eyes opened with surprise.

'I guess you've got all that on video.' I got up ready to go. I suppose I felt exploited. He watched me with real interest and he could certainly work up an atmosphere. Of course I should be angry but I didn't want to have any emotions in front of him. My reaction could wait till I was alone. Never be vulnerable around potentially dangerous people. I'd learned that living with my mother.

He picked up the electronic key and threw it at me. I caught it, put it in my bag. 'Have you got a lot of stand-ins? We could really have some fun.'

'How did you get off drink, Patrica?'

'I'm sure you wouldn't be interested.'

'I wouldn't ask if I wasn't.'

So I told him about Doctor Strigner and how the system did work. Doctor Strigner had saved my life and if this well-heeled surveillance specialist wanted to send him patients that was fine. I just hoped Doctor Strigner would charge double. I told him about the hypnotic exercise and how you did it yourself several times a day and when you stopped drinking there was no withdrawal. Drink was in the universe but somehow you never saw it. It had nothing to do with my life. What made J's eyes glaze interested Tycoon.

'Do you know someone with that problem?' I asked.

97

'I'm interested in you. You've been through a lot and you've come through it. People getting through adversity always interests me.'

He sounded as though he knew too much about my life. He couldn't have got all that from a simple look down the Mills and Boon employees' list.

'Why did you want to meet me?'

'Perhaps our paths have crossed. What do you think?'

I was sure I'd never seen him. Even drunk I'd have remembered him.

'I remembered your name. It was you I wanted to see. Not J. You can do better than him. You haven't gone through all that to end up listening to put-down all day. D'you know why he does it? You're competition. He's jealous.'

Mills and Boon fashion he looked into my eyes deeply then held out his hand. 'Have a good journey back. We'll be in touch.'

And in true Mills and Boon fashion we didn't fall from grace. Our goodbye was chaste. He walked with me to the public corridors, didn't enter them himself, didn't want to see the people.

'Goodbye, Patricia.'

Patricia. He'd given me back my name.

Chapter Sixteen

When I got to J's house to say goodbye the Daimler was reversing towards the high electronic gates. 'Get in. I've got to drop a casting note off at the Beverly Hills.' The gates swung open, swung shut. I gave him the lost key.

'Someone found it at the hotel. They didn't know who it belonged to.'

'Well that's a bore because I've just gone to some expense installing a new system. All I can say is you're not lucky with keys.'

As it was my last day he didn't want to quarrel. He suggested a drink in the Polo Lounge. We'd been quite close if a little scrappy during my visit. 'I'll be over before the summer,' he promised. 'And next time you come here make sure you have a real holiday.'

He made me wait in the foyer while he swept up to the reception desk. He asked for the manager who appeared before he'd even finished the sentence.

'Mr J, sir.'

J's voice was low as he mentioned a girl, an English girl. I crept forward pretending to watch the florist freshening up the dahlias. I realised the casting was not the celluloid variety. 'So I thought

99

maybe she could work in the reception. She's very presentable and all that.'

'Absolutely, sir, Mr J. But the position is quite filled at the moment. But we could keep her phone number certainly.'

J's voice became a low growl like an amorous tiger. The heavy gold cigarette case was out. He chose a cigarette and snapped it shut. The manager swung forward, lighter flaring, but J preferred his own, a chunky gold type with status like the case. There was a lot of gold about. 'But I've already intimated to the girl that she could work here.' Then he mentioned the names of some of the famous he was bringing for dinner, the following week. They, it seemed would be gratified to see this girl sitting in reception. Something came up about the obligatory green card. J continued his strange bargaining. It seemed he was trying to get a fourteen-year-old girl a job because of favours she'd done or was prepared to do.

The manager's face belonged at a funeral. It was now in folds of grief, his eyes like lost dollars remembering all the little gratuities this well-known gentleman had bestowed on not just the staff but him personally. I missed the rest of it because the declining filmstar and her companion came out of the Polo Lounge and greeted me warmly. She wanted to option the book and I was very pleased but thought I should keep it to myself. J would throw buckets of cold water over that one. I explained I was getting a plane to London so could my agent handle the deal. Ageing filmstar said she'd talk to him.

J was now beside us and kissed filmstar's cheek and said she looked better than the last time he saw her. He was never fulsome with his compliments. She mentioned *Quark*, hungry for a part. J promised to call her, then took my arm and led me to a number two table. No flutter of notes today.

'What's all that about? She wants to option your book?'

I closed my eyes, resigned. He knew everything except that Robert Hartman wasn't Irish.

'Waste of time.' His eyes green and candid, a lovely green. 'Not bankable. And she won't give you anything much for it.'

'So what was all that about rearranging the foyer? Employing girls under age?'

'Why not?' He tossed the menu to one side to make room for the real business – drinking. 'She'd look pretty sitting there. Prettier than what they've got.'

'Does she have to work in a hotel?'

'Not a hotel, honey. The Beverly Hills Hotel, yes. She likes stars and she'd see plenty here.'

I thought sitting in reception looking at stars was the tip of the iceberg of that particular job.

'Did you convince the management?'

'Not entirely.' He flicked fingers for a waiter. 'But I will. They haven't seen her yet.' To the waiter he said, 'I'll have double bourbon and she'll have an eggs benedict.'

The agent, snubbed about the fur coat, wouldn't do the option deal. At first. So I mentioned Robert Hartman. A stiff corrective silence followed. 'I only don't want to get involved because this particular lady won't put down real money. It will be so little that taking my percentage would be – well, robbing a child. It would be better if you dealt with her direct. There's no need to involve Mr Hartman in this. I'll do the deal if you want and forgo my commission.'

I was dying to ask about Robert Hartman. I gave the agent my London number and he said he'd call me.

There was a traffic hold-up at the airport and I saw Colin Diamond leave a cab and walk towards the National building. I was on my way to International. I called him and he rushed back, pleased.

'Come to New York. Come on. You can go back that way. I'll show you around for a couple of days.' He seemed freer and lighter and full to the brim with positive. I phoned the kids and said I'd be back the day after tomorrow. We changed my ticket and he paid the excess then we went to the bar and drank freshly squeezed juice and coffee. Now the deal was off his back he was no longer cautious. He told me about his clients' list he was building. 'I've got into something big. I wish I could share it with you. But it's too hot.'

I asked him how he'd met Robert Hartman.

'I heard about him through a guy at Universal Artists. Just a rumour. I heard he wanted in at UA, but they weren't buying. So I thought, what is there that he can pick up immediately and make a lot of bucks from, and not be rejected and be grateful to me. It was there, right under my nose. Those romance books. I thought an automatic hit would become an automatic hit film. So I walked into the Mills and Boon New York office and they liked it.'

'If it was that good they'd have financed it themselves.'

'They never spend their own money, those people. So when they knew Robert Hartman wanted to invest it seemed a good match. Of course he wasn't the easiest person in the world to get hold of. But I'm in strong with' – he mentioned a movie superstar. 'And that got me in the penthouse. I never did get the hang of him. He's got to be Organisation. Got to be. What did you find out?'

'Nothing.' I could have added, only that I like him.

Chapter Seventeen

When we got to JFK airport we shared a taxi to Manhattan. It was
a glorious arrival, the light just right. Then into the shadow of the
streets was like entering a forest from a fairy-tale. I could see at once
it was a place that could go either way for you. I remembered a one-
time travelling companion from Morocco saying, 'You have to find
the right way to arrive in New York. It's more than just taking a
plane to JFK. It's to do with how you are on a spiritual level.' In his
case he arrived in New York from South America. He drove up
through North America and arrived in the Bronx. That was right
for him. He stayed there six months and it was all magical. He even
got some of it on film. The schemes he'd tried over the years so he'd
arrive right! He worked for a while for Wim Wenders and asked for
something in lieu of wages. He detested wages. So he asked the
director for a one-way ticket to New York. He felt that was the right
way. Then he saw the latest film he'd just worked on and said Wim
Wenders had gone commercial. He detested anything commercial.
So he gave back the ticket and went on an uncommercial journey to
South America. It was deep in a forest somewhere, looking up at the
huge trees, that he knew this was the moment to look up at

skyscrapers. My way in was simply JFK and a taxi to Manhattan. That fitted me spiritually.

Colin had urgent business at his office. He was in trouble but hiding it, so I didn't insist on going with him. He'd made calls from the airport trying to get me into a moderate Manhattan hotel. Everywhere was full. There was a convention and not a room to be had in the whole of town except for one on Broadway, which was not the one to stay in. That had vacancies so I said fine, no problem. He arranged to call for me in a couple of hours and we'd have dinner.

It was a huge old hotel and at first I liked it. Along one side were grilled windows rather like railway station ticket offices, and travellers stood in lines waiting to book in. There was the reserved and unreserved section. The huge foyer was full of men. I stood in line like the notice said and then I realised the man behind was touching me up and the one in the next queue was trying to rob me. The man in front was complaining bitterly to the one in front of him. 'I'm only here because every room in Manhattan is taken. It's this or Penn Station or the cemetery. There's not one but two conventions on.' Other straight men had the same story. The less straight were in line because the place was cheap. I dealt with the crime problem behind me and to my right by going to the desk in the middle of the hall behind which sat the undermanager. I told him his clients were giving me a bad time. He said, 'That's life. Join the queue.' I stood another ten minutes and it was hot. Then a woman pushed ahead of me. She wanted immediate release of her jewellery from the safe. The clerk behind the grille – and I was beginning to see why they needed all that protection – refused to give it unless she paid her bill.

'But I have, sir.'

'You owe an extra day, ma'am. We've been through this already.'

'But I was supposed to leave this morning but my husband died up there.'

'Maybe, ma'am, but you still didn't vacate the room before ten so I have to charge you an extra day plus city tax.'

'How could I vacate the room, sir, when he was lying dead in it?'

'You still have to pay for him.'

'But he's dead.'

'But he's in there.'

I thought I wasn't going to like the hotel. At the next grille another desperate woman couldn't pay at all, due to the theft of her credit cards and money.

'You should have put them in the safe for good keeping, ma'am. We're not an insurance company.'

Dramas held up the queue and I got to the grille after standing forty-five minutes. I wanted the best room they had. There was no best anything. It was double, single, with shower or not. So I booked for one night and was given the key. The porter grabbed my luggage and stuck it on a full trolley. It was the first quick action I'd seen. He had a huge protuberance on the side of his head. From some angles it looked as though he had two faces. Yet he smiled. It was a good day. A midget handled the other luggage cart. The cluster around the lifts was like a store at sale time. Everything hot, old-fashioned propeller fans hung from the ceiling and spun slowly. The hotel was decayed but it had been something once. The porter dropped my luggage off at a room in the three thousands. We'd covered miles of ill-lit corridor. His hand was held out like a beggar's, waiting, patient. Two dollars made it go away. 'Keep your door locked, lady, at all times. And keep the chain on.'

I entered a typical room with shower. It was seedy. It was the enth degree of seediness. People had died there, would go on dying there. I distrusted everything about it. The bed, the chairs, the shower, the door.

New York was a flamboyant mixture of old and super-modern but I didn't realise it then. I didn't know what to expect. I didn't expect touches from the 1920s and 30s. I dialled room service and ordered a vast number of things to cheer myself up, then I cleaned my face. I didn't unpack because the cupboard scared me. It wasn't because it was musty and unclean. I couldn't get the air-conditioning to work and the window was a slit in the wall. Its view? An airshaft. Twenty minutes passed and I rang room service and the same person replied. I asked where my order was. 'On its way.' I picked up the menu and added a portion of french fries. I gave the room number again.

There was a banging on the door and I opened it eager for coffee and fruit juice. Two security guards looked disapproving. 'Never open your door. Keep it on the chain. Always ask who's there.'

'Excuse me. I called room service and my order still hasn't arrived.'

'That's called "Waiting for Godot".' They strolled off laughing.

I shut my door and locked it the requisite three times and put the chain on. The metal notices dating back from the 1930s didn't exactly give a feeling of security. 'It is advisable for guests to keep this chain on while occupying the room'. 'Guests are requested to double-lock the door for their own safety'. The door bristled with locks and chains and bolts. In the middle, however, was another door, closed by a simple latch. I opened it and there was a space with a message in tin, also from the 1930s, advising guests to hang clothes to be cleaned in the space and the valet would return them in the morning. The outer door of this cleaning arrangement was also opened and closed with a simple latch. It led straight on to the corridor. Anyone, except a large intruder, could ignore the huge safety precautions on the main door and enter through the cleaning door. Simply by lifting the latch in the corridor and opening the outer door, putting a hand through the space where once clothes waited to be cleaned, lifting the other latch, they could enter the room. So I tried it. Within two seconds the security guards were back. They travelled in pairs like cops in the Bronx.

'I was just testing your security.' And I told them it was odd to worry so much about locking a door when in the middle there was this other smaller door with no precautions at all. It was nothing more than a burglar flap.

They looked at me unblinking.

'You know. Like dog flap. Anything could pass through this.'

Burglars and intruders however were only interested in big doors with lots of locks and chains. Little doors did not interest them. I asked to be moved to a room with an all-in-one door. Forget the cleaning arrangement.

The security guard shook his head and relatched the cleaning door. No one would think of that if I hadn't. 'Go back inside, lady, and observe the safety rules.'

I sat on the edge of the bed. I am sure the quilt had not seen cleaning action since the cleaning doors were in operation. It didn't look filthy because the pattern and colours took care of any combination of filth. The material felt exhausted. It would fall to bits at the first spin of a cleaning machine. And I got depressed. I thought this could be me in ten years, twenty years, except without the choice. Confined in the room alone. I called Colin's number, engaged, so I took a shower. The towel was no bigger than a man's handkerchief but it hadn't been used. Walking across the bathroom floor barefoot was not pleasant. The plastic tiling was so dirty it was greasy. The shower water was yellow. Also it was cold.

When Colin arrived, all sparkling and fresh, I clung to him, I was so relieved. 'I've got to get out of here.'

'But it's one of the spots of New York. It's history.'

Then he took me out on the town and that's one thing Colin could really do. In Times Square, for one moment, I did feel I was in another place, not earthbound at all. It was the sort of freedom I'd been searching for all my life. The crush of people was terrifying, then I went beyond the terror and there was a hungry jubilant atmosphere with a drift of desperation, not unlike New Year's Eve in a dodgy city. And the noise was huge. Blasts of light, music, crimes, all the sadnesses of the world were in that square, and the pleasures. And I could imagine from such a crush of extremes you could literally be expulsed upwards like a pea out of a pod. This was the platform to real travel, the space kind. The sex-change hookers gathered around Colin with their gravelly voices and amazing make-up and gold laughter. We could have been on Mars, with these strange tall, painted creatures. And from the cars their guys watched and counted their tricks. It could be dangerous because Colin was playing not paying, but Colin chose not to recognise direct danger. He was very, very positive and that transmitted itself to possible aggressors. To knock down all that positive and turn him into a victim would be heavy work. There were easier, more vulnerable people.

Afterwards I said I felt really high.

'Not surprising with all that grass around,' he said.

'I disagreed.

'You breathed it in. Grass, Leb, angel dust, not to mention their chemical gear.'

Colin was the agent for anything 'literary' coming out of Times Square. One pavement sex star had already scribbled a life story and Colin was making it comprehensible. He pointed out the rooms where snuff movies were being screened, films showing live sexual assault, then apparently, actual murder of young girls. Rumour had it the girls' bodies would then be sliced up and disembowelled for the satisfaction of the voyeur Jack the Rippers in the audience. The girls mainly came from South American villages, from starving families only too eager to be offered money for their daughters to be given a chance of stardom hundreds of miles north. They only got the one chance. It seemed to me, standing in Times Square, that nothing new really came up. Jack the Ripper atrocities, the slave trade, torturous Oriental-style deaths for an audience, plagues, poverty, addiction. But in Times Square the pressure made reality crack a little and we could all have toppled in, sins, the lot, into the whirling black dizzying space normally only arrived at by dying.

Colin decided to go to his favourite smart Italian restaurant on the East side. It was calm and safe and he'd been there with Shelley Winters.

'So you do know her?'

'I'm doing business with her.'

Tonight he looked like a 1940s filmstar. Sometimes his face seemed to go through a chemical change. He'd have made a great magician.

'You her agent? Surely not.'

'I wish that's how I could put it.'

I was pleased with the restaurant and said so. An orchestra played, there was a mound of something white in the middle like a huge glistening wedding cake. There was a lot of greenery and trellises and privacy. A fountain splashed over some stones in the corner. Colin said he wanted me to relax totally and enjoy myself. Absolutely no sweat, not with him. That sort of talk always made me alert. Something unrelaxing always followed. Was he going to say he couldn't pay the bill? He said, 'Can I trust you?'

'Sure.' I was far from relaxed.

'You are a friend. I'm in worse shit than I thought.'

Discreetly, I felt in my bag. There were some notes but they could be one dollar for all I knew. American money all felt the same. The waiter came across and Colin selected a lot of dishes. He was going to sink so it was going to be big. I urged him to go for the cheapest, just one. Then the owner came across and Colin was pals with him. He asked Colin to try the speciality and brought a sample. Colin said it was OK. He'd been born in Little Italy so should know.

'I can see you're a little shy with ordering,' said Colin. 'Have anything you want.'

'What kind of a piece of shit are you in?'

'I have really smart ideas. That one I had about putting romance on the screen with Robert Hartman was great. He wants to be in pictures. The guy really wants in. But Hollywood's not easy. You come from nowhere. Who are you, they say. They've got to check you out. Even with half a billion dollars they've got to check you.'

'So what's that I heard about Robert Redford sitting in his kitchen?'

'Every star wants money, more money. Clint Eastwood, Beatty, Coppola. Hartman's knocked around with all of them. They're not going to say no to a guy with stars in his eyes and 300 million bucks in his pockets. That's what he's worth personally before he even starts totalling the business profits. So I financed the LA deal myself. Air ticket, phone, hotel, car hire. I was there three weeks.'

Adversity didn't diminish his positive attitude. He told his story brightly as though he were pitching an idea. His appetite didn't suffer. 'My agency is still young but it's got potential. For instance, I've got one writer whose first book will net $150,000 on an airtight film deal. And I've got the Stones to agree to do a book.' He meant the popstars this time. He was getting so cheered up and optimistic I reminded him about the money lost. Had he invested in a show? It could happen. I could see super-optimistic people really believing in something like a show.

Colin got up, full of energy. 'I'm going to trust you, so I'm going to show you something unbelievable.'

We took a taxi uptown and got out by the Pierre Hotel. In one of the streets opposite the park he stopped under an awning. 'Tell me a secret so I have something on you.'

I couldn't think of one.

'What's the worst thing you've ever done?'

'Lost my love.'

'Did you sleep with Hartman?'

'No.'

'Tell me something about him that he wouldn't want known.'

'He's shy. He wants the top people to accept him. He's afraid of rejection.'

Colin sighed noisily. 'Didn't you get a gander at any of his business transactions?'

So I told him how when Hartman sent the Irish thug out on the town to impersonate him he got J and me on video. That had to do.

Under the awning security men waited. It was a luxury block and needed all the protection it could get. They knew Colin. We were escorted up to the seventh floor.

The lift stopped and there was only one exit, directly into apartment 7. A maid waited. She was pleased to see Colin. The apartment was palatial and there were several paintings Colin said belonged to the French Impressionist time. The sculpture was all real too. Colin went straight into the bedroom. I followed and there, propped on the bed, was one of the great stars, a legend, a cherished memory from my childhood. If she saw us she made no sign. Kindly Colin stroked her hair and kissed her cheek. She was clean and beautifully made-up. Colin talked to her as though she could understand. He wasn't afraid of infirmity. The maid brought him an iced tea and asked what I wanted.

'I needed that deal with Hartman,' said Colin. 'It wasn't some ego bullshit. I'd have picked up something like $30,000 minus the ten I laid out. It would have come close to twenty. And I'd have been solid with him, on the payroll for other deals. He liked me because we're both Italian.' He smoothed the legend's hair. 'But life doesn't always work out, does it, sweetheart? The deal went down putting my life in danger.'

Then he told me his troubles. They made my life look like a luxury cruise.

Chapter Eighteen

I spent the night lying on top of the sheets. The dubious mauve and black coverlet was on the floor. The lights were on, all of them, so I could see the insect parade that shared the room at night. Outside, the town was noisy and I found out New York never sleeps. And you don't sleep because it's all pounding away, a dynamo, and you go with it. The electric high gives you no choice. I expected to be attacked. All my chains and bolts were on. I had a chair wedged against the cleaning door. I watched the doors, both of them, expecting some crouched figure to come leaping in. It was Paris and the bad days all over again. But it seemed to me I was possibly a lot safer than in the swellest hotel. As far as I was concerned I was usually safer in the places that were supposed to be dangerous, which got me round to thinking about Tycoon. That widower in black, exuding money and power from a dozen penthouses across the world. And with him it would all be luxurious and taken care of, and amongst it I sensed great danger. And Colin with his appearance changing, subtle as quicksilver. Was it caused by fast-changing sugar levels or inherited from his father or did he house multiple personalities. He too, in the ambience of the bedroom, became a threat. Next I'd start worrying about London and my bills and how I'd get by. Little things like how did I bring up the kids. So I escaped back to the happy time when I had José's love.

During that ecstatic time on the winter journey to the south, José and I stopped in Tarragona. We sat in the deserted ampitheatre watching men picking each other up. Boys in plastic jackets, businessmen dressed in suits, creeping in and out of the actors' entrances. The performance naturally didn't take place on stage but was hidden in the crumbling airless tunnels where two centuries before the actors used to prepare themselves. The men arrived alone, would leave alone. Sitting entwined with José only emphasised the men's loneliness. I suspected José had occasionally got by in Paris much as the plastic-jacketed youths were getting by in Tarragona.

José possessed me. I possessed him. He mothered me, fathered me. He was a warm blanket around me. I ached for him, he filled me up. At last I was cherished. I'd found the one my soul loved. In honesty, I don't think another person could have brought that love down. Not his mother or the French sculptress. Only something, some quality in us could have destroyed that which in retrospect I see as a gift, a loveliness given to poets and the very young. A piece of a beautiful star had been broken off and put in our hands. And of course in the higher realms, bits of star would be used wonderfully. But José and I couldn't handle it and it got all fucked up and after a while its light went out. Occasionally, during the happy days when we were living together in the fisherman's cottage in Puerta de la Selva, I saw love as a rose in full bloom, fragrant, the best rose of its kind. But in there amongst the luscious petals was an unseen worm secretly destroying the rose and soon its bloom would be gone. The worm was my ambition. I wanted acclaim. How could life having babies in Catalonia, unknown, compete with Hollywood? Another time I saw the worm as José's dishonesty. He needed a smart Barcelona life like his rich cousins had. He wanted to frequent the houses of the bourgeois wealthy. He believed that would hide his failure.

We had a way, both of us, of not growing up. We were open to everything, hating responsibility, encouraging delight. He wanted to stay the child. That's how he saw life then. Maturity happened rather quickly in my case. One summer night in London, the phone call. 'I'm going to marry Nina.' He hadn't said that. He never gave himself uncomfortable lines that would cause trouble. So I'd said, 'Are you going to marry her?' And he'd said, 'Something like that.'

At least the let-down hadn't happened in the Broadway hotel. I could have ended up as one of their regular stiffs.

In the morning, before I left for the airport, I asked the undermanager at his desk in the middle of the foyer, what was the matter with room service?

'Room service?'

'It never arrives.'

'But we don't have room service.' He pointed to a coffee bar at the side of the hotel. 'That's all the service we got.'

'Then why take orders on the phone. Who answers the phone?' He didn't know.

'Who answers room service and takes orders when there is no room service?'

He thought I was another nut. 'Lady, get a coffee in the coffee shop, OK?'

Colin came with me to the airport and said the Hollywood agent had extracted $2,000 from the ageing moviestar for a six months' option on *Harriet Hunter*. It paid my trip and I took some extra money home. I was pleased.

'But you can't do the script,' said Colin.

'Why not?'

'Because you're not American.'

I thought about Tycoon. Why did he like me? And what was that about Gerona? The hidden quarter? Why was he interested? Was Hartman the real Tycoon or was he mad? Madmen always wanted to be the doctor and he would have borrowed Irishman's patter for the penthouse appearances. I found out Robert Hartman was the real Tycoon. He got what he wanted. He got a large chunk of Hollywood. He bought into the studio about to do J's *Quark*. Although it was a few years later he obviously hadn't forgotten J's rudeness, because the first thing he did was bounce him.

Chapter Nineteen

I shared the big dusty house in Kentish Town, London with the kids
and Phil, who taught history at a polytechnic. We'd been together
since the early 1970s. We were no longer excited about each other
but couldn't face up to it. We didn't fuck any more. We didn't know,
either of us, about relationships where people didn't 'do it'. Sex had
always seemed to be the end-all, the beginning of everything. If you
didn't do it everyday you were missing out on life. We found out
eventually there were other things – intimacy, shared experience,
memories, loyalty, familiarity and respect. Phil had moral qualities
that I admired. He was on the side of right, whatever that was. He
wasn't a right-wing shit like the man I'd been with before, who
believed in the US invasion in Vietnam and still believed in it even
when the Americans no longer did themselves. Phil believed in
people and their rights. He was a lot of things, including nice to me
and loyal to my kids. I still would have left him at a drop of a hat for
José.

The Tycoon sent a card from the Cannes film festival. 'There is
a bed here in Cannes if you want to visit. There's always a bed in my
house for you.'

I couldn't go because I didn't have the money to get there. Also what would I be doing in Cannes? That was the kind of thing you could feel very left out of if you didn't have a film or any success.

On impulse I took my book *Harriet Hunter* to Lauren Bacall, even though it was under option to someone else. She'd just finished her run in the musical *Applause*. I got backstage but nowhere near her. So by using J's London connections, without him knowing, I got her address and put the book, with a note, through her door. I didn't expect to hear anything. And I didn't. But I'd followed my impulse and it meant that that dream was settled. The $2,000 came through from the option payment. I did not believe the modest descending star would get it set up and I was ready to believe anything. But I was grateful, because the money that was left over after the trip kept me going for a few weeks, while I wrote my next Duckworth book. Their advance could not keep me going. It was well into the summer of that year when the money ran out. I could not get anything going. I couldn't get any journalism, script rewrites, loans, advances. I remember going to an agent and suggesting writing a real tripe book for money. And he said, 'It's just as hard to write a bad book as a good one. And they're as hard to sell.' That stayed with me.

When they cut the phone off and the bank stopped believing my lies, I went to the Social Security office in Kentish Town Road. The street was hot and smelt of fumes and rubbish and it was full of tramps and madmen and alcoholics passed out on the pavement. That day it seemed I was the only one around who was upright. And the truth of my life came out in that grim office. I was an unsupported mother with two kids trying to be a writer. I had no real income. I hadn't had a hit. I was nowhere. I wasn't even in paperback. I had to wait with the unfortunates for hours and by the time I'd finished waiting I was one of them, and the woman behind the counter, protected by a grille like the foyer of the Broadway hotel, said I'd have to be investigated. I couldn't walk in and ask for money. So what! My kids couldn't eat. I looked middle class. Surely I had friends who'd loan me £5 for some food? It wasn't a question of £5 for food. It was all the weeks to come.

'Well, writing's a tough profession. Perhaps you should consider some other kind of employment. How many people live by writing? Let alone bring up children.'

I was in cloud-cuckoo- land or whatever they called it in the Social Security office. I think it was Pie in the Sky. She concluded her speech by saying an officer would call around and check out my hard life. I could see Phil loving that. He had stiff middle-class values when it came to government intruders. I crawled out into the blunt heat of Kentish Town, that garbage-pail street, and spent my last money on a lipstick, a real red one to cheer myself up. And I imagined J's reaction to my SS visit. I imagined it all the way home and laughed like one of the street lunatics.

I told Phil I didn't have any money. The rows about that sort of thing were always grim and lengthy. He accused me of extravagance. Of course I had had money. I'd got a great advance on *Harriet Hunter* and got drunk on it. Then I'd spent another advance getting off drink. Then I'd gone to the States, for Crissake. He meanwhile sweated hour after hour teaching in the polytechnic to students, half of whom were fugitives from reason, when he could travel the world freely like I had at fifteen. I reminded him he was thirty-eight. He always compared his life to mine, during a row, whatever my crisis. He always came into the picture somewhere. How did I say I was bored with him? I couldn't say either that I spent money because I was sad. Domestic disharmony never did me any good. I threw some shit about, didn't win, then backed off and tried my ex-husband. He said, 'Fuck off. I've got my own problems.' And I tried Duckworth and, with a hugh sigh, the director lent me something for the week.

Once money was in my hand when I was in such tight circumstances, I had to spend it recklessly. The less I had, the more I spent. It was only when I finally had real money I started taking buses. Next step, the bank. They didn't like writers in there, not unless they were displayed at airports. My lies literally dropped dead of exhaustion at the bank manager's feet. No go with the overdraft position. So I ran from debt to debt, and didn't open the door. The kids were *au fait* with that one, and said I didn't live there any more. Sometimes when I wasn't sure who was knocking, after all it was conceivable good news could come to the door too, I'd take my shoes off and creep upstairs and look out of a top window. If it was a creditor I'd say the entrance to the house was next door. And he'd go next door and bang and shout and no one ever came because it was empty. And for the real bad guys I had a red curly wig and I'd open the door and say I was the *au pair* and the lady of the house was out of the country doing something really glamorous which was what I should have been doing if life was in its right mind. Times of adversity came and went like the seasons, and during them I'd always vow I'd save. I'd become a straight with three building society accounts. Sometimes I'd borrow a friend's small children. I'd have them cluster around me at the door. The electricity board responded to that one. They always gave me an extra week before cut-off for the sake of the kiddies.

We always ate, the kids and me. There was always food on the table however bad the debts. And bad times made me write. During the 1970s I did a hell of a lot of writing so it must have been bad.

And in the bad August that followed I got a letter from New York. Lauren Bacall's agent had read *Harriet Hunter* and loved it. Then the star herself had read it and loved it and she was coming to Europe and wanted to meet me. They'd option it immediately. It had taken three months from my putting it in her door. It turned out it was the door of the wrong house but the owner knew her and reposted it. And I saw that if I couldn't get to Hollywood, Hollywood would come to me.

It was about the time I had lunch with Bacall in Knightsbridge that I knew I had to see José Tarres. Reaching out for him was the return of some incurable disease. Its only relief, seeing him. I tried to ignore it. I put on a big make-up and tried to look like a winner. Bacall was one of my heroines, one of the adored ones of my adolescence that got my mind off Albany Park. I'd seen *To Have and Have Not* and *The Big Sleep* so many times I knew each frame by heart. Everyone I knew was curious about Bacall. Perhaps because she'd had such a marvellous love affair.

At the lunch she looked incredible. If she wore make-up, it didn't show. Her voice was husky, low and magnetised everyone in the place. Her two English agents sat at the table to hear what I had to say. We spent an hour deciding how to go about filming the book.

I was to get the first crack at the screenplay. Then she asked me about myself. I'd much rather have asked about her. I said, quite irrationally but in fact with more relevance than I realised, 'I hate my past.' She asked why. I said, 'I had fun then. It makes the present kind of dull.'

She could have said similar, after the beginning with Bogart and all the success. But she was someone who took the day as it came. J had once asked her how she felt now if she saw the old movies with Bogart. Desperate? Nostalgic? Perhaps she couldn't bear to watch them. That's what he wanted to hear.

'Oh I watch them. And I think wasn't I beautiful?' And she'd laughed, a real, full of humour, generous laugh. J didn't have one of those, of course. We spoke about him in passing. I could tell she didn't like him. He was too critical. But if he directed the film it would get done. He was always bankable.

We left the restaurant together and people stared. She was on her way back to New York. She loved the book. She'd get it made. My judgement was right, she said. Oh yes, the book was for her.

Fortunately the ageing moviestar in Hollywood did not want to renew her option. She hadn't got anywhere. Everyone she showed it to wanted it for their girlfriend or wife. Ponti had seen it, wanted it for Sophia. But he'd only do it if I could get Sophia on every page of the script. As written, the book produced the filmstar in the flesh in the last third. Unthinkable for Miss Sophia Loren and Mr Ponti. Three-thirds or nothing. I was happy to stay with Miss Bacall.

Chapter Twenty

When I was fifteen, in the summer, the Residencia Internacional was full of Catalan businessmen and French tourists passing through. In the winter it was cold and dimly lit with just the regulars huddling around the black stove with the black pipe curving into the ceiling and the smell of woodsmoke. It was the winter I remembered. The friends would come and sing songs around the piano on the ground floor and on Saturday night there was dancing. The smell of olive oil and perfume filled the rooms and the street. Smells bring back the passion. Smells are powerful. It was always mysterious, that place, and of course I was young. Sometimes the sun made shadows on the walls like beautiful, complicated letters. There was a language already written. Perhaps if we'd known how to read the writing on the wall our lives would all have been different.

In the old days I kept longing for a hit so I could be with José. I'd have the money so he wouldn't have to spend his days scouring Catalonia, and something in me would be satisfied too. I considered Lauren Bacall was the hit. High on her enthusiasm I went back into José's life. Her approval gave me the right. The privileged feeling

I had meeting her, writing for her, sent me straight back to Gerona. Straight, that was, in my mind. I couldn't just go there because I had to have some idea of my reception. What if he was happy with Nina?

After the Bacall lunch I'd sent two telegrams to his mother's apartment in the Calle Forsa asking him to phone, reverse charge. Then I waited. Why I expected him to ring I didn't know. Because I needed him to do something didn't mean he would, as well I knew from the days in Paris, waiting at the Gare Austerlitz, broke, and he never did arrive on the 8.05 train from Spain. In London I was stuck, trapped to the phone waiting. For over twenty-four hours I waited for José's call. It was the most important thing in my life. The sun blazed outside and lit up the dust spinning by the bookcase. During those stuffy wasted hours it was obvious José could live quite well without me. It seemed that I still loved him. Age, even maturity, couldn't take the joy from those first years in Gerona. My soul stretched back. My body felt in bits, a sure sign of depression. Anchored by the phone, waiting, I was washed out as though by some secret illness.

Just to arrive in Gerona after hours of travelling, after upsetting Phil perhaps irrevocably, and to find José not there, to stand in the Calle Forsa, trembling with exhaustion and hear, 'The newly weds have gone away,' would be infinitely worse than waiting for the phone to ring. Nina of course would have got hold of the telegrams. She'd have torn them up. The pieces would be small. José didn't need me. He could live perfectly well without me, always had. The *Teléfonos* was open till 10.00 p.m., if he got the telegrams. Then it occurred to me he might love his wife. I gave an animal growl of pain that terrified the cats. My nerves and grey face drove Phil from the house. And I knew, that August during those dead hours in the dusty house, that if I didn't somehow stop the all-consuming passion for José, something terrible would happen.

I tried to make the best of it, the waiting, like someone in goal, lying in the living room by the phone, head in a patch of sunlight. I remembered the second time I'd met Nina. He was trying to pass her off as someone's girlfriend and everyone was embarrassed, except me. I was always optimistic.

'Nina is a sculptress. The statue in my *barraca* garden is hers. You wouldn't think these delicate hands could make something solid would you? But these hands are strong.' He lifted them up and was familiar with them. The hand-praising speech meant he was with her.

I'd eaten an apple, drunk some water. In a minute I'd do ten minutes' dynamic yoga. My standards wouldn't go, however lousy I got to feel. Now, I thought, he'd be coming home to the Calle Forsa. He'd get my telegrams, go straight to a phone. How my mind lied. Five p.m. I thought things couldn't possibly get worse, then the kids came back and started quarrelling. Chris, obsessed with football results, told me the score in a voice well engrained with the worst aspects of comprehensive school. 'Fucking score! I'll change my fucking side if this goes on.' He wanted to use the phone, even picked up the receiver. I kicked him so hard I made his 'beloved side' look like a lot of flakes. I filled up with anguish. It came on suddenly, then I phoned Luis at the Arc Bar. I gave him two reasons for José to call me, one with death in it. Luis said he'd deliver my message personally.

How many calls did I have to make? How much money did I have to waste before he could be got to a phone to make a reverse-charge call to London? If he couldn't get to a phone, and there were thousands all over Catalonia, was it worth wasting a couple of hundred pounds going to see him?

I couldn't sit in the sun in the garden because I was too far from the door and I wouldn't hear the phone. I wouldn't hear it anyway because he wouldn't ring. I knew that now. Even the phone seemed to be waiting. No more nonsense with the everyday stuff like the kids' friends and creditors. It was a beautiful day and the wind in the tall trees sounded like the sea, a wild sunny day like ones I'd spent with him. Couldn't I feel alive except when I was with José? If I couldn't live without him what was I going to do? It seemed terrible to put something before life, to love something more than life. I was in London, half dead, in debt, out of love. He was the one sunny thing in me.

The next day it became clear he'd settled for his French girl who did battle with rivals by flatly refusing to leave his side. Even so, José could get to a phone. I was being chucked by silence. If that didn't work he'd leave Gerona, taking the French girl with him. But he was no match for my love.

The phone did ring then and I started towards it as though it was some squealing prey. Robert Hartman said, 'I'm in London at the Connaught. Would you like to have dinner with me?'

But I was on my way back to Gerona. My mind was already there.

Although I got off the train in Gerona the next day I didn't go to José's mother's flat until dark. I spent the day walking. He was always the first person I saw when I came into the town. But now Nina was in town too, and she rearranged, even magnetism.

At half past nine in the evening I knocked on the door and his mother said he was away, many kilometres, with his wife. She closed the door.

I sank on to the stone landing and the automatic light clicked off. He'd gone. It felt as though half the lights of the world had gone out. I stood up, banged on the door and told the mother the first amazing thing that came into my mind.

'Lauren Bacall, the film actress, wants to hire José's little house the *barraca*, for a film.'

The mother said he was away in a place that sounded like Latvia but she'd heard of Lauren Bacall. Introducing another woman had taken her by surprise. She did not shut the door.

'What a shame. Miss Bacall's location manager is waiting in the street. What a disaster for José. He'll lose all that money.'

'Well, it's possible he could be here tomorrow.'

My heart soared. 'What about tonight?'

'Even tonight.' The mother's eyes gleamed. Money had a revitalising effect.

'You mean he could be here say in one hour?'

'It is possible.'

When I went back down into the street I was weightless. All pressure, tiredness, even age had gone. Luis was out in the night. He was still silky and malicious. His eyes were magnified many times by pebble glasses. Gossip was now his life. Nothing happened in the town that he couldn't exaggerate.

'I have just seen him and his wife. Of course you knew he was married.' It was obvious from his expression he hoped I didn't. 'They have gone towards the *barraca*.'

'How is he?'

Luis hesitated. 'You knew him at his best.'

I went down the stony winding path to the *barraca* and the wind started rolling across the hills. Through the hedge I could see the little house was shut up. It looked as though it had been silent for months. The garden was overgrown. I wouldn't have been surprised if I was dreaming. I'd been there so often in my dreams.

I went back to the mother's flat. He opened the door. All the happiness we'd shared was put back in place. It wasn't lost in the endless aching silence caused by Nina's arrival in his life. His face lit up, eyes heated up. I hadn't been looked at like that for a long time. He kissed me as I went in. The kiss was polite, anyone could have seen it, but his eyes, they were deep in mine. The wedding had taken nothing from me. I was made whole. I was healed. He led me into the reception salon and his hand brushed mine, lingered. I felt strong. I was weak with joy.

Then he brought in his wife and we all sat down, very correct, on high-backed antique chairs. He was very polite to Nina, put his arm around her, included her in every nuance of the conversation. At first. I sat opposite and talked madly of film-making in the *barraca*. Thousands of pesetas were mentioned. Lauren Bacall's name flowed through every sentence, giving it grace. José murmured something about being very grateful. Yes indeed, he adored Bacall. She was true cinema. Nina nodded fierce agreement. I couldn't look at her. She was there at the corner of my eye, a huge sponge taking his thought, his energy. José knew nothing about the urgent telegrams announcing this momentous piece of luck into his life. Nina turned shellfish pink. She'd torn them up. I could see the mother squinting in the doorway.

When the film lunacy came to an end there was a pause. It was time for me to go. I stayed and I said, 'Let's go out.'

He agreed rather too quickly for Nina's liking.

We had a night on the provincial town, a heart-breaking replica of the ones I used to have when he was single and celebrating my return to him. We started off in my favourite restaurant but I was too emotional to eat. Nina's fingers kept creeping at José, his thighs, his arm. In the end he brushed them off like an annoying insect. They had the same insistence. They reappeared at his neck, his ear. Nina was the cashier counting every exchange he made with me, every compliment, even a smile did not go unnoticed. I'd only seen her a few times. She had a sheep's nose, a gamine hair style and a way that could be described as *très gentille*, if you had nothing against her. I had hoped the marriage would be an immediate disaster but between José and her there was a definite tangible something. Her eyes were all over him, forever searching his. They too, like the fingers, jumped up and down his face, over his chest, like an outbreak of insects. Then she kept fussing with his arm, his hands. He let her touch him. I'd lost.

We went to Luis's bar and José got going on the brandy and the past. At one point he was so overcome he forgot what he was doing, which year he was in, and ran his hand up and down my leg. Twice he muddled her name and mine. The more excited he got, apparently about the 1950s, the icier Nina became. She loved him the way I did. I could see that. I understood her jealousy and potential violence. It would be her or me in the end.

Luis was radiant seeing the three of us together. He was the perpetrator of savage rumours and he didn't like it if the town was at peace. He had the yellow disquieting eyes of a wolf, camouflaged day and night by tinted glasses. His manner was excessively gentle and encouraged confidences. No one ever saw him eat or drink or sleep. He seemed to survive on cigarette smoke and gossip. He kept refilling Jose's glass. He wanted him to make one real big mistake and he could live off it for a month. Nina wanted to go. She was anxious to get José holding her, inside her, hers. He held her hand as we walked down the narrow street to his mother's flat. He said again how marvellous it was for me that Bacall was in my life.

I thought it odd they lived with his mother and not in a house of their own. After all, Nina had the money. José said, 'Will you be here tomorrow?' He said it inoffensively as though to a stranger. And I looked at him and knew why I'd been born. I'd come into the world too early, chasing José. And the price had been intolerable. And now to make a kind of correction I deliberately held back. In the things I wanted I made reason to delay. I didn't feel ready for Tycoon. You lost things that way. Suicide came next, the way I was feeling.

Because I hadn't booked a hotel I stayed the night in his Calle Forsa apartment. It seemed odd that now he was married I could enter with no trouble. The mother said nothing. In the morning José prepared a breakfast. The mother was in bed. Nina was in the bathroom and the noise of the shower was loud but he made warning faces every time I tried to speak.

'I need to see you,' I whispered.

'Be careful. She hasn't slept all night.'

She came to the table smelling of scented soap. Her face was the same colour and texture as the pale bread rolls and she had smudges under her eyes. I wondered if there was a medical problem. Kidneys for example? The film project had died down in the night, like a gale. Sometime during the sleepless hours José had seen through it. He gulped his coffee and said we should all meet at the tavern in San Daniel for lunch. He got a ghastly prune-coloured velvet jacket from the cupboard and said pointedly he had business at the town hall. When he got to the front door she ran up and kissed him on the mouth. I waited a polite interval so she didn't think I was going to follow him, then left. Mama was getting up. A lot of banging and swearing. I was glad to miss that.

I did consider going to the town hall but we'd always met by chance. If I'd looked for him deliberately I wouldn't find him. The magnetism didn't work on that level. I went purposefully in the other direction to the modern part of town. Our communication wasn't on the level of messages, requests, telegrams, demands. The wavelength it was on was dreams and coincidence.

I almost bumped into him as he came out of the jeweller's.

'I thought you were supposed to be at the town hall?'

'I said that to reassure her. With Nina we have to be very careful. She is not a woman of the world like you.' I wasn't sure how he meant that.

'Come and have a drink, José.'

'For one minute. No more.' He tried to sound reluctant.

We went into a modern bar with a lot of chrome and loud music.

'Your story of a film gives at least some credibility to your visit.' We looked at each other and laughed. 'Nina said you'd invented it to see me. It sounds too much like the sort of thing I make up. Perhaps she thinks I made it up for you. Oh God! She's upset by you. She says there's a strong sexual attraction between us.'

'Isn't there?'

'Listen. I don't want to hurt her.' He was never more full of moral inclinations than when he was about to be immoral.

'Will we be able to spend at least some time together? Will we?'

'All right. For an hour.' His swift submission took me by surprise. I realised he meant then. It was in fact the last thing I felt like doing. I wanted to talk to him and try and secure the future. He wouldn't go to a hotel or out of town or anywhere near the Arc Bar. He decided on the *barraca*. He drew me a plan which took me almost to the frontier just to avoid the Calle Forsa and Luis. If anyone did recognise me he told me to say I was working on a film location. 'I now have to be seen doing the things she thinks I'm doing.'

Because I avoided the dangerous street I ran into his two American friends, Richard and Jane, who were buying vegetables in the Barrio Chino. Whether they liked the brothel area or the vegetables were cheaper I didn't know. The Americans had fallen in love with Gerona in the mid-1970s and had bought a house near San Daniel. However, they'd found the Catalans a stand-offish lot and it had taken José to draw them into the life of the town. José had approved of Richard's painting and had given him his first exhibition when he was director of the government art centre. I was therefore surprised to find the Americans less than friendly.

'We don't see him much,' said Jane.

'Why not?'

'I suppose we don't approve of him.' Jane was sultry and looked like Jean Peters and could have made it as a star in Hollywood. But she'd taken fright at something in Tinsel Town and between a day and a night left for Europe. She did have plenty of money and dressed glamorously, in clothes obviously purchased further afield than Gerona. She said she'd never go back to America. She didn't want anyone in the business to know where she was. She wanted a private life. That's what she said. Richard had been a lecturer at Harvard, and he said nothing.

'Why don't you approve of José?'

'He pulls the wool over people's eyes. He promises you the world. He'll change your life. It's all fantasy.'

'Perhaps it's lies,' I said.

'Not lies,' said Jane. 'He means to do it. He's always letting someone down and people get hurt.' I saw then she was talking about Richard. 'There's a million José Tarreses in New York. They're all going to change the world. We knew what he was, straight away.'

I doubted it.

'He lost his job at the art centre.'

Nina would hide his disgrace, I thought. Her way of life would give him credibility, a shell around the soft mess of failure. 'Doesn't the new wife realise what he is?'

'Of course not,' said Jane.

'Is he happy?' I almost died asking that one. Richard didn't look happy. His good-looking face twitched, indicating that his wife should shut up.

'He doesn't understand Nina. He has no idea what she is. There's more there than he knows. As long as the family chauffeur keeps coming for him in the big car and the servants make him feel good at the father's house that'll be enough.'

I was so relieved Nina was gauche. I think I'd have died if she'd been attractive.

'She's jealous of you, of course,' said Jane.

'Me?'

'She thinks you're in Gerona even when you're not. It's a joke. She can't let him go anywhere alone. He tells her he's going somewhere and opens the door so she gets her coat and says she'll come too. He's not going where he said at all. He's going somewhere altogether different, somewhere innocent but he doesn't want her always with him. Sometimes he needs to be alone. But she gets that coat on and holds his arm and he has to go to the first place. He hopes of course the physical thing will die down.'

'Physical thing?' I sounded as though I was in pain. I'd known him for twenty years and it hadn't died down with me.

'She'll wake up one morning and see him for what he is,' said Jane. 'At the moment she refuses to see it because she's in love. And he'll go on with it. They'll have children, then her father will have to give in and buy them a house.'

'But she's not pretty.' It was my only defence'

'He's nearly fifty. What does he expect? He's lucky to get her.'

'You think there will be a child?'

'Of course.'

I sat on the pavement, quickly. I never could deal with shock, however much I got.

'It's getting for a quarter of one,' said Richard. 'Where did you go in America?'

'LA. New York.' I spoke absently.

'And you're in the film business?' He looked at his wife, pointedly.

'Don't worry,' I sighed. 'I wont tell the *LA Times* Jane Graham is hiding out here. Anyway, they've got new excitements. Every month someone else. You know how it is.'

'Some people don't forget,' and Jane laughed and her teeth stuck out attractively.

I asked about José's wedding. I might as well get all the pain at once. Jane gave a shriek of joy. She didn't get the chance of such a bitchy exchange, not in Catalonia.

'Was it in a little church in the country?' My voice was so rundown it was barely a whisper.

'It was not! It was an affair at her father's house. Two thousand guests. I've never seen anyone as happy as José. If he could, he would have bottled the essence of that wedding day, all the important guests, the journalists, the staff. I've heard of the radiant bride, but my, he was glowing!'

'José's OK,' said Richard laconically. 'He could have made it in politics but I guess it didn't work out. It's ten of one, Jane.'

'She came along at the right time. Just in time,' said Jane. 'But she'll kill him. I hear he has to do it five times a day.'

I thought she'd kill me if she said anymore.

I ran up the dozens of worn steps to the top of the old quarter. The cobbled streets were uneven, chewed by time. I appeared in the Paseo only briefly before dipping down the little-used path to the *barraca*. The Paseo, gossip mile, where Luis the Wolf watched and waited.

Further along I could see my rented house. How right that house's voice had been. Nina got his glitter.

Chapter Twenty-one

He let me in, his eyes nervous. 'If anyone knows, it will be the end.'
He gave a Spanish sigh, full of shrugging shoulders, tossed hair then
started making the bed. He prepared it, tucking the sheets in neatly.
He was preoccupied, practical. For a moment it seemed he'd
forgotten what he was arranging the bed for. I felt inept as though
I was with him for the first time. Undressing was awkward and
lonely. He undressed the other side of the bed. I was far from sure
I wanted to do it. Knowing he still cared was enough. But I lay in the
bed beside him. We hadn't been together for so long I had to
rediscover him. It wouldn't, I realised then, be the ecstasy I
remembered. His body was slacker. We didn't fit together anymore.
We made love but there was no love in it. It was staking a claim,
collecting a debt, anything but love. The most violent thing about it
was our perfumes. Mine, Ma Griffe, and his, a Spanish eau-de-
Cologne. They mixed together. My mascara smudged on his
shoulder. Nothing much else was left on him. He got up abruptly
and peered through the shutters.

'What's the matter, José?'

'I don't know. A feeling.'

We spoke in whispers.

'I feel very bad about her. I have not once been unfaithful.'

'She's rather possessive, isn't she?' I tried not to whisper.

'Only when you're here.'

Naturally I wasn't buying that. Then I asked the big one. If the answer was yes I'd go and stay gone. 'Do you love her?'

'She loves me.' He turned and looked at me sitting naked on the bed. Then he smiled. It was the first tender thing he'd done.

I said, 'My life without you is empty.' I realised that was true.

'My position is not what it was. You must understand that. So get going now. The way you came. Make sure no one sees you.'

The cathedral bell boomed through the small room. He counted. 'Did you really want to marry?'

'Patrice, it is nearly two. Hurry.'

'Did you?'

'She was very good to me when I was depressed. I lost my position at the cultural centre. Political reasons.'

He threw me a comb. 'Do your hair.'

'She knows you don't love her. That's why she clings. Always touching, touching.'

He tried to make the bed look as though it hadn't been used.

'Do you think of me at all?' I asked.

'I always think of the past. It's very important to me.'

'Shall I come and live in Spain?' I went on touching him with words, trying to reach what I wanted.

'Life here is very hard, Patrice. I have not changed. This town has. There is nothing for me to do anymore. So she is a solution.' He dressed quickly, angrily. These days the shoes didn't have holes in. I hated the prune-coloured jacket. It didn't suit him. It was like bearing Nina's flag. 'You left me, remember? You left and took the boys.'

'Come on, honey. You were already with her. I may have been drunk but I wasn't blind.'

'There was no money.'

'I didn't realise you were so concerned with money.'

'Patrice, I risked my life for this town in the old days. And now they won't even give me a job.'

I could see the revolutionaries had gone out of style. He had the same habits and patterns as when he was an idealist with Quico Sabater. He couldn't adapt to the modern changes and the town didn't want him.

'Did you want to be with me? If we'd had the money.'

'It's no good thinking about that.'

I didn't know whether to kill him or love him. I went over and held him and we made love again. It was right that time. I hadn't lost José. I could do anything knowing that. The magic that bound us was still in place.

Later that day Jane told me José was opening up a restaurant. 'Off the Calle Forsa. He's opened up a street which has been closed for years.'

'So he's got money all of a sudden?'

'But of course.' Jane was enjoying herself. 'Someone else's money. What changes?'

So Nina had cracked open her inheritance and he was into the pile, up to his elbows. I was therefore surprised when Jane said the money came from a young local man.

'He's been left a fortune so José got to him immediately and made him his partner. He ran round and round like a dog around a bone until he got it.'

'But the father's put a stop on the spending,' said Richard. 'When I passed there today the door was decidedly shut. And José's got seven Andalusian workmen who want to be paid. That's trouble in anyone's language.' His voice was lazy and Southern.

'Who is this young man?'

'Juan Serrat.'

I'd never heard of him.

'The young man supplies the money, José the ideas,' said Richard. 'If you see José don't mention we talked about him.'

Before I left for London I was determined to see this new venture. Of course José wouldn't like me there. She'd be there. But Gerona was part of my life. I'd actually reached thirty-five and that gave me the right to stand on anyone's street I chose.

The eighth-century alley had been opened the previous month

and was little more than a dust-filled gap with steep broken steps. Workmen were clearing rubbish. The entrance was half-way up through a narrow arch. I asked a workman for José Tarres. He didn't understand my pronounciation and shouted a name and the cultural minister of the province appeared, then the deputy minister of Catalonia, then a type from the town hall and two journalists, and when I was well surrounded by all the factions José would most want to keep in ignorance of our liaison, he appeared. He was aghast but kept it to himself. He made some kind of introduction. I was Charlie Chaplin's daughter-in-law. He sounded formal as he introduced me which made them all suspicious immediately. They knew I'd been his lover.

'This is the Jewish Centre, to be named Isaac the Blind in honour of a renowned Jewish mystic. We are excavating this ground which was once the centre of cabbala and mysticism in the thirteenth and fourteenth centuries.'

'To build a restaurant?' I asked. The men laughed.

'Not at all,' said José.

'That's what I understood,'

'It began as a restaurant but then my good friend Juan Serrat and I made discoveries. We have uncovered the treasure of the Jews.'

Workmen were laying a Star of David in marble on the courtyard. These were the seven Andalusians who wanted their pay cheques.

'Isn't it marvellous,' said José. 'Jews and Arabs produce the most horrible wars all over the place. Yet here in Gerona it is the Arabs who create for the Jews their symbol. Here in Gerona we are at peace. Perhaps here is the promised land. The lamb lies down with the – '

'Lion?' I suggested.

He caught sight of the minister who'd fired him from the art centre. 'Snake.'

I asked him how he'd begun this enterprise. It was all new to me.

'How did they begin it? The Jews? An angel appeared to them in this courtyard and sometimes the light falls in such a way I am persuaded that has happened to me.'

'Are there any Jews living here? In Gerona now?' I'd never seen any.

José could hardly be scathing enough. 'We are all Jewish.'

'Really?' Now I was surprised.

'Ninety per cent of the Catalans have Jewish blood. Because at the time of the Expulsion many Jews accepted the offer of the church to become Christian converts and stayed on in Gerona. So this town is full of Jews.'

'Do they know it?'

He hated challenging questions from a woman. And I could see he was beginning to take the whole thing personally.

'They sense it. Their heritage is no surprise to them.'

The minister of culture murmured against my ear. I'd forgotten our audience. When I was with José no one else existed. That hadn't changed.

'Forty per cent,' said the minister discreetly. 'On the blood question. Ninety per cent misrepresents the Jewish influence.'

I felt he didn't like any part of it. Jews had sprung up like mushrooms right in the middle of his Christian Arab patch that he sold to the tourists. Was it just a spectacular revenge because he'd fired Tarres? But he was prepared to be liberal, to balance somewhere in the middle until he saw which way public opinion went. And after all most mushrooms had a very short life span.

'Do you think Jews will be welcome here in Gerona?' I was trying to describe Hasidic Jews.

'Of course we in Catalonia welcome all religions, all customs, however extreme.'

Not when I'd first arrived, I thought. My dress sense got a lethal response.

'So they can continue their Jewish way of life, their religious practices in a Catholic town? Food restrictions, bathing?'

'But of course.' The minister was magnanimous, but then he was a minister. He'd agree to anything as long as it wasn't going to happen.

I realised Jews had not been exactly prevalent in Catalonia. José said it was because the time had not been right. In fact the memory of the Expulsion had scarred Jews even to this day and it was still not a popular country.

'This will become the new Jerusalem. We will revive the

splendour of olden times.' José spoke with great charm and the journalists scribbled it all down.

The minister looked as though he deeply regretted firing José from the art centre. As we stood there an electrician and his mate brought in hundreds of different sized light bulbs. At night the courtyard would blaze with a glory only José and someone else's money could provide.

Jewish mysticism appeared in Gerona in the Middle Ages. In the closed quarter off to one side of the Calle Forsa several generations of mystics, while in trances, could receive a vision of God. Cabbala practices were complicated, secret, and, I imagine, something like LSD trips but with great clarity, and intention. They weren't just getting out of their heads. The secret practices were handed on only to those evolved enough to use them with respect. The memory of that constraint stayed with me over the years that followed because I think José Tarres took into his little earthly body some mystical cabbalistic power – he may have sniffed it in with the dust from the excavations or it could be still existing in the stones. José said that at night they made a noise like singing. It's the only way I could explain his survival. No one could have got away with the stuff he pulled. He'd definitely tuned into something.

Jews had been known in Gerona in the second century during the Roman occupation, but José said they'd most certainly been there earlier. In the fourth century they were banished from the city and lived in the nearby villages – Besalu, Mont Juich, Ampurdan, Vilajuiga. Remains of their synagogues and ritual baths still exist. In the ninth century they were invited back to Gerona city by the ruling counts who found them more entertaining and cultured than the locals. They were allowed to buy twenty- four houses surrounding a communal courtyard in the shadow of the cathedral. After the Expulsion in 1492 this was closed by order of the Church. Some said it was cursed, others that the mystical practices left influences, and as the town had turned on the mystics so the result could turn on them. The cruelty and suffering of the Expulsion undeniably left terrible memories.

The Jewish quarter had always produced the best craftsmen of the province, the most qualified doctors, lawyers, teachers, so when they were gone the standard of Gerona life dropped. Today's Gerona inhabitants, the historically minded ones, think of the Jewish presence before the Expulsion as an exceptional and happy one. Apparently there was a good relationship with the town's-people. I personally couldn't buy that. I'm no historian, but why did the Jews lock themselves in at night? The huge door leading to the Calle Forsa was closed before sundown. And why did the Jews have doors leading house to house so they could make a quick escape, if the social life was so happy? Maybe that's just me. I see these things. My interpretation doesn't have to be right. It certainly infuriated José.

I asked him again how he'd got into this Jewish business. He said it had just come into his head.

'It usually takes a little more than that. Has someone suggested this to you?'

He dismissed that one.

I couldn't understand this sudden fix on the Jews. As far as I knew, he'd never met any. At one time he used the word Jew as an insult. About a previous business partner, in reality she was a siesta partner, he'd said, when she wouldn't pass him half the profits, 'She's so mean and hard and uninteresting. She's a Jew!'

I had to find a chance to talk to José. I drew close to him as he opened the boxes of light bulbs. 'I don't want to harm your marriage. I just want to know if I'm still in your life?'

His eyes begged for silence. Nina was crossing the courtyard. When she'd gone a peace settled and I could be persuaded that these men of light had lived here on a spiritual dimension we'd certainly forgotten, if we'd ever known it.

Chapter Twenty-two

After making love with José in the *barraca*, the lunch with Nina had been difficult. Happiness was obvious to anyone. It couldn't be hidden and I was full of it. We'd sat at the long table in the taverna. Nina, with her gauche looks and eyes that missed nothing, the new wife, twenty-three but not young. José was trying to be on top of things. He was kept. No holes in the shoes. He was writing poems again. His wife's family collected him in a chauffeur-driven car. The image was holding together, except for people who knew him. At one moment he gave me a look, almost of respect. How I could destroy him! One familar move, a salacious glance, and that would put paid to the chauffeurs and poems. I believe he thanked God during that lunch that I was no longer drinking.

I had to ask myself if I really understood him. I'd always thought he was left-wing, an idealist. Now he seemed establishment, all for the bourgeoisie. I was still for people doing what they wanted. He was all for conformity, the right style, the right time, correct behaviour, proper dress. That word proper was creeping in rather a lot. To misunderstand someone's politics was a serious flaw. What else hadn't I understood? His coldness in the last years? Never any gratitude for anything. He'd even started wearing pyjamas in bed. What part did taking them off play? I thought the new way of life would kill him off. But he found a way out quickly. He found the Jews. Gerona, I realised, had changed too. There wasn't as much music. There was a self-satisfied smell. Plush leather goods filled what used to be the old-fashioned *tiendas*. Old-fashioned was non-existent. Gerona could be London. Anywhere.

Thinking more about the lunch, I suspected it had not gone as smoothly as it seemed. At one point José poured me a glass of wine and I pushed it away and he said, 'Oh yes. Patrice has given up drinking. I am proud of her. She is determined. I like that in a woman.'

Nina pushed her plate away, the food uneaten, and she looked like a big eater to me. I tried to belittle my conquest of alcohol. 'No, no,' José insisted. 'You have done something. And you are beautiful again because you have triumphed.

Nina sighed violently.

There was noise at another table. Workmen were excited because someone had seen a vision at the back of the cathedral.

'D'you think it's true, José? I asked.

'Why not? Just because we can't comprehend something doesn't mean it doesn't exist. I'd hate to think that what we understand is all there is.'

My love for him was back, visible to the whole restaurant. Nina went to the lavatory and I said, 'Come away with me. You know we should be together.'

So he suggested the Hotel España in Barcelona, our old meeting place. Later that evening he'd slip away when she was with her parents on the coast. We could pass a few hours together.

She came back to the table and folded her napkin over and over, methodically. I didn't like anything about the movement. José paid the bill. He seemed unaware of his wife's mood. He put his arm around her as we walked to the door of his mother's apartment. He said he had to take a siesta. I said I'd go on to Barcelona, so kissed Nina on both cheeks. This was goodbye. Over her head, José looked at me. We belonged together. He smiled almost bitterly, acknowledging it.

'Barcelona then. I'm sure you will find all you're looking for.' He waved goodbye. For an hour I'd walked in the streets of Gerona, high with happiness. The past was there on every corner, in every street, recaptured, undying. I thought, what can I do with so much joy?

In Barcelona there was only absence and let down. I left the city and walked on the stretch of dirty beach in front of the fish restaurants. The tide was out and everything on the beach looked withered. I knew now he wouldn't come, would never come. His leaving me for the young girl had been like a sea going out, leaving me dry and stranded.

Every approaching Spaniard of middle height was José. I called his name. A man turned round. Nightmare feeling as I saw the face was almost José's. But hundreds of Catalans dressed like he did, walked as he did, had the same hairstyle. Because I wanted to see him I forced a resemblance on every man that passed.

José had said it wasn't physical with Nina but she had that quietness that comes after erotic passion. She had a self-satisfied air too – something was going on. I didn't quite believe Jane Graham's story of five times a day, but that could be envy.

When he said he'd marry Nina I had wanted to kill her. People thought I was joking. I supposed I was joking. Jealousy poisoned that summer.

I kept seeing her young squat body, the way it always gravitated towards his. She wasn't happy unless at least one part of her was touching him. She wasn't really happy unless he was inside her, making love to her. I'd understood that in one horrified glance. I understood the French girl because I felt the same. Even now he was obliged to lie.

'Of course I don't have anything physical with Nina. Why should I lie?'

Lying, to Tarres, was breathing. I thought of her artist's ear-rings, her ragged sculptress's sweater, all the unseen masses of money, the shy pretty eyes.

I could smell the sea now. It always made me feel better. I'd been with José on that Barcelona beach, early one morning in winter. We'd sat outside a café drinking Cinzano and watching the sun come up. That was the golden morning. Joy like that was untouchable now. It could only be mourned.

Nina with her blunt bourgeois body, her greedy love, her bank balance, had taken him away.

I moved off towards some fishing boats and sat between them, hidden. I remembered the beach at La Escala. I'd gone there for a holiday with him, years before, and the joy of that day had been such that I'd never looked at boats and sand in the same way again. Fishing boats brought back instantly the winter sun, the loud wind, his beauty, his flapping coat. What had once been joy, how it could turn and hurt? I'd been so happy that morning on the beach that the only thing to do, to give it expression, had been to try and fly. In my dreams I could fly. The wind could have lifted me if I'd found the right way to let go. I felt gravity could somehow be evaded. Happiness could do it.

The beach at La Escala had also been deserted. I remembered the dark coarse shrubs, almost torn up by the wind. The trees bent to one side like umbrellas, blown inside out, some snapping, others uprooted dying, and José stood and watched me trying to fly. The wind lashed the sea higher up the beach. The sand was brilliant. It was sunny, wild, loud that day.

The village had seemed empty. The dark narrow bars were untouched since the beginning of the century. There were unexpected beautiful things, tinted photographs of women in long skirts with piled hair, gas lamps, engraved mirrors. Tourism hadn't plundered the village. The wind howled round the streets like a monster and the people stayed inside, their shutters closed. José said the wind had saved the village and it would never be modernised. The smell of woodsmoke was heavy and perfumed and made his eyes sting. Shadows made dramatic patterns on the dazzled streets, a mysterious language of signs, solid as any three-dimensional thing. All of it was heightened, ignited by José's presence. 'We should live here,' he said. He pointed to a house next to the café-cinema in the main square. 'That is now empty. A good writer lived there. And it will cost nothing.'

He didn't say who would pay this nothing. We had a future. I could have had him. I never trusted him. I sat desolate between the boats. The recent happiness at noon had been nothing, an oasis at most. The sand got paler, night was coming. At one time he'd wanted me to have his child. He'd made love savagely. However much he did it the desire didn't go. How did I allow that spoilt little rich girl to make such an impression?

I got up and hurried away from the beach. I didn't want to see boats anymore. At the hotel they told me Señor Tarres had not arrived. There was no message. They remembered I'd played that scene before. I went back to the Ramblas. 'I'm old because of him. I've spent my life, wasted it, waiting for him.'

Around ten the criminals and sex hunters came out and the Ramblas was full and dangerous. I became deeply depressed, not because I was being accosted but because I wasn't. I was past my best. I considered killing myself but I saw it didn't solve anything. Eternity stretched forwards, backwards and I stretched with it. You didn't go anywhere when you died, except into another structure. You'd had thousands of those. Killing yourself was no more than cutting your nails. A mad woman howled in a side street. Because I felt truly terrible I reached out to the one person who might help. On impulse I phoned Robert Hartman at the Connaught. I didn't expect he'd still be there. I said I was having a bad time. He asked for my number in case we got cut off.

'I wish I could be there with you. I'd look after you,' he said. 'Go and have a meal and think of me. I'll send you some loving thoughts. Then go to bed and think of me. OK? Then tomorrow come home.'

For a minute I didn't know where that was. Gerona? Albany Park? Hollywood? He meant London. He wouldn't be there when I got back, however. He flew to New York in the morning.

I sent a letter to José before I left. I assured him the marriage was a suicide. That girl would suck the very life out of him. She'd take his soul if she could. I concluded with some good advice. Leave her now. It was one of those effective letters all right. She opened it.

I walked the night, from one end of the city to the other. Instead of remembering the sexual love, the binding together through pleasure which was almost pain and the harmony that came afterwards, I tried to make sense of his changing attitude. In Paris he'd changed and that was years ago. He never quite had innocence after that. There were different layers to him. One good, family good, community good, then love of women, ego, selfishness, greed. Then another good layer, kindness, a mystical link. Where did he exist? Was he like a mole burrowing in the deep bad layers coming up for an occasional excursion to the good surface? Whatever – he was a failure. And now he'd lost his magic and let me down.

When I next saw him he was enclosed in his marriage, part of Nina's world as the Jewish excavations were part of his. History was being taken in large chunks and recycled through his poet's mind. It would cause a little difficulty. Medieval was going to cover a lot of ground. But at last he'd found who he was. An impresario. And now he had a real show to put on.

Chapter Twenty-three

I went back to Hollywood in 1979 because I had a National Film Finance grant with director Michael Lindsay-Hogg to write a script and get it into preproduction. Michael was busy with *Brideshead Revisited* for Granada TV and *Whose Life Is It Anyway?*, the stage play. So I took the initiative and chose an actor and got the story sorted out. Michael was happy as long as it was wild enough. I felt up, good about myself because I'd set out to get something and achieved it. I didn't know then but I was going to soon enough, that insecure people *have* to get there. Everything else is in the slop pail until they've made it, except they never make it big enough to quell that aching nothing inside. But for once my insecurity and my ambition were hand in glove, which meant for a time I was harmonious. The rejections and disappointments I'd gone through in my work were shaken off by this new chance. Twice my third Duckworth book, *Having It Away*, had been near to being filmed. I'd done several versions of the script and at least four directors had been attached. It had seemed so certain. And I so needed it. I believed a film success would equal Gerona and what I'd lost. One thing I had learned. Don't spend the money until you actually have it in your hand. Money in someone's head was just in their head.

J was busy on *Quark*, the final preparations. He had a dazzling line-up of stars. He didn't tell me this. He wouldn't waste professional news on an outsider. Any glory I thought I might have was swallowed up in two sentences of icy realism. Then he actually spent time explaining the studio system which directly excluded me and the NFFC. I said I'd go to the alternative Hollywood, down to Zeotrope studios and find Coppola. They were non-conformist enough down there to let people in if they liked your ideas.

'You do what you want, honey. Zeotrope, incidentally, has gone bust.'

So I got my career out of the way and we settled down to play backgammon and everything was all right. For him. J was the sweetshop of my childhood, full of dozens of longed for treats. Yet even with money I couldn't even weigh up a quarter of a pound of dolly mixture. So I asked a direct question. 'I need a Hollywood agent. Can I be introduced to yours?'

'Swifty wouldn't be right for you.'

'Why not?'

'Because you're not known. Ditto the Lantz Office. I don't think Robbie could come in at this stage?'

'But where are all these lucky breaks people get out here? If you've got talent it gets you a chance, right?' And I flopped out the pile of English reviews of my books.

He closed the backgammon board. 'We're going to have tea with Christopher.' He meant Isherwood. He lived over in Westwood and the drive would take thirty minutes. J wanted to avoid the traffic. 'He'll tell you, by the way, what I try and tell you but you don't listen. Even Christopher, who was known when he arrived, could not have written in the English way. You'll find he writes as though he's a native of California.' He fingered the small scattering of photocopied reviews. 'He's got plenty of these too.'

The next day, as I was sneaking away from Mulholland Drive to do the forbidden, see an agent, I saw Colin Diamond going into Hamburger Hamlet. I got out of the cab and joined him. Last season's problems changed for others like a suit of clothes. He didn't refer to the vengeful Hell's Angels. The forged diary was still on ice in the legend's bedroom. He still looked after her.

'Do you have a deal with her?'

'No.'

'Why don't you get the rights to her biography?'

'They went years ago. She only asked one thing of me. "Just make sure I die pretty." I owe her that much. She was my idol as a kid.'

His new problems belonged in Hollywood. His top writer's book was being filmed but the studio wouldn't let him on the set.

'Why not?'

'Because as his agent I try and look after him.'

That seemed to include Colin stopping the camera, changing the dialogue, directing the director. 'The book is based on the real thing, right? A true happening. They don't realise it. They're up to their arses in libel and I'm simply trying to save them.'

'Didn't they realise it was based on fact?'

'Are you kidding? They wouldn't have touched it. Fact is always more sensational than what you make up. That's the trouble.'

'Whose story?'

He laughed. 'Don't worry. It's not Robert Hartman's.'

Also, Colin's latest affair was about to be revealed in the *Enquirer*, the local dirt sheet. The husband wouldn't be too pleased. 'And I was only trying to help her. That's how I got into it. She's incredible but screwed up. She could have been big. She got offered two major films but she's self-destructive. She started going to a shrink. The next thing, she's having an affair with the shrink. She goes every afternoon and she talks about herself for five minutes and the shrink spends the other forty-five screwing her. And what do you know? He sends a bill. She won't pay it. So he says he'll sue. So she says she'll countersue. I go and see the shrink and he says if he didn't send the bill the husband would be, well, curious. Shrinks are not known for their generosity. And the husband's Mr Big around the town, politically. She's beautiful, she's amazing, I love her but I can't save her.'

I asked about Tycoon. Colin hadn't seen him. If he heard anything he'd let me know. I hadn't spoken to him either, not since the forlorn night in Barcelona. I didn't remember nights like that. My

145

rule, only remember the good stuff. That meant I didn't have to have a long memory. But it meant I survived.

Colin paid for the hamburgers, even though I had money. 'I think you're going to get in the fast lane,' he said. 'I've always had that feeling about you.'

I met a producer who worked at Zeotrope for Coppola's company. They were real film makers. In other words, they got on with it. The producer, Lauren, said she could get me into Cop. She'd got through reading my latest book in galley, *The Siesta*, which was coming out in England at the end of 1979. Cop would go apeshift for it, she said. Now that was very good news indeed. To go from floor level at Mulholland Drive straight up to Francis Ford Coppola was the time to open the champagne, if I'd been drinking. Of course *The Siesta* was about José Tarres. If I couldn't have it, I wrote about it. It made up the love deficit.

Lauren kept buying me Mexican food and showing me Hollywood. And it was incredible actually to sit next to someone who could say, 'Martin Scorsese. I know him. I go roller-skating with Jack.' (Nicholson.) She said she loved the character of the man in *The Siesta*. That was José. 'I'd love to cast him. I've got ideas.' She named two of my fantasy figures. 'It'll go,' she said. 'It'll be a go film.' So I'd brought José to Hollywood after all. Before I got too happy I asked about the rumour that Coppola had gone bust.

'That doesn't mean anything to someone like Cop. For some people it's the end of the story. For Cop – it's everyday. A breathing space.' She shrugged.

She was hard, with a big hard smile and perfect grooming. Normally I wouldn't like her at all and she wouldn't like me. It was amazing how close you could get when a bit of ambition was involved, a few shared dreams. I even liked her white running shoes. She made some calls and I walked down to the sea.

It was a funny sea. It only really became something up past Malibu, near Zuma beach. There was a lot going on, jogging and exercises, roller-skating, karate, meditation, the dynamic kind and the still kind. Then I saw a man running, running very fast along the water's edge towards me. The speed was incredible but he didn't slow as expected. He went even faster until it was wild, free, incredible anyone could move so fast. Then he turned cartwheels over and over in the hard wet sand. And I saw his face, only in movement. I knew it was him. He saw me too but he didn't stop. A last cartwheel, then he plunged round and ran back the way he'd come. He stood out from every other runner on that beach. Because he was free. I wrote about it, the man running along the seashore. And when I wrote about him I understood him. He was only wild in places he loved. The city was his enemy.

Lauren joined me and I asked if she knew him. She hesitated as though his name was not unfamiliar. 'Robert Hartman. I should know who he is.'

I told her where he'd been running and I hurried her off in the direction he'd taken. I sped along the sand for nearly ten minutes but didn't see him.

The next day I got flowers at my modest hotel. So he'd found out where I was. The message, 'From Gerona. Our Immortal City.' No signature. I tried to reach him on the Rodeo company numbers. They'd never heard of him. Even Irish was lying low. He wasn't known at Ocean Park either. I asked at the gate, phoned the management.

Up at J's the phone never stopped. He got the superstars, the presidents, the financiers. I got Mr Romance. That hadn't changed.

Colin said to tuck some money into my belt for a dinner in Malibu. There was an incredible director that I should meet. He would be superb for my NFFC deal if Michael Lindsay-Hogg was too busy. This man would immortalise my writing. All I had to do was pick up the tab on a dinner. I could see my film money sliding into Colin Diamond's dynamic dreams. And I'd have nothing left except the memory of incredible people.

'Why are you so cautious?' said Colin. 'It's not like you.'

'When I had no money I had nothing to lose. These days I feel careful.'

'One dinner. It's not even your money.'

'What d'you mean? I got it.'

'It's the British Government's.'

Colin knew the background of money sources in countries other than his own. 'A tab at dinner. You'll never get this chance again.'

'Does he have a name?'

'Of course he has a name. Having money doesn't suit you. I do all this for you and you carp over a few bucks. Orson Welles.'

I made the mistake of not hiding my excitement from J who said, 'Orson will do anything for a dinner these days. He's broke. You won't raise a buck on him.'

I turned venomous. My ways were not his. Not top drawer but they worked. Anonymously through letter boxes I stuck my books. OK I waited months but my intuition was right.

'Don't get so aerated, honey. You'll have hyperventilation or something and we'll have another medical crisis. And you know doctors never visit in LA. They just will not come out.'

'You could have given Bacall the book. Just like that.' I snapped fingers. 'But you didn't think it would work out. And now it has what do you say?'

'The same as I did before. It won't happen. You should have posted it through Elizabeth Taylor's door. She gets backing.'

I thought he would in time kill me off. I'd hyperventilate right up to heaven, and join Jean Harlow and James Dean, hopefully.

'I could have gone to Elizabeth for you.'

I didn't remind him he'd said the little book would never make even a little paperback, leave alone a movie.

'But it's too late now,' he said dryly.

'What out of the multitude of "too lates" are you referring to?'

'Your book. Betty will have shown it everywhere. It will have been rejected everywhere. So it's no good to Elizabeth.'

'I thought for a minute you meant it was too late for us. You and me.'

He gave a green-eyed cynical look and the pool hissed. Of course he was attractive, he didn't age. No effort required there. He just had a fortunate hormone system.

I dressed in a yellow silk suit and called a taxi to take me to dinner with Orson Welles. I made myself look as good as possible. Orson might not appreciate it or even notice but it was worth the effort if J suffered. I clicked around the pool to the gap in the hedge on spiky-heeled shoes, glamorous and sinful. I expected to hear, 'You never look like that for me.' He said, 'Are you having dinner with Orson to discuss this Betty Bacall option or just to eat?'

'No, J. I have funding from the NFFC in England. That's how I'm out here in LA. It took care of little things like the eleven-hour flight.'

'What, the little Duckworth book, you mean? *The Siesta?*'

'I mean the fucking NFFC project.'

'You know you're something of a phenomenon. How many writers out here have three books in film development? You should telephone Variety. They'd certainly make something of you.'

'Why don't I phone the *Enquirer* and tell them what you get up to in private? Let them make something of you.' I wanted to cry. Catch me crying. I longed for Tycoon then, just to stand there and do my fighting for me. 'The director is Michael Lindsay-Hogg. He's well known in the theatre and television,' I said.

'Yes, I know his mother.'

'You'd do better knowing mine,' I snapped. 'Then you'll see what I'm going to grow up into.'

He sat looking into his pool as the lights of the city came on below. 'I think you're a very good short-story writer.'

'I'm going to get there, J. However much you try and stop me. And one day you're gonna say, she did well for a short-story writer.' I turned and began a dignified exit, the suit made gold by the night. But a lone coyote was waiting in the last bush, waiting for J to be alone so it could approach. I saw its baleful dustbin eyes and raggedness. The night allowed me no idea of its size. I gave a piercing scream and J sped round the pool quite ready to defend me against any marauder. 'It's in the bush. A beast.'

He held me, stroked my hair. His hands were full of caresses for the misguided friend–lover who thought she was going to make it. He watched me go down to the gate and get in the taxi. It was all his, twinkling little lights of Hollywood, like candles on a cake. And I wouldn't get one slice of it.

Chapter Twenty-four

Colin said Tycoon was invisibly involved in a lot of movies. 'He's big but the profile's low.'

'Is he with anyone?'

'Who knows? He might be with the government. He's no stranger in Washington.'

And I thought about his special surveillance of J in Mulholland Drive. Of course my reaction was the oddest thing about it. I hadn't got angry or made any significant protest. But later in London it had started to worry me and I felt he should be avoided. I didn't understand obsession at a distance.

'He eats all over the place. Sometimes at a really good hamburger joint downtown. Now that's smart to know about that. Sometimes he entertains a lady at the Dome or Spargos. But that's business. The ladies say he's well mannered and quiet. Show him your new book. Tell him about the finance money. Give him good news. He always believed in you.'

'But how can I see him?'

'Show up at Ocean Park. Tell them at the gate who you are. If he's not there leave a note where he can reach you. Keep it business. I'm not psychic that I know of, but I think with him it's only business. It would be a mistake to go for more.'

I told Colin that going for more hadn't occurred to me.

'Yeah, well some big ego ladies have tried. Nothing doing. In fact it screws up the business benefit.'

So I decided to leave it to fate. If I was meant to meet him then I would. Why buy pain? There was enough around for free.

I thought the tiny agent with the furrier father-in-law still represented me. I got a horrible reception. He'd not forgotten the beaver lamb mock coat. It still mocked him. He looked at my clothes but there was nothing to worry him. He said nothing doing, not on *The Siesta*. Not on anything. I'd gone behind his back and given my previous book to Bacall. That showed I could handle my affairs myself. He didn't have time to waste so would I please leave. He was very angry. Could getting it wrong about a bit of fur make you that upset? Then my film agent arrived from England and she spoke to him. She said, 'I can't make them out. You can't trust them, these Hollywood agents. They're all over you one minute and hostile the next.'

I said it could be an identity crisis because the British were beginning to mean something at the box office. She said, 'You can't trust any of them.' She didn't trust the Lauren deal I'd half set up at Zeotrope. 'Don't you realise they always say yes. A yes is only a maybe. Be real.' And within two hours she'd sold the option on *The Siesta* to Caroline Pfeiffer, a producer at Island Alive. Once again I was to go home with full pockets. It evened it up for me, with Gerona. I'd brought José to Hollywood, because he was after all the point of what I'd written. *The Siesta* was about my inability to stop loving him. The murder in it was just a fictional extension, I thought. After a while Los Angeles and the wishworld became one. It was the fusion between the real people and how I wished them to be. Caroline Pfeiffer wanted Roman Polanski to direct *The Siesta*. 'If it was a perfect world, he would,' she said. 'It's created for him.' He was lying low in France after the teenage girl scandal at Jack Nicholson's house. My French agent in Paris, Marcelle Simon, was very close to his business manager and they arranged to leave the book by his bed. Even the French thought Polanski would direct

The Siesta. But perhaps he didn't read books in bed. And by then he was absorbed with *Tess.* Anyway, he never came back with a response. Once again I didn't get to do the screenplay. I was too English.

Colin dealt with his problems by making out he didn't have any. The worse the adversity, the bigger the V sign. He opened a huge office in LA and it was his 'fuck off' to the world. He would go down in a big, beautiful total way with his new office. However, his attitude and energy refused to see it as financial suicide. If the world was against him, why should he be against himself too? If the shit hit the fan it was bad enough. Why be down? He'd had a wobbly childhood like me, except he came out strong physically. And he wasn't a solitary person. He'd had to bring up six brothers and sisters. To be nice, I said he could be my Hollywood agent. How many mistakes are made through kindness? So we went to Swabs drugstore and he drew huge beautiful plans for my future that I could believe in.

When I was in Hollywood I felt nourished and secure and no other existence was possible. This free person in shorts on a bar stool in Swabs was what I'd become. I even forgot the children. I operated in Hollywood, at my best. José was not there in my mind either. Everyone has their own Hollywood and other people's were not so pleasant. 'It does me good here,' I said to Colin. 'There's nothing like a new patch.'

'But you never do any writing.' This was true. I hadn't even noticed. I liked it so much I was too busy living. London suited the writing because it was a neutral place. I didn't sense such excitement in the streets that I was tugged out of the door every five minutes. Colin toasted me with black coffee. 'You're going to be a star. And I'm going to be twinkling right along beside you.'

Every morning I was greedy, not just for food but for the textures of the room, the voices, the street sounds, and I couldn't wait to be out there. Every morning began with sun, abundant room service, looking through the huge LA papers on the terrace, finding out what was going on. I concentrated on advertisements for yoga, meditation, health, beauty. This was my stepping-off point to a glorious sphere, mental, physical. I tried to get in for the LA

Symphony concert conducted by Carlo Maria Guilini. J hated music so wouldn't come. Colin said I'd never get in but he came with me in case there were returns. There was a long queue and I never got to see Guilini but I did see Tycoon. He arrived in a dark suit, elegant, self-possessed with half a dozen well- dressed people. One was an opera singer. He was whirled amongst his sophisticated group to the stalls. I left the returns queue, too ignominious, and walked towards him, knowing I wouldn't speak but not able to stop walking. I hadn't seen him up close for two years. And he turned to check in one of the women's coats at the last minute, a long velvet-fur trimmed number the tiny agent could have got his nose into with safety. And he saw me. No smile.

A perfunctory nod. The coat was taken away and he got a ticket. I stayed where I was. He almost joined me, hesitated, went back to the woman. Then he turned and made a telephone gesture. Then he was enclosed in the privacy of his group in the stalls.

And I knew I had to make it. It wasn't just fantasy time. I had to be there.

Colin slept in my room on a bed called a rollaway, unknown to the management or J. He decided the room-service waiter was a potential very big star so the breakfast bill dropped by half. 'They've all got ideas,' said Colin. He was trying to get Orson Welles to write his lifestory. He was also busy fixing my film. The one with the film money attached. He left to do business at the office at ten. I sunbathed because I was waiting for the phone. I remembered the T.S. Eliot poem by heart. When I got to the passage about the rose-garden it sent a shiver, a thrill, even, through the parts of me subdued by food.

Tycoon rang at eleven and asked if I'd been to Gerona again. I didn't want to think about that, not in Hollywood.

'But they've opened up the closed quarter. You should be there. It's your town too.'

I doubted it.

We agreed to meet at a coffee shop opposite MGM. I hadn't noticed before but he had a solitary's eyes. He asked about my life and I told him the good bits. I asked about his life and he told me only what he wanted me to know. 'Buying, selling, as usual. Mostly buying in this town.' He said the movie business was on change. Videos were coming in, cable films. It was becoming anti-Hollywood. He ended on an up note. 'But quality will always win out.'

We went to an early dinner at a fashionable in restaurant on the Strip. I think it was there that I noticed that wherever he went the same two guys were always at the next table. I took them to be bodyguards. Because I was going to have to leave for London I wanted to know this man. Questions were a lousy way to know someone, but that's all I had time for. I asked about his life. He wouldn't discuss it. I touched upon his personal life. He said he didn't have one. I broached the subject of his dead wife and made my first bad mistake. He took in a deep breath and it shook a little, not unlike a death rattle. I said I was sorry he'd had such a loss. For a moment I thought he was angry. His voice was gentle, however, when he said, 'I don't think it's something we should get into if you don't mind. I don't as a rule.'

'Why not?' I said it because I was on the spot. I'd made a mistake and had no way to back off unless I burst into tears. But I was not a crier.

'Because I can't lightly discuss such a loss. It doesn't belong at this dinner table. I'm sorry.' And he sat, all closed in, remote. Subject over.

'Don't you think other people have to go through loss too?' My voice shook. It wasn't the dead wife that upset me or his disinclination to talk about it. I was upset deeply because he did not have a personal life. At least when I asked. It meant he did not want me. 'Doesn't it occur to you that I could have lost somebody as well?'

He gestured with a hand, beautifully. 'I am very sorry for you. But what can I do? You can tell me about it.'

And I told him about José and how I'd lost him to the rich little French girl. 'And that's a death. We have to look at each other over a death. It's over.'

'It sounds as though the fires have gone down but the embers still glow, no? I am sure you won't let him leave your life.' Then he touched my hand. 'Please don't be offended. Of course you have suffered.' Then he asked about J. He was fascinated by his life, his eloquence, his education and breeding. He asked a lot about J. Then *Harriet Hunter* got some play. I said Bacall hadn't got the money yet. When we left, the two guys at the next table left too. Robert Hartman drove me to the hotel and asked again about Gerona.

'I suppose it's hard for an outsider to fit in there.'

And that reminded me of Jane and the husband whose name I'd forgotten. And I would have mentioned them but I didn't.

'Do the foreigners get a chance there?'

And then I couldn't mention them. I remembered she was on the run and didn't want any part of Hollywood and stardom ever again. It was no more than a feeling but I was sure that if Robert Hartman wanted someone located his surveillance would take care of it.

'I think outsiders get a lousy time,' I said. 'It's a hard place to crack. How do you know about the Jewish restoration?'

'Some Spaniards have discovered that the closed quarter was the Jewish centre in the Middle Ages, where certain mystical practices were carried out. Books have been written about it. It is quite interesting historically.'

'Did you read it in the paper?'

'I believe I did.' He smiled in the darkness, his eyes darker than any darkness. 'We'll be in touch,' and he let me out of the car.

I was glad Colin was waiting in the room. I felt choked with misery. Mine? Robert Hartman's? Of course I wasn't fabulous enough, successful enough for him. And if I didn't watch it I wouldn't be young enough. He'd put me on the outside even in a place I loved.

Colin said, 'He's still besotted with the wife. He tried everything to save her. He took her to Lourdes, had her blood changed. Treatments were flown from Russia, prayers were said in the Vatican. He stayed with her day and night. She was a marvellous pianist. She died at thirty. I think all his activity prolonged her life. It might have been kinder to let her go.'

'Who told you this?' I was sure Robert Hartman hadn't. The film legend had, in the days when she could still remember.

'Then his son, a brilliant scientist, shot himself. Blew his brains out in New York. I don't know how he deals with it.'

I said how fascinated he was by J.

'Well of course. J is it. Royalty. What is Robert Hartman? Sicilian gutterboy.'

So J was educated and classy and all Robert Hartman wanted to be. Yet Robert had given his love and dedication to a wife and tried to save her. J had three failed marriages and saved spiders.

Chapter Twenty-five

J made up our Orson Welles quarrel. He listened to one half of a cassette of my first radio play, due to be broadcast in 1980. He only managed half. He looked as though he was manacled to the chair. Good behaviour killed him. Then it was down to the health store for a bumper present of good things. He smiled a lot and wanted to do whatever I chose. I preferred him, unfortunately, when he was normal. He asked if I wanted some jewellery.

'Jewellery?'

He thought I was sneering. 'Well, you are unadorned and that's unusual in women of your age.'

Jewellery! I wanted a film, a literary success, to be a household name, to love and be loved in return, to become evolved. Jewellery had never occurred to me, except on that catastrophic train journey to Barcelona to see José before the marriage. And the middle-aged woman with the hair like corn in moonlight had worn rings. And the amber one had made me hungry.

'You need cherishing. I could cherish you,' he said.

'Do I?' I thought he might have a point.

'Definitely. Your boys need a father.'

157

"They've got one.'

'I bet they don't know it. And you'll get into bad company if you're not careful.'

'To whom does that remark refer?'

'Your friend at dinner last night. You were seen. I wouldn't play around with him.'

So I asked what he knew about him. He certainly knew about webs and catching flies but then he understood spiders.

'But surely he tells you about himself, doesn't he? I wouldn't like to think of you just getting into the company of someone questionable.'

Was he questionable? I didn't know. 'What has he done?'

'I don't know personally. One hears things. I hear he buys people into this town. He arranges an entrée for those who couldn't get in otherwise. He's also originally from the East. And he's dangerous.'

'The Mafia you mean?'

'To women.'

'Does he buy them?'

'He might. He might well. But the ones he doesn't buy don't do too well. Someone got quite upset and well, she took an overdose. And now she spends her days at the psychiatric office.'

And I was sure she was Colin's friend. For once the two worlds crossed.

'She is awfully pretty,' he said.

'Is she married?'

'She is,' he said promptly as though giving the right answer on a quiz game.

'Well perhaps she should stay with her husband and out of trouble.'

Everyone kept warning me. The trouble was I couldn't get anywhere near him.

J had the last line. He said my evening at Spargos with Robert Hartman must have looked like a scene out of a Mills and Boon romance.

'It's a shame they couldn't get him on film. He'd have been perfect for the hero. Dark, unapproachable, hotly sexual, lethal but held back for the right person.' J chuckled for a long time over that.

'Are you gay?'

'Just realistic.' He squeezed my hand. 'Your life could be a lot easier if you were looked after. I don't mind your tantrums. I like it abrasive. I loathe absolutely women who keep trying to please.'

It was all yes in Hollywood. I never heard no. *The Siesta* was already about made except they didn't quite have the finance. Except they didn't put it like that. So I suggested to Caroline Pfeiffer she try Robert Hartman. She'd not heard of him. 'He backs movies invisibly. He's on my side.'

Coppola, it was rumoured, had also read *The Siesta* and absolutely adored it – in rumour parlance. I went high and fizzed over. Nothing came of it.

On the night before I left, Robert Hartman phoned to say goodbye. He asked if I needed anything. I needed his approval so wanted him to read *The Siesta*.

He asked if J had been nicer that visit.

'Why don't you bug him and find out?'

He laughed. 'Perhaps you don't need it nice, Patricia.' There was a pause. I thought we were taking a sexual turn here. What should I say? What I said could kill his interest if he had any, so I changed the subject. 'I'm not in his world. I am always on the outside.'

'So am I,' he said softly.

I wanted to see him, didn't know how to ask.

He said, 'We'll see each other again.'

I did see him later that year at the opera in Paris. But I was with my agent and he was with a very pretty young girl. He didn't look on the outside that night.

I thought the pretty ones came unstuck quicker. They expected more. And that's when life got troublesome. The pretty ones ended up, dozens of them, like the wrecked cars at the sides of the freeways all over Hollywood.

Chapter Twenty-six

The house in London had no heat except small dark blow-heater fires like little dogs panting, and there was a broken pane in the french window. Chris had kicked it in during a moment or two of adolescent violence. The animals, two cats and three dogs, went to and fro through this gap into the garden. I always intended to get a flap made. A flap always reminded me of the Broadway hotel door with its cat door in the middle. When winter came it was survival time. Wrapped in blankets to watch TV. Crouched against the breath of the blow-heater to write.

My life in London was always the same. I did the shopping, made the meals, washed up, walked the dogs, did my exercises, and wrote. Sometimes I wrote twelve, thirteen hours a day because there was nothing else to do and the house was too uncomfortable to be in. The only thing was escape. Mine was writing – then the cobwebs and the peeled walls would recede. Also I was obsessive, ambitious, and writing was a way out of this huge Victorian mollusc shell in Kentish Town. I couldn't move in the normal way because there was no money. The glamorous clothes stayed in the cupboard and only came out when I aired them in the sun or on a trip abroad.

People visiting the house always cheered up. In comparison it made their place the Ritz. I must say they weren't so cheerful when I acquired something a little more stylish in Hampstead.

The house was a prehistoric cave, huge, echoing, with sudden misty unexplained lights. Quite often lost street characters would bang on the door and want in, thinking it was a squat. After a while the authorities didn't call because they thought it was abandoned so we never got billed for gas, and Phil spent nights of anxiety wondering how to reverse the meter and what would happen if he got caught and would he lose his job?

The house had no heart. Except the telephone. After a while we all had a way of living and it was separate. Phil stayed behind shut doors reading, working, listening to music. I was on the same floor at the back, writing. The kids were on the top floor, each with his own life. Guests stayed in the attic. Downstairs was never used, except to store furniture and cook. We never took meals together. I'd prepare the stuff and everyone would take it off to their own room. Except Phil who prepared his own. He seemed to get some strange excitement out of eating food long past the stage of being edible. He'd scrape off mould, spoon away clots and curdles, break off the withered and the spotted. He was deeply offended if anyone threw away a seeping lettuce or fungus-coated loaf. I thought it was a response to my wild spending on travel and those 'good times' he accused me of having. But he had an incredible digestive system because it all went down and stayed down. He knew it was strange, this food hoarding, and wanted it kept in the family. 'Whatever you do don't tell my mother.' She was elegant, sophisticated and very, very clean. He kept her away from that house.

The day José said he was marrying Nina my heart broke. I forgot about it. My heart remembered though, because I could no longer feel anything sexually for Phil. It just evaporated. We tried for a while to get it back, then gave up. I felt it was bad for your body to force yourself to sleep with someone you didn't want. I was sure it made you ill. Why it came out on him and not José I do not know. I suppose because he was there. However, I kept my LA dalliances to myself. I was still nervous of him, of his anger. I lied. And so did he. He certainly had plenty of extra action. We should have split then. But we stayed together and our relationship changed into something familiar, like two old animals roaming together around the huge house. At best I was very fond of him and when he was in trouble I realised how much I did care for him. I didn't live with Phil. He was the man with whom I shared my life. And the house, echoing our stagnant relationship, sank lower into the rotten soil and twisted, and bits fell off. Yes, the house and everything in it became stagnant and there was not one thing I could do about it. Except try and make money.

He could easily have left me. When it was clear José was still in my life, if only as a heartache. He stayed because he didn't want to move. Change frightened him. He had a funny sort of respect for me, for the dodgy times I went through. I counted with him mainly because I did what I wanted. He watched my way of being alive and it gave him ups and downs by proxy. He didn't have to go and put himself on the line. He didn't enjoy it because it meant he was three-quarters asleep instead of being fully, if dangerously, alive.

J visited England and got very excited by the house. The broken pane in the backdoor stayed with him for days. 'You'll feel that in the winter. If we get a really cold winter what are you going to do? Can't you get it boarded up and put in some central heating? No, I suppose you can't. Not a house this size. And how are you going to clean it?'

'I'll get a cleaning woman.'

'I can assure you you won't.' J examined some broken floorboards by the lavatory. 'You wouldn't get a Latvian peasant cleaning in here. I don't know how you are going to live through the winter. I hope you've got a good doctor. Fix these floorboards. Some guest using this lavatory could have an accident. Especially if he'd had a drink.' He was thinking of himself. He liked surfaces flat and secure when the whisky set things spinning. I think he saw the house as a huge saga film on a level with crossing Siberia in LA sunclothes. He found a handsome spider hanging from the bathroom ceiling. 'That'll have a hard time in the winter too.'

Chapter Twenty-seven

I wrote the NFFC filmscript and called it *Don Salino*'s Wife. Essentially, a script is a hundred pages long. I turned this one in at 180 pages and was asked to cut it. I started work but it became even longer. Somehow I didn't think I was going to get my second half preproduction money. Michael Lindsay-Hogg was busy putting on *Whose Life is it Anyway?* in New York and wouldn't be free to film anything until the following year.

I also wrote radio plays, journalism, a TV play, a documentary, short stories. A lot of it was rejected so I rewrote and turned it in again and in the end most of it got accepted. Everything for me was hard, except in Hollywood.

My sex life was fantasy and Robert Hartman was the star. I created a whole life with him. Sometimes he came into my mind so clearly, I supposed he must be thinking about me. He appeared in my thoughts, hovered there, then was extinguished like a spent light bulb. How I wanted him to take me into his life! I'd be a reborn person then. But I still wasn't free of my association with José. It, too, came into my mind.

After I left Michael in the 1960s I lived with José in Puerta de la Selva. There was the hard summer and the soft summer.

During the hard one, at the end of the 1960s, I was full of a brazen optimism. Even now I can see myself in the Spanish sun. It's like looking at a separate person, not a friend, more a relative that I don't particularly like but understand only too well. The heat pressed me against the wall, the sombrero tipped over my eyes, the street dust stung my bare feet. My mind was without thought, body without sensation. I was part of the wall, the heat, the afternoon. José was standing on the balcony of our rented fisherman's cottage, the baby Timothy in his arms. We didn't have money but he was able to turn the children to advantage. It secured him credit all over the village. That afternoon the owner of the butcher's shop below was hosing down his doorway and telling José what a marvellous son he had. José didn't deny it. He chose that moment to ask for credit and got it. Michael had said José had charm, a *joie de vivre*. 'I'd like to have what he has. You can't acquire it. You either have it or you haven't,' he'd said.

During the soft summer we walked along the beach to the next village. An act of love had put our bodies so much together that even walking produced a sort of pleasure. There was a powerful lovely smell of flowers which grew at the edge of the sand. The houses of the village were stacked against the mountain like playing cards. Umbrellas over the beach café tables were flung up by the wind like tulips.

I looked at him, remembering how we'd made love that afternoon. A pang of fierce happiness shook through me. He was thinking about it too. 'Come on. Let's go back and have a siesta.' His smile was wicked and lovely.

Towards the end of the hard summer the *tienda* owner rattled up the slope on his motorbike and opened the butcher's shop. The sky was angry, speckled, and there was rain over the mountains. The kitchen was full of stillness.' Good people have lived in this house,' José said. Like a hand, the stillness folded over the words, snuffed them out. We sat together peeling vegetables. The kitchen soothed all thought of future, all questions, held back the future. I felt then as I had when I'd first met him in Gerona. In those days I used to do something I wasn't ashamed to call living.

Later we noticed the car with the Belgian number plates was back. It was parked outside the butcher's. Sometimes its owner washed it, or polished and mended it, but his eyes were always on us. He was the detective and he got the dirt. I got the deal. It came down to survival. I had to eat, the kids had to eat. José had no money. I went back to London to divorce.

The next time I saw José he was cooler. He was beginning to see his life must be resolved from another direction.

He came back to me in thought as I sat in front of the panting blow-heater, my body stiff and exhausted from typing. And I had to see him again. My mind kept retreating to the hard summer and the soft summer as I went through the interminable Kentish Town winter – all that J could have desired. Icy winds whistling through the broken panes, frozen pipes. The spider didn't make it. I did.

In the fisherman's cottage the living room had been small with a low-raftered roof. It held the air, the smell of another century. It had bottle-green doors with panelled glass windows and against these hung white pieces of silk stitched with broderie anglaise. Hanging low over the table was a lamp consisting of three bulbs like bulging pears which could be brought low by pulling a weighted chain. José said the lamp was over a hundred years old.

'It's still in the last century, this house,' he said. 'It has no need to change. Don't you love it?'

'As long as you're in it.'

Making love wasn't what brought us together. Sometimes I believed our souls loved each other. Why else did I keep having to go back to him? I was surprised I lived the way I did, forgetting him so often, being with other men. Then up he would rise from the deeps of my dreams.

The Siesta got some good reviews when it came out just before Christmas 1979. I considered that was enough of an up to lead me back to Gerona. I needed a key to enter these days. Success was the key.

I walked into Gerona and the past, the esctasy, came back. It had nothing to do with circumstances. It was some chemical thing. The cathedral, catching all the light of the late sun, seemed to hang over the town. I'd never seen it look like that but Gerona never ran out of surprises.

I expected to see him. I walked without direction along the narrow streets, up the stairways, across the bridges. He should be there. It was the hour when people were out walking. They didn't dress up any more because they were always dressed up. Hardship was all in the past. I regretted my past behaviour with Nina. It made going to the flat in the Calle Forsa difficult. I should have been diplomatic, but how diplomatic can you be when you're in love?

I took a room at the Hotel Centro, the last old hotel, with huge lofty rooms and peeling paint, old-fashioned bathrooms with pedestal sinks and china cupids. The place had housed my love for José, soothed my pain, given me hope. Mostly the rooms were unoccupied, their blinds closed, doors slightly open. And in the vacancy there was a definite lingering sense of a time gone, of romance heady but undeniably gone. And it made me sad because wherever I went in the town it would not be found, or in the country, or perhaps whatever place I visited. And if I should find it, could I hold it? Could it ever be more than a sweet tantalising fragrance in an out-of-date hotel? There were long, pale green winding corridors and a palatial silent dining room, with moulded ceilings, turn-of-the-century clocks and lamps. It stayed this way because there was no money to modernise it. It had a smell. I sniffed for it immediately. It was still there, musty, slightly perfumed. The wind howled around the ends of the corridor, banging the shutters and the hotel sign creaked and swung. The breakfast room was full of oily greenish paintings. The table cloths were bleached by sunlight, the huge china coffee cups gleaming, gave off a pale milky light in the dim room. There was nowhere in the world I'd prefer to be.

They knew me at reception, remembered the times I'd passed through Gerona with the children. So I asked about José. They never saw him. If he was in town they didn't know about it.

My room was pale green, the lace curtains made the light soft. For a moment there was the cold thrilling damp atmosphere I remembered. Then it was gone and I could be anywhere. I was trying too hard. I was looking desperately for joy. I stood on the balcony and looked along the street, sniffing deeply. Even the smells had gone. There should be heat, vibrance, music. When I was first there the days were scorching and 'Johnny Guitar' was played everywhere. People used to be out on the street and the smell of olive oil cooking used to hang around in the heat. It all seemed to have got colder, especially the people.

I considered going to the apartment in the Calle Forsa. What could I offer this time? Another film deal? So I went to visit the American couple in San Daniel.

Jane was dressed exquisitely and her husband whose name I could never remember was levelling a granite floor. He'd transformed the stone house into something cosy and warm. How I could have used him in London! Jane's hair was curled, her face radiant. But who saw it? Except the husband. They still didn't mix, it seemed. They made me a hot drink and Jane did the talking. I had the impression, although the smiles were on, they weren't exactly thrilled to see me. I trotted out the old Lauren Bacall film locale story. I thought it wiser to stick with one piece of good luck, even though it hadn't materialised, rather than move to another, for instance *The Siesta*, which might have more chance of actual success. But why confuse them? I could bring out *The Siesta* reviews but then I'd look like some door-to-door salesman. I stayed with Bacall. Yes, the film was coming along fine, a lie, and we would be filming in Gerona, false.

'So you go to LA?' said Jane.

'A lot.' I modified that. 'Quite a lot.'

She poured herself a huge Scotch and looked thoughtful.

'Will you ever go back?' I asked.

'Never.'

'So Gerona's caught you too.'

'It's real here,' said Jane.

I thought that was the last thing it was. I got real. I asked about José.

'He's fixated on Jews. Daily he takes over houses and apartments around that courtyard on non-existent money. He must be into debts so colossal it's going to be the salad oil swindle in the United

States all over again. He spares no expense. The lighting for a start is beautiful but cost thousands. It took a local firm – how long was it, Richard?'

'They were in the best part of· six months.' He laughed laconically. 'They've still not been paid.'

'Why not?'

'He's waiting for the Jews.'

'He's got the most marvellous bar. The counter's from Granada. It's engraved wood embossed with gold.'

'Bar?'

'He's turned part of the place into a bar restaurant, just to make some money. It's the only thing making money.'

'Will the Jews come?'

'Oh I expect so,' said Richard. 'But will he recognise them when they do? He's never seen a Jew. He keeps finding signs and artifacts. If that doesn't work he'll turn to miracles.'

'The government's furious,' said Jane. 'Because this time it's a sensitive choice. I mean, before it's been activists, then the gypsies, then artists. But now he's taken it out of Spain. Now it's Jews? What next?'

'Juan Serrat's father still won't come in but he'll have to in the end,' said Richard. 'So will the sister. She's got money. Otherwise the whole thing will go down the plug and Juan's inheritance with it. It's called throwing good money after bad. Serrat and José run from bank to bank looking for loans to pay the workmen. You can't say *mañana* to an Andalusian. He'll slit your throat. I said to José he should go immediately to the Department of Culture and demand some aid. After all he is promoting Catalonia.'

'Not a chance,' said Jane. 'They know José.'

'If you see him,' said Richard, 'don't tell him we talk about him like this.'

'What will she do that for?' said Jane. 'She's not here to upset him. It's not that we don't like him. It's just he always takes the easy way out.'

She poured another drink and I asked how Jane filled her days. She replied 'Happily.' Then I told her Gerona was known, even in Hollywood. How it was surprising they were the only two

168

foreigners. And I described Robert Hartman and how he'd known about the closed quarter. And Jane went shaky. Richard got up and stood beside her. He couldn't offer her a drink. She was well into those.

'I didn't realise you were that into Hollywood,' he said. 'I thought you were just kidding a bit to impress Tarres.'

They looked at each other and made a decision. 'How well do you know Hartman?' asked Richard.

'Hardly at all.'

'You've not said anything about us?'

I was sure I hadn't.

They decided to trust me. They had to. 'Jane was married to his son. He worked at a weather research centre. A scientist. One day he took his life.'

'He blew his brains out,' said Jane.

'And Jane had a really good career beginning in films.'

'So I got out of there,' she said.

'Why?'

'Because I was already in love with Richard and we were – well, we hadn't dared have an affair because of all the surveillance Hartman's people specialise in. But Jamie, his son, must have known. I think that's why he took his life. I don't know whether or not he'd left a note but I figured Hartman would come after me. So Richard and I just ran for it. I dyed my hair red. It used to be gold and long. A change of name. We came here. We're not married.'

'But Gerona! I mean he knows about this place.'

'So it's the one place he won't look,' said Richard. 'If he's looking.'

Remembering how cute he was with J's electronic key I thought he could do something simple like find his daughter-in-law. Even with a change of hair colour. It all sounded OK, the story. I didn't believe it.

Of course I tried to get my fill of Hartman information. She said she never saw him when she was married. It was all business with him. Even Jamie didn't see him. He had to become a corpse to get that one's attention. She felt Robert Hartman might have been responsible for her original entrée into films because she did the

169

screen test with a superstar and that suggested a favour returned. So I assured them I wouldn't give Robert Hartman their greetings from Gerona. How could I? I never could find him. And in return they'd play me down to Nina if they saw her.

The next morning I fell into José's company in the bank. He was standing at the Spanish transactions counter while I changed money at the foreign desk. He was accompanied by a tall well-dressed young Catalan, Juan Serrat. They'd been refused a loan. I caught the tail end of it. The refusal didn't seem to get José down. He indulged in some banter with the clerks and got them laughing. He was smiling a lot, two teeth at the side were now missing and the lustrous black hair was not as I remembered. For the first time since I'd known him, he looked ordinary. He greeted me by saying he had to pay his workmen. It was always the same story. I offered him 6,000 pesetas. I had 20,000 but before he could decide one way or the other Juan Serrat declined the money. But he was impressed with my gesture.

I told him about Bacall and the film and made my visit sound like some sort of location hunt. José remembered the Bacall story from the last time and as I was still saying it, maybe it was true. 'She is a legend. Incredible. When is she coming here?'

I said anytime. In fact the whole deal had now fallen through and she would never be coming here. I hated J to be right, but her company had not raised the finance. The book was now out of option and fancy free.

José was busy with the fantasy, he had it well between his teeth. 'I will give a banquet to honour her. She will be our first guest, at the centre of cabbala.' I said it was lucky because she was Jewish so might appreciate it. As I spoke I thought José and I were the two people who could have made a true union and here we were propped up by all these other people. As we left the bank I tried to arrange a meeting. Frantically he indicated Juan and his eyes widened, 'dangerous'. So I publicly said I'd visit the Jewish centre later and Juan shook hands and started walking away. José hung behind. 'Nina must not know you are here. Which hotel are you in?' He said he'd be there within an hour.

I put on dark glasses which I supposed made me invisible and walked around the old part. There was a place called a pub with loud music and Scottish beer. A lot of the old places had gone. Chez Beatrice was now a pizza bar. The Hotel Residencia Internacional was still boarded up and covered in decaying posters. An old woman stepped in front of me and started shrieking. I thought she was the local madwoman until I heard my name. 'I think it's disgusting you come here trying to break up that marriage.' It had to be José's mother. Age had made her unrecognisable. In comparison the Residencia Internacional was in good shape. 'That sweet girl. You'll be repaid, never fear. You'll go to hell, you selfish slut!' She waved a cane in my face and I thought it was time to move on. Her curses shook along the street after me, reverberating wall to wall. I thought if Nina hadn't known I was in town she did now. Everyone else did. Mama was still doing her town crier act denouncing me, so I entered the Hotel Centro over the back wall.

In *The Siesta* I'd written about Nina.

She was in his life and had changed everything. Barriers had been put up, letters intercepted, telephone messages sneeringly destroyed. The relatives ganged together. 'He doesn't live here anymore.'

'So where is he?'

'India. Sweden.' No place was too fantastic to keep him away from the English girl.

How right I was.

I could understand why Nina would hang on to him. He'd given her correct little existence, where everything was overprotected by her parents, mystery. He'd given her pleasure beyond her schoolgirl imaginings. Life was sensual when he was in it. She couldn't wait to be in bed with him. I could see that she was impatient with every other life function, even eating.

The cathedral bell chimed every quarter of an hour, day and night, and was echoed by lesser clocks across the town. I always had to wait for him, even when I was fifteen. 'Wait for me in the Savoy café. I'll be there at nine.' And the cathedral clock would break up the hours intermittently. Ten. Eleven. He never explained why he was late. He didn't avoid explanation. It was just that nothing substantial seemed to come out of him.

Today I looked curiously young. Had I reached back to the person he'd first loved? We'd never fulfilled that original promise, made good our chances. Perhaps I was really two people, not complete identities but overlapping ones. And the deeper one belonged to José and that was why I was often in such anguish to see him. I had to have him back. I'd run away with him if necessary.

He came in as the bells chimed 11.30. A knock on the door and everything in the room jumped. The lace doilies on the sofa and armchairs slid on to the floor. 'You look good,' he said. 'You're looking – ' he snapped fingers – 'up.' He hung the doilies back on the chairs and sofa.

I thought he didn't look good. Perhaps things were not going well for him but I was more concerned with his receding hair and the softening and shrinking in his face. But then being in love was a selfish business.

'Listen. With Nina we must be very careful. She's dangerous.' He took off his clothes swiftly. 'She had been raging all night. Somehow she senses you are here.' He got on to the bed, made a cut-throat gesture.

'Bullshit! She's not the type. She is far too greedy and grabbing.' I thought of those clinging little hands.

'Why d'you think I couldn't get to Barcelona? I left her parents' house to join you. I said I was going to Tarragona on business. She ran up to the bathroom and locked herself in – it was awful. Now I feel death all around me. I am never wrong about these things.' He shivered. 'Then she got the letter.' He lay back, hands behind his head waiting for me to undress. 'What a fucked-up day that was. She went rigid like one of her sculptures. I spent half the day with her in the clinic. How could you write such a letter? Have you no sense?'

'I was sensible enough if the person it was intended for opened it. I had no idea she was so free and easy with your mail.'

'She reads everything. You be careful. Now I will have weeks of her bad thoughts.' I was going to be blamed for everything but he still stayed in the bed waiting.

'Why is she so suspicious if you're so happy together?'

'It's only when you're here.'

'I find that hard to believe. Two days every two years? Leave it out!'

When he held me I knew I didn't want to be famous and successful. I wanted the past back. I wanted to be the runaway dressed in black who crossed Spain, barefoot, without money or fear, who saw José Tarres on the steps of a local hotel. I'd never been more what I was meant to be than in those days. Having lovers, having kids, knowing rejection, failure and some success, getting old, wanting things like money, respect, had somehow made me veer away from that real person still inside me. He stroked my body, remembering it.

'In my dreams I reach out for you, Patrice. And I find you but you've changed. Don't change.'

The love had come back, just. After a while so did his worries. He said, 'We must not be seen together.'

He got up and put his clothes on in the greenish light.

'Why don't we get out? Let's go to Istanbul,' I said.

'We will. As soon as this business with Serrat is finished.'

'No.' I could see a lot of sense in a quick get-out.

'I haven't any money for that. I've put all my money into this affair with Serrat.'

So I said I had money. A lie. He put on his shoes and I could see his neck twitch. He wasn't saying no for once. It was a nervous tic. I thought that real life had caught up with the golden boy and it was proving to be a strain.

'I can't just walk out on Juan. He put his trust in me and – '

'We've all done that.'

'You were the one who left, Patrice. Not me.' Quick as a whip. 'With the children. You were supposed to stay a month.'

'If I'd stayed you'd still have married her.'

'We'll never know now, will we? It was a solution to my life.' He shrugged and put on a brand-new beige winter coat. I was glad it wasn't the prune velvet jacket. It looked as though he'd chosen this one himself.

'You always wanted the good life, José. How does it feel?'

'She loves me. She's loyal. You were impossible in those days.

The drinking, the extravagance. I never knew what you were going to do next.'

'Be poor. That always came next.'

He kissed me briefly and was gone. The door closing made the lace doilies slip gracefully off the armchairs on to the floor like a lot of debutantes fainting. Normally such a sight as a lace doily would make me laugh but I was a million miles from laughing.

Chapter Twenty-eight

I left the hotel by the normal entrance and walked straight into Juan Serrat who asked me to go with him to the Jewish centre. As he was paying for the place I reckoned it was an invitation I could accept. The stairway was now finished and there were pots of plants at the bottom. Juan's father, Papa Serrat, an old bowed figure, was sweeping fallen leaves off the star of David on the courtyard. His smile was angelic. He was doing a beautiful thing. I realised he'd had to capitulate and throw in his whack of money.

There was a bar to one side with locals in a line drinking and salons where tables were laid with expensive cloths. The rooms were private. It looked like a house of rendezvous. I smothered my first impression and admired everything. José was showing around a group of businessmen. A house with a tower loomed over the patio.

'What's that?'

'That is the house of Isabella Sans-Gomez,' said Juan.

José greeted me formally. The businessmen ordered some drinks. Nina was hanging a cage of doves at the side of the courtyard.

'The birds of peace,' said José.

Then she turned and saw me and her eyes were far from peaceful. But after the letter I'd sent there couldn't be even a pretence of goodwill between us. Her greeting was sullen and she hung on to José from that moment and did not let go.

'We have found the treasure of the Jews here,' said José.

'What does that mean?' asked a businessman. 'Gold?'

'Oh, something far more valuable,' said José. 'Their heritage. In this courtyard they travelled further into the possibilities of human experience than anyone has before or since.'

The businessmen would have preferred gold.

I asked José about Isabella Sans-Gomez.

'She made all this possible. She gave me permission to open the street. She had facilitated all the dreary legal procedure so we could buy the area.'

'But who is she?'

'The goddess of Gerona. She's lived here all her life. I'm surprised you ask.'

Nina's hands were all over his arm. He swept them off but they were back somewhere else. Of course Jane was right. He always took the easy way out. If she made a fuss he'd let me down. That's why he hadn't come to Barcelona the last time. But because he was weak he couldn't tell me to go away, neither could he make her happy. He didn't love her. I knew I should simply leave and let the marriage die.

'Isabella Sans-Gomez is our patron. She has been more than generous. She has given deeds and licences without payment.'

'What was here before?'

'It was closed. But the whores could get in from the other street, through a broken wall. This was just bare ground filled with rubbish and dilapidated houses. The whores, the ones who couldn't get a position in the Barrio Chino, brought guys here. Also gypsies slept here. And a man came every night at two in the morning with a shovel and dug and dug, looking for the treasure of the Jews. Poor Isabella Sans-Gomez never slept one night through.'

I could see the point in letting José have a few legal points for nothing. At least she slept nights.

'And the moment we began our excavation the light changed.

176

Isabella said it came down in pale blue shafts shot with silver. It will bring back the cabbala.'

Nina nodded fiercely.

Gerona had a marvellous atmosphere as long as it was unsung. I thought José and the demands of his now gaudy ego would brutalise its mystery.

'We have concerts here of Sephardic songs and the whole town comes to listen.'

'I hope they pay.' I couldn't resist it.

'They pay 300 a ticket. They would pay 3,000. There are so many the courtyard is overflowing and they hang over the balconies and the music floats across ancient Gerona and the birds join in. It's impossible to describe such a wonder. But for one or two hours life is right.'

They showed me around the buildings. There were three storeys of beautifully decorated salons surrounding the courtyard. There was a well, a restored medieval cooking oven untouched since the Jewish occupation. Below that began the excavation which would yield the real stuff, the testaments, the vessels and maybe some money. Guys didn't spend all night digging for nothing. A synagogue was almost complete with a Bible donated by a Jewish foundation in Germany. Everything was ornate and lavish but an expression of José Tarres' taste rather than Jewish culture. It wasn't anything like the glory of the Hotel Residencia Internacional. It didn't have the love in it.

'Here is the mortuary, the dormitory, the area where they slaughtered the animals. This is the ritual slaughter block. This is the hospital. That the bathing area,' and we trod over stones, passed through broken walls, and there was the real treasure, the sun stone.

'That,' said José, 'is the reason you came to Gerona. That is pulling to it what it desires. It has for centuries. It sends out its invitation.'

It was a pale oval with markings on, lying tilted. I asked if it was Jewish.

'Before. It belonged to the sun-worshippers,' said José. 'The cult of Mythra. Nina says it gives her energy. If she feels depleted she only has to put her hands on to its surface. At night it sends out a wave like singing.'

There was more historical stuff which I was supposed to look at but all I could really see was José and Nina. They were a couple showing off their new house. In practical matters they were well suited. There was a definite rapport about the refectory table. Between them they positioned it perfectly. Maybe the sun stone would so re-energise her she could keep this ageing man.

José suggested we have lunch. He made sure Juan Serrat came along. The boy would do for me, act as blotting paper to absorb any overflow of emotion at the table. We climbed some spiral stairs and arrived in the bar. Beyond that there was another considerable network of palatial salons with *chaise-longues* and sofas, and cunning lights and marble floors. It reminded me of a luxury brothel. Nina disappeared.

'Are you going to be converted?' I asked José. 'To Judaism?'

'I was born a Jew,' he said. 'How else could I find the key to all this?'

He crossed the courtyard and deftly lifted back a branch loaded with winter blossom. He fixed it against the wall to advantage. And in that moment I saw what José was. He would show even nature to advantage. He could make the least moment significant. He made life beautiful. He remained, his hand lifted making sure the branch would stay. And we all watched him. That was the way it was.

'Truthfully, when did you get the idea for all this?' I was suddenly furious I'd been so left out. 'Since you left the art centre? Before?'

'It's been in my mind for years.'

'Well you've certainly kept it to yourself.'

'But only now can I begin. Now is the right time.' And he listed the local visitors, the messages of support, the huge plans for the future. I cut through any more proud talk by saying, 'But where are the Jews? It's very impressive what you've done, but it's nothing but a beautiful cradle. Without the baby.'

Nina's sculptures filled the place like detectives watching our every move. His eyes demanded silence. She was out of sight but she could be listening.

She came out wearing a huge make-up, a replica of mine. Even her hair was done the same. I took it as a compliment but even after the life I'd had I could be screwy where enemies were concerned. She was in fact sending me up but the joke was private. Just for her and him.

I realised there was a lot more to me as a person than I'd supposed. It took a lunch with Nina to show me that. I now saw I was a person of qualities, the grown-up kind like patience and mercy, because I didn't kill her. I saw her strong, clay-moulding hands all over him, possessing him, showing that he was hers. Of course luck attracted yet more luck and even at the table in the frugal tavern, where one would think nothing could get to you, along came a local journalist kissing her hand, praising her. Then he wrote a cheque. It seemed he'd purchased a piece of her sculpture. She slipped the cheque into José's pocket, a gesture nothing on earth could have made me do. Her eyes searched for mine and blazed with the pure pleasure of winning. What was hers was his and in return he was hers. Her cheque slipping into his pocket was a sexual act. For some reason I remembered the bad times in Paris waiting for José. I remembered trying to get money so he would have a room in which to sleep when he finally got off the night train from Spain. Any money I made was in Pigalle. I picked up Algerians to eat, then ran away. After one repast in a sordid backstreet I hadn't run fast enough. When my host caught me he said he'd cut my throat. He'd paid for my meal so he got my body. I remembered the knife, its pressure against my windpipe. It made me gag, sickly. He took the knife away, jabbed it against my back as he walked behind me towards a sex hotel. 'I paid. I get you.' Pigalle philosophy.

I'd begged the Algerian to leave my clothes on. I wanted to be pure for José. Twenty years later I still wanted to be pure for José. He was ruining my fucking life. Because of what I felt for him I was sitting opposite a smug young chick who hated me as much as I hated her. I was always losing. Nothing changed. It used to be his mother. I could see my life hadn't been successful because of José. And then the French bitch took him when I'd gone through so much.

I ate the lamb and bean stew, the crème caramel and talked about art, or whatever rubbish she was on about. Juan Serrat had beautiful manners and passed salt, pepper, oil, poured wine at the right times.

'Where are you from?' I asked Nina.

'Paris.'

That figured. All my worst times were in Paris.

José was full of cabbala talk. What I knew about it had come from the encyclopedia in Shelley Winters' house. It wasn't a lot but it was still more than he knew.

'We have found it again. It will be restored to its rightful place. The centre of cabbala is here with us.'

'But I thought it was in New York and in some parts of Jerusalem.' I was sure about that.

'No,' said José decidely. 'The cabbala is here.'

Nina couldn't nod her head ardently enough.

'Are you going to get in touch with these existing groups?' I asked.

'Why should we? We have it here,' he said.

And she nodded emphatically, her eyes gleaming with spite.

'So it's sort of on the side of the Calle Forse up some steps, the cabbala?'

They both nodded.

'It's been waiting for us to unearth it for hundreds of years.' He talked about it as though it was a piece of stone, not an idea.

'But who's going to teach it?' I wouldn't have been surprised by this time if he'd said himself.

He said, 'The Jews will come and amongst them the right teacher. The vibration of our centre will attract Jews from all over the world.'

'But don't you think you should let them know? I know this must sound ordinary, but what about letters to synagogues and foundations in – '

'It's not neccessary, Patrice,' he said. 'You don't understand because you're English.'

She gave the tiniest laugh in the world but we all heard it. I'd stood in too many dole queues and scrubbed too many floors and fought off too many creditors for this scene.

'I think you're crazy. You're spending his money' – indicating

Juan Serrat who didn't dare open his mouth – 'to build an institute of cabbala and rabbinical studies and you haven't involved one Jew. I mean, how do you know what a cabbala centre is like? They may have all kinds of requirements you haven't thought of. They may not even want a building. I'm not too sure about the bar. It seems to me cabbala is in books and it's passed from person to person, even now. It's secret. It doesn't rely on a physical site but the people involved – '

'Wrong.' José sighed. 'It was here. It is still here. Nachmanides, the greatest cabbalist, lived in our courtyard. So you see it is a shrine and the Jews will come back to Spain to their past and pay homage.'

I knew it was wrong but there was not one argument I could put up against him. It seemed to me it had already been done. A perfection had been reached and recorded. Who today could better the mystics of the medieval time? And if they were around would they come to Gerona to do it? 'How will you make money out of this centre?' I asked.

'Money!' José scoffed. 'I do not want money. I am returning to the Jews what is theirs.'

And Nina did some more nodding and her violent sneering eyes waited for me to be hurt.

'Patrice doesn't understand,' José told Juan Serrat. 'But I cannot argue with her. Because she is an old friend.'

Nina yawned a couple of times, then took José's arm. Siesta time. I stayed with Juan Serrat and discussed Judaism, something I'd never done before. Really I was curious to know how José's marriage was, how often he slept with her, if he was unfaithful. In other words I wanted to hear that he still loved me.

Juan was respectful and pleasant but there was one drawback. I couldn't hear what he said. After a while it all flowed together with not enough consonants. Then I realised it was due to drink. The after-lunch brandies had simply washed them away.

'So you're happy doing this restoration?'

'Very.'

'But it must take a lot of money, Juan.'

'What is money when something like this is at risk? You can't equate money with history.'

181

That sounded like one of José's lines, the ones he used for other people's money.

'Has he put money in?'

Juan nodded.

'I didn't think he had any.'

'His cousin underwrote his loan. And there's some land.' He meant the *barracca*. 'We can always use that as a guarantee against credit.' Like me, Juan was quite happy with the future. José had a way of making it attractive.

'But surely your family, your father for instance, must be worried about your money. I mean, this is an unconventional business scheme.'

Juan said his father wasn't worried. On the contrary, proud of what his son and Tarres were doing. It had begun as a quite ordinary venture. A bar casino. Then they discovered it was the site of the Jews. They found coins, passover bread, scrolls. Juan had another drink and the list grew.

'But if it's for the Jews don't you think the Jews should be involved?'

'They will at the right time. When José says it's the right time.'

After his next drink I brought up the subject of the marriage and Juan said they were happy.

'Don't you think she's very young? She is at least twenty years younger than him.'

'When you're young you can love more and you have more energy.'

I stopped that conversation before it got painful. Juan had inherited a hundred thousand pounds. In the end José got his hands on all of it.

I couldn't decide if I should stay or not. Was there any point seeing the man I loved being with someone else? My instincts still said she'd bought him. She'd come in at the right time, when he was down.

I went for a drink at Luis's bar Arc. Luis was now unhappily married with seven children. He'd never written the book he was going to begin over twenty years ago. But he was rich. He began by saying that my presence in Gerona was not a good idea.

'Now José has to be a conventional husband. Good behaviour doesn't suit him. You shouldn't come here.'

'How about boredom?'

'José's not bored. He's got Serrat's pile to go through, then Papa Serrat's, then the sister. Then he'll start on Nina. He can't get his hands on her money yet because the father is watching.'

'Doesn't he approve?'

'Absolutely not. But what can he do? She has to have her way. They tried everything to stop the marriage but she is spoilt. But José will find a solution. He'll give her a baby and that will be that.'

My eyes, my whole being shut with horror. Luis, suspecting he'd gone too far, tried comforting me. 'He's not happy like he was with you in the good times. He's a different person. But the town changed. Our politics have changed. He's obsolete. So he has to get by.'

'I don't remember a good time. Just a lot of lies.'

'He doesn't lie. They're fabrications. They're real for him.'

Luis asked about my life in London. I said fantastic. I think I even said I was married to a filmstar. I was considering killing Nina with the medieval weapon hanging behind Luis's bar.

'Of all the beautiful girls he could have married.'

Luis shook his head. 'Why would they marry him? They could get less fanciful men who pay their way. Who wants to marry Don Quixote? All she had to do was get rid of you.'

'How did she know about me? I was tucked up there with the kids in the cursed quarter, half pissed most of the time.'

'The Americans Jane and Richard would have told her. She stayed with them at night while her studio was being built. She was determined to get him. It was in her face the first time she saw him. You must be careful of her. I think she will do anything to get you out of the way.'

I thought of the intruder in the rented house. The man who looked like anyone with a white shirt, maybe pink in the darkness. He wanted in. And Chris, Tim and I speeding through the night half naked. I mentioned it and Luis remembered.

'Nina is not the innocent, believe me. She is not what she seems.' ·

I had to hide in doorways and alleyways waiting to speak to him. First she came out yawning and replete after a busy siesta. She crossed the bridge to the modern part. Then he appeared with Juan Serrat and they started up the steep steps to the excavations. I called to him and he turned. How I still loved him! Reluctantly he crossed to me and I said I must speak to him. He said, 'She could see us.' I said she'd gone.

We sat behind the pale lace curtains in the Hotel Centro. We belonged so much together, joined in everyday things like sitting in chairs. I couldn't envisage a life without him. It did not seem logical. I told him and he didn't disagree.

'What shall I do? Have a threesome? Put you with her in the bed?'

'Do you have threesomes?'

'Well, I have. Why not?' He stood up to peer between the curtains down into the street. His mother was trundling past, a big baggage of hate. 'I once picked up a couple on a train. It was quite extraordinary. I'd gone to Barcelona to have dinner with Nina and her parents and on the way back I stopped off in the Gothic area for a drink and got delayed, so I missed the last train to Gerona. The only one left that night was the *Talgo* going to Paris, but it's expensive. It left at midnight. I had absolutely no money, but I got on because I couldn't spend the night on the station. I went into the bar because I thought when the ticket collector came I could say my ticket was further on with my wife. And I got into conversation with a Scandinavian couple. She was elegant, so beautiful.' He paused, remembering her. 'So we had some drinks and they asked me to go with them to their wagon-lit. First of all I had her, then he had her then I joined in and Gerona went by and the next thing I knew we were at the frontier. I thought, shit, I'll be in Paris next. So I got off at Port Bou and had to get the first train at 6 a.m. to Gerona. It was an incredible time with them.'

I wasn't believing any of it until he said Port Bou. I remembered the night he was supposed to be in Tarragona but had a ticket in his pocket from Port Bou.

'When was this?'

'Oh years ago. Before I married.'

'When I was living in the rented house opposite your *barraca* with the kids?'

'Yes, that's right.' Quite innocent, not thinking.

Nina would have killed him for that. 'So that's what's called business in Tarragona.'

He still didn't remember his lies.

'It's that something between us that Nina hates. She goes on about it morning and night. You see it, she sees it. What can I do?'

'Do you see it?'

He shrugged. 'I hate possessiveness.'

He'd certainly chosen the right one for a wife. I asked him to take a few days out of his marriage for me. That's all I asked. He believed she'd settle down eventually then, maybe, just possibly we could meet somewhere. I immediately arranged the somewhere that night. So he said we should take Juan Serrat and his car and get out of Gerona.

'Is that what you want?'

He sighed.

'You don't have to. Do you want to? It's up to you.' I was beginning to see that if you gave people a choice they more often did what you wanted. And they had the illusion it was their decision. He said he'd come for me at eight.

It was almost like the old days.

Chapter Twenty-nine

Juan drove us up into the hills surrounding the city. I said I was hungry.

'We were always hungry,' said José. 'Don't you remember?'

'But we were young then.'

Then he talked about the night in Tossa de Mar dressing me up as a gypsy as though it were a cherished memory. I'd read the palms of the rich friends and they crossed José's palm with gold.

'Why use a party game to get the money?'

'Make fun of asking and you get more.'

I could have used that in the Paris streets.

'Did your mother know about your political side?'

'Of course not. I was a poet.'

'I didn't mind being used, incidentally, but I'd like to have been told. I'm not made of glass.'

Juan didn't know what we were talking about. He probably wasn't even born when the activist Quico Sabater was a legend.

He drove to a small *typique* restaurant and we ate outside under the trees. Chickens ran in the grass. A sweet sound of church bells crossed the field. Juan ate quickly, then went inside to watch football on television. The night came and José and I sat listening to the leaves rustling, a silvery sound like young bells.

'It's OK here,' he said. 'Everything gets on with its own life. Trees, sea, birds.'

'And the people?'

'People fuck everything.'

We stayed in the night, not speaking. His arm was over my shoulder. We sat effortlessly together, in harmony with each other and with everything around. The harmony flowed one to the other and circled out into the night endlessly.

Juan came out and said it was nearly ten. And then José remembered Nina.

'I think by the spring we'll have a Jewish quarter settled,' José said. 'Then let's meet in Barcelona and take the boat to Turkey.'

'We should go now or we'll lose it,' I said.

'You can't lose what really belongs to you, whatever you do.'

Who was I to disprove fairy- stories? 'You could come to London. After all, you got there before. When I was married.'

He understood the significance of that.

'When you insisted I leave Michael. Did you think we could have a life together?'

'We already had a life together. Just because we didn't see each other didn't mean one wasn't going on.'

'So will you? Come to London?'

From the beginning I'd wanted to get him away from where he was, from what he was doing. Because he was mine.

The lights had come on in distant Gerona, a cluster of sparkling colours, a beautiful adornment encrusted with jewels. Long ago some unaccepted lover had adorned the nakedness of the city, celebrating its mystery and uniqueness. I too would have to make an offering in the end. I would not get away untouched.

'Remember this place because we've been happy here,' he said. 'Like the day we took the cart full of ice to the sea.'

I could see the chunks of ice gleaming in the sun. The cart had been drawn by a slow brown horse. José had worn a dark blue shirt, and around his neck a golden chain.

'But do you remember it?' I asked.

'Of course.'

'So the past matters to you?'

'Infinitely more than the present.' And he really looked at me then, his eyes passing through my clothes, my skin, all the frivolous things that could change until he located what had first attracted him, a feeling of pleasure that was not unfamiliar. He said we'd known each other before and had met up again for better or worse. Reincarnation didn't even come into it.

His words linked me to him, bound me more closely than any ropes or chains or even embraces. And I knew I'd never be able to leave him. All I could do now was expect compromise.

'When you are happy in a place that happiness goes on existing. And with you I have touched happiness. What do you think?' he asked.

I wanted to mark the moment with some sign, write a message, leave a token so the moment would be remembered for always.

When we got down into Gerona I prayed he'd come away with me. I prayed in all the sinful places. Not the cathedral or the churches. Too many prayers got sent up from those and I'd never get a look in. Then I walked, reclaiming the town and all the streets and cafés where I'd been happy, even the ones that had gone. I'd got him back.

That night a voice in my dream kept saying, 'He always lets you down.' I thought it was Emilio the football coach from the old Residencia Internacional Hotel. 'He can't let you go altogether. You represent the wild adventurous side of his nature, but it's dying.'

I had breakfast in the gloomy room with the huge white cups. I counted my money again. There was enough for his train ticket. He said we should get the ten o'clock train. I was absolutely sure this time he meant to leave with me. But was it for London or Istanbul?

I'd always felt that life appreciated the grateful ones. And because I'd recognised when I was happy, I celebrated the moment with all my possibilities of pleasure and energy. Like when I'd been on Paradise beach with José in the 1950s or with my Auntie Amy in Portsmouth when I was a child during the war. Because I was appreciative life would see me all right. It's only when you didn't recognise your happiness that you were really in trouble.

I paid the bill and waited downstairs by the flowerpots. I felt no guilt about taking him from Gerona. But she'd produced the solution she'd been desperate for and the prison door clanged shut. In the night she'd told him she was having his baby.

Chapter Thirty

When I got back to London I started a new novel, *The Rose-garden*, which was eventually published as *The Unforgotten*. Trying to get it published was an experience none of us involved would ever forget. However, it was my favourite book, perhaps because it was about Tycoon.

I also began a play for the National Theatre in conjunction with Radio 3, *From the Balcony*, about a Portuguese nun. I also began a film treatment with editor Jim Clark for Don Boyd about people committed in Bedlam in the nineteenth century. The only 'also began' I didn't get into was the personal stuff. I did not answer José Tarres's letter. I had to give the future a shape. I had to make an ending now because I daren't believe ever again that a life with him was possible.

I decided that when I came to the end of this gigantic pile of writing, which was nothing but lunacy, seeing it all had to be delivered in a few months, that I would devote myself to myself. I'd be solvent. I could therefore buy clothes, improve my looks, go to health farms. I'd travel. I'd meet people. I'd be stimulated. I'd marry and I'd never think again of José Tarres of Gerona.

The man I had in mind to marry was Tycoon but that seemed like a long shot. However, after what I'd been through I could do anything. I promised myself that, after hearing the news of Nina's pregnancy. I sat crouched in the street by Gerona station and all the sorrow came out, like being sick. I'd lost. Somehow I'd let that which belonged to me slip away. And then I sensed Los Angeles calling to me, a siren across the world, with its desert voice. And I thought of Tycoon. I knew he valued me. However, the feelings I experienced sitting sickly by the station were such that I promised I'd never get that low again.

To make it all seem positive I did use it in my writing, especially the Portuguese nun play. This particular nun had the misfortune to fall in love with a type not unlike Tarres. It seemed that even in nunneries in the old days you weren't secure. If sin wanted to reach you it found a way. So what chance did I have crawling around in Pigalle half my youth? It did help me write about the nun. I think I gave her a little extra. Seeing José Tarres on the steps of a Gerona hotel was the same as the nun seeing the soldier. 'It was from the balcony I first saw you ride by.' 'And now a passion from which my heart expected so much can give it nothing except separation. Will I ever look again into those eyes in which I saw so much love, which brought me to ecstasy beyond sense and loosed in me a craving for sensual joy?' I saw that writing was an odd experience, not at all like life. Alive in the words, I ceased to matter. My surroundings receded too, which was lucky seeing how they looked. It was only when I stopped writing that I realised in what a squalid tip I spent my life and how ill and exhausted I had become.

When my Dad died in November 1981 the only place to go for that sort of thing was Gerona. But I couldn't go there so I went to Hollywood. Bacall had given up on *Harriet Hunter* and I felt deeply let down, not by her but by logic. She was so perfect. And for a brief while it was resuscitated because Verity Lambert wanted it for Euston Films, but the board or finance or whatever it is that stop people doing what they want, didn't like the idea of money going into Spain. One thing about my life in those days, I could never be disappointed about anything for too long. There was always some new bitter rejection on its way. I did suggest to Bacall she approach

Robert Hartman but she got him muddled up with someone else of Italian origin. 'I wouldn't touch his money,' she said angrily. Her tone implied she did not trust his money.

The *Harriet Hunter* option was taken up by Alain Chammas who was in partnership with Richard Dreyfus, the film actor who was making the movie version of *Whose Life is it Anyway?*. He told me there was a type of flu going around. It had no fever but you felt very bad – I knew. I had it. And it kept coming back. The superstars could call this illness what they chose. When I said 'recurring virus' the doctors went crazy. How the hell can you have flu every week? I didn't know. Except I was having it. 'You haven't even got a temperature. It's in your head.' I found out later many viruses produced a very low temperature. It certainly wasn't in my head. That was already full of its own kinds of shit. I started to lean on Valium. For me it was alcohol without the disadvantages. I tried to keep this flu from J because he did not respond well to sick people. I was his guest. At one time I did say I felt too ill to go out. I sat huddled by the pool, a raggy dusty outcast like one of his beloved coyotes. But what went down well with wildlife did not apply to women. He strolled into the brilliant winter sunshine and saw me looking 'unHollywood'.

'What's all this?'

'I don't feel good.'

'What, a woman's thing, you mean?'

'I mean flu.'

'Impossible. It's not the flu season. No one gets ill this time of year.'

'Well it's something that Richard Dreyfus says is flu.'

'You know something, honey? You're the sickest person outside of a hospital.'

The remark made me mad enough to stand up and act well. I just hoped one of these days he was going to get something, a normal person's illness, a toothache, just to make a balance. All he ever got were sneezing bouts. A dozen sneezes blew out whatever bug was trying to accost him. Then he'd grip on to a carton of Vit C powder and fizz up a potent dose in water, wash it down with Scotch. End of episode. I didn't have to wait long for revenge. After his viper remarks about my state of health I found him, the following morning, wringing the top off a new carton of Vit C powder. Without bothering with a spoon he tipped a liberal amount into a glass of water. There was a lot of dithering hands and shakiness and some of the powder spilled on to the floor. Was it a hangover? Of course he didn't have those either, he said.

'Not feeling well, J?'

'Definitely all right.' He gulped the fizzy remedy and I saw his eyes were baleful and red rimmed. A bug had got in.

'Perhaps you've got flu. Like I had yesterday. Oh, but it's not the season.' I sounded very nice.

'I just said it's nothing.'

He padded off to his tyepwriter. The typing was slow. Then silence. I saw him creeping into the bedroom and sliding between the sheets.

'Would you like me to get you something?' I was nice, very nice.

'I would not.' Very prompt. 'I just thought I'd work in bed today. Like Proust.' He picked up a pen and a sheet of paper.

'Why don't you just give in and lie down? You know you feel terrible.' I brought him hot lemon tea and soups. I treated him the way I'd wanted him to treat me. When I left to go shopping he said, 'Better get some aspirin. As I never need it I haven't got it.' Then he said, 'Is this how you feel?'

'Lately, yes.'

My virus recurred for over five years. J got rid of his in two days. Apparently it clung to your cells. Something to do with the protein. It left no trace, not for the X-ray or the blood department, so it got no respect. It was considered psychological until everyone started getting it. Some scientists said the viruses came from out of space. They hit a particular territory and the vulnerable ones got them and kept repeating them. I didn't bother to tell J that one. He was impatient with every unseen aspect of life. The mystical drove him to a frenzy.

Alain Chammas had an exotic two-storey suite off Wilshire. He'd been the head of Warner's or Columbia in Europe for years and now wanted to produce his own movies. He was starting with a movie starring Dreyfus and Susan Sarandon. He had good plans for

Harriet Hunter. It was being scripted by an Oscar-winning writer. He wanted Charlotte Rampling for the main part. He knew films. He watched them constantly in his home movie theatre. Also, he liked having a good time. Party games, house guests, nice food, excursions. He was very social. A lot of the Italian directors visiting Hollywood stayed with him. He was good friends with Bertolucci and Antonioni. Everything he said about filming *Harriet Hunter* made sense until one day he put the projector on and said , 'Watch this. Our male star.'

As the part was that of a history professor, intellectual, introvert – Peter Finch came to mind but we couldn't get him for obvious reasons – I expected to see a clip of George Segal or, if we were really lucky, de Niro. Whatever was up there had to be clever, respected and history-loving. So I could be forgiven for being a little taken aback when John Travolta came whirling on to the screen. Alain let me watch a couple of minutes of dance then snapped off the show. I was quiet because I'd realised years ago that strange things happened when you needed finance.

'I thought you'd be surprised,' said Alain. 'He's not everyone's idea of a history lecturer.'

'Is he intelligent?' I asked cautiously. 'I mean in everyday matters.'

'I'm intelligent,' said Alain. 'Because he's the biggest box office there is. We get finance like that.' He snapped his fingers loudly. It was like dry twigs snapping. It wasn't a healthy sound. Two servants came running but he didn't want anything. He was just excited. 'I can see by your face you're one of the minority who didn't go mad about *Saturday Night Fever.*'

I'd not given myself the chance. I hadn't seen it. As far as I was concerned Travolta looked primeval. The dancing meant nothing to me. With his face and those close-together eyes he looked to me like anyone's idea of a dancing baboon. I wasn't even sure he could speak.

'Just one thing, Alain. Can he play a historian?'

'Of course not. We're changing all that. He'll be a dancer, not a teacher. I'll get Gene Kelly to arrange one of his great numbers for Travolta. One of those Spanish ones. After all, it's set in Spain. And

we'll call the film *Tango* or *Boléro*. We'll get Bernardo to direct.'
He meant Bertolucci. 'Right now Travolta's on a fat farm in Santa
Barbara. But he adores Bernardo and wants to meet him, so we'll all
drive over there and pitch him the idea. I know it's not quite what
you've written but this is movies. Let's be sensible.'

I didn't think anything about it was sensible. But in that moment
when I could have said something I realised I didn't own the
material. I'd been given money and now Alain owned it for a certain
time. Also it was senseless to fight Hollywood. Things got set up,
perhaps not in the best way but they got made. To start objecting
would only take energy and I wouldn't win. Anyway, I had the
original book – that was my work. If anyone ever wanted to read it
after seeing the film they could go to the library. And I got paid. I
learned my lesson in a couple of seconds and never forgot it. It came
in useful later on. Some of the things that happened to what I wrote
were beyond sensible but I never did a thing about it. My attitude
outraged other writers. To them I showed a lack of taste, care,
scruples.

We never got to the fat farm with Bernardo because Dreyfus flew
in from New York. He made a provacative speech on TV that
startled the town. It was about himself, how he saw life. It was
brave, eloquent and didn't kowtow to the approximate moral code
of LA. He looked fifty. He was thirty. Life had whitened his hair.
Alain's new idea was that we should all fly to Vegas and play poker
for a night and a day. I hung back because I didn't have that sort of
money. Alain tried to persuade me. 'Come on. Richard has money
now but it doesn't mean a fucking thing to him. Five years ago he
couldn't even afford to buy the cards to play poker.'

We aimed for the airport but ended up in a hamburger joint.
Dreyfus was highly articulate and had plenty to say. He wasn't
someone you got close to because at sometime he'd been in exile,
maybe in his childhood. It was a cold place, endless, with wolves
howling all around. It had stayed with him. If you got close, you paid.
Alain eyed him with fascination. He adored wildness as long as he
didn't have to do it. He could get close because he understood him
and mothered his talent. He knew all about the cold place which the
ladies slipped up on so innocently.

195

We were close friends at that time, Alain and me. It took *Harriet Hunter* being rejected all over again for that friendship to break. He blamed not the script but my book. 'You never licked it. You had the story but you never got the ending.'

I think what really had gone wrong was *Fedora* being released. I personally thought it was an incredible film. But it didn't make jingle noises at the box office so films about movie stars were out. My Paris agent then gave *Harriet Hunter* to Romy Schneider who was bankable and did want to do it. But she unfortunately died. Then it strayed at last, like a bad lost foal, to its rightful owner, where it should have been in the first place.

I tried to use the time after my Dad's funeral as a holiday, but the nun play had to be delivered and Don Boyd wanted his *Bedlam* treatment. I sat working in the hot winter sun by the pool. J came out to see what was going on. I kept quiet about the film stuff, just kept it all literary and low key. But he'd seen the producer's name on the treatment title page.

'You don't want to touch him. He's just done *Honky Tonk Freeway*. Just about broke EMI. I am not sure it will recover.'

'Well he can't break me. I've got nothing to lose.'

'Don't take him out for any dinners. I know you get persuaded into that sort of thing.'

'Why?'

'Because I hear he never has any money, only credit cards, so you'll have to pay his taxi home as well. And this is a big city. Taxis can cost twenty-five bucks.' My way of life amused him but then he didn't have to live it. He thought I looked thin and strained and my weight was down to 7 stone 7. Looking after my mother during the bad months had a lot to do with that. He told me off for letting myself go. He didn't have much time for death. After all, he'd seen enough and it happened to everybody. I wasn't in mourning for my father. I was glad he was at peace.

I found out my winner's attitude, cutting out what didn't suit, wasn't foolproof. It didn't take care of the loss of my Dad. Because my mother had had terrible problems during his dying I hadn't had the chance to mourn him. I'd put her into a hospital, then a nursing home, dealt with his funeral, got the plane out of it to LA. Finding out 'cut off' didn't work was my first bad night in Hollywood. I'd just had dinner with Alain Chammas at a fashionable place in the canyons, crammed to the brim with stars. Jack Nicholson, Hal Ashby, Warren Beatty. So I got a look at them close to and they carried on with their own lives. Alain was all excited because Dino (de Laurentiis) was setting up again in Hollywood. Alain didn't drive so we waited outside for a taxi to his place. Suddenly I sank to the pavement, my world in disarray. I didn't know whether to throw up, scream, piss myself. I needed to drink water. But I couldn't speak. Everything had gone. So, as Chez Valentino was nearby, the taxi took me there.

J was out and I asked Alain in because I felt too unstable to be alone. After a bottle of mineral water and another Valium things took a brighter turn. I offered Alain a drink. He didn't. Then J came in. Now of course he had to be Alain's hero. His cinema fantasy. First of all Alain was shocked because he had no idea he'd ever see J in person, and more, that I knew him. The occasion was equal to four John Travoltas all saying yes. Alain told him what he thought of his films. He knew them all, frame by frame. He spoke reflectively, asked questions, showed a lot of common sense. J always liked that. He could get the fancy talk in the cinema review mags. A lot of praise came into it and J was warming up. He didn't like strangers in his house, not the two-legged kind, but this wasn't the usual businessman. This was a movie buff, a connoisseur and soon they were deep in conversation. I was totally excluded. I didn't have to be the centre of anyone's world but I did feel after twenty minutes someone should talk to me. I did make a statement. It took time to think of it – it was ignored. Then J saw his new fan was without a drink. 'Don't tell me she hasn't even offfered you a drink? Oh, that is too much.'

The 'she' was hostile.

'I did,' I said. 'He doesn't drink.'

'Don't be silly,' said J and poured Alain a man-sized whiskey. Alain accepted it. He'd have drunk piss for his hero.

Now I hated them both equally. I got up and said I was going to bed. That was OK too. A little more of the 'she' came from J. Then Alain had the sense to remember he needed me, at least till he had the script written. He said I was a very talented writer, original, stirring, with plenty to offer. J gave a horrible wince and decided it was time for Alain to go home. I knew I wouldn't be allowed to die until I had two Oscars minimum. Nor would J because he'd have to see it. Even if I had to scrape him off heaven's ceiling he'd see it. I knew then that Tycoon had been right. J wasn't just putting me down. He was actually competing with me. He was jealous.

Alain realised he'd been a little selfish with his hero-worship and tried to include me in the evening. I said I'd call him a taxi. J wouldn't hear of it. He'd drive him home.

I went to bed, too furious even to shut my eyes. The wild night life prowled. There were hunting screams and mating cries, then their hero came back and the night was full of purrs. J stood amongst them like Francis of Assisi, patting a few racoon heads, murmuring praise to long furry things. He came into the bedroom, his eyes glittering, and chucked down his cigarette case and lighter.

'Always offer a guest a drink, Patrice. Maybe it's out of fashion in Kentish Town but we're sort of used to it here.'

'Did you have to take over my guest?'

'Someone had to. Why should he be bored to death?'

I picked up the long gun by the bed. It was supposedly there to shoot pheasants. It wasn't pheasants tonight. I pointed it between his eyes. The pool was about to get its first murder.

J tried to save his life by saying I was upset about my father.

'Bullshit! I'm upset by you. It's not "she" by the way. It'll be "it" next. One week of domesticity with you has turned me into a murderess.'

'Think of it this way, Patrice.' He sounded reasonable. 'That gun won't kill me but it will kill your career. And you've worked so hard. Now all you need is a good agent and tomorrow we'll talk to Robbie Lantz. He's in town.'

My arm stiffened, wanting to kill, finger on trigger. Two bullets would put that cynical, critical, woman-hating brain to sleep. But then a cool breeze got up. But for that perhaps I would have killed him. I'd heard it somewhere, in some film, that line. Weather always had an emotional effect on me.

I didn't wait for a taxi to take me to a hotel. I ran down the winding canyon road towards Sunset Strip. I was barefoot but I had my credit card. That was one up on the Gerona days. I was reminded of the intruder night when it all ended with José. But instead of a rough winding path, this was smooth and belonged to the super rich.

When I couldn't run anymore I sat on the road above LA looking down at the Strip and beyond, over all the pulsing lights to the ocean. I realised they were all gone, all those who had given glamour and dreams, and it was nothing but a patch for estate agents to get rich in after all. And then I thought of the other one who gave dreams. But if I went to Gerona I couldn't see him again either. I'd just look at a lot of streetlamps, twinkling. And my Dad was also gone. And he'd given me dreams once, about the sea. When I was a kid and he was home on leave he told me about the sea and the places he'd been and he'd bring back silk pyjamas from Japan and ornamental secret boxes from Egypt. He too had a magic in those days. So I said goodbye to him from Hollywood. Then I got up and walked to the nearest hotel, full when they saw my lack of shoes. So I got a cab and went to an airport hotel. And they gave me the wrong key. So I spent ages blaming myself because it wouldn't allow me to enter room 2440, and what it was about me that had such a perverse effect on keys. At reception they gave me another key which got me into the room and I wished it hadn't. The room promised me eternal loneliness. You think Albany Park was bad. That'll seem like a penthouse, promised the mauve and green room. Everything was dead. The air, the carpet, the bed, the blank TV set. I took a shower for something to do and the plastic curtains hadn't shut properly and when I swung them open I looked down into a small pond. The wall-to-wall bathroom green carpeting was holding on bravely but then the water started to win. I went into the bedroom. It was like walking over a soggy field in Kent. Never lose anyone again. A Gidion Bible waited on the night table. I didn't dare touch it. I knew it was there for suicides. Nina didn't lose anyone. She sat smug in his mother's flat wearing her wedding ring, he wore a matching one, and every day put them closer together because the baby grew between them. The love object, it stopped the inevitable death of the marriage.

I spread towels over the soggy carpet and expected to get shit from the occupants in the room below. I decided to deny it. I looked out at the night. Unlike New York, these windows opened. I missed train stations. I knew LA had one but I'd never seen it.

Train stations had played a big part in my affair with Jose. In the old days the train from the frontier to Gerona took over two hours and was always late. He'd be waiting on the platform, black coat, white silk scarf, black eyes, warm smile, hopes, deceits, and before the train stopped, before my body moved, my soul would leap out to him. Those moments held me captive now as once I'd held him.

The hours of travelling, the tiredness, the difficulties leaving England and finding the money would be shrugged off unnoticed as soon as he touched me. To see him opened up a new world full of colour and I used to believe entry into this bright place was only possible through him. It turned out I was right. I'd climb down from the train and the lies would begin before the first kisses were over. His beauty and warmth, all the good things in the end made him bad. But he could have done something marvellous in those days. Everyone expected it. Yes, I'd had the best of him.

In the last years he'd been unreliable about meeting trains. Was it the fault of the new oversized station glinting like an airport or the fact that Nina was in his life? The old station had been built when the railway first came to Catalonia. There had been a dark cool bar where we drank bitter Cinzano and every time we met it felt as though we'd never been apart. The time that had separated us didn't exist. I forgot loves, friends, duties. It got me into trouble often. Buffets were good places to talk about the future.

I knew, as I was experiencing the beautiful things, that they were more than just happy chance. These were tokens from fate, receipts, not to be forgotten. You've had your fun. Now pay. I looked again at the Gideon Bible, considered approaching a church. But God is supposed to be everywhere. Not when I needed him.

Chapter Thirty-one

J was sitting thoughtfully by the pool when I returned the following morning. He said immediately, 'How did you stop drinking?'

'Why?'

'Because I'm going to have to. The earth moved. Just now.'

'I thought that only happened in Hemingway books when you were having a good time.'

'It all moved, all of it. I've had too much to drink.' He shivered.

In fact there had been a mild earthquake. I was too depressed to notice, he too drunk. I heard it on the TV news but didn't tell him. I felt too mean. The previous night's row meant nothing to him. I didn't offend the real things. He'd recently had a mistress to stay who thought she'd please him by killing all the ants in his kitchen. He caught her pouring boiling water over these, the real guests. He was so angry it put his blood pressure up. It was the first time in his life that had happened. My lifting up a gun was just playtime.

Until he too found out about the earthquake, the time was spent on instant reform. He questioned me closely about the deadly enemy. Did I have d.t.'s? Had anything like that happened to me? Used I to drink anything or did I have preferences? I'd liked beer and wine but when the alcohol level reached a certain point anything goes. So I'd throw down gin, vodka, and would have had meths if it was around. I didn't slip suddenly. I was born needing a drink.

I remembered again Tycoon saying J was jealous of me. I asked about his work. His writing, for example. Did he enjoy writing scripts?

'No.'

'So why do them?'

'Because I do them reasonably well and that gives me some feeling of accomplishment. But a script is not more than an architect's plan. A script is not after all the building.'

'But you make the films.'

He did not feel creative then either. He was no more than a dance master getting the actors through the dance of false life. It had nothing to do with life.

'Life?'

He didn't want to talk about it.

'Did he want to write anything else?'

Yes, he did want to write a book. So why didn't he? He looked pained then. 'I can't. I'd rather not talk about it.'

'But you're one of the best film makers going.'

'If you have no self value it doesn't matter what you are.'

It turned out he thought the creative stuff was missing from him. What he didn't realise was he had to be a completely different person for that. He had to be on the edge, even slightly mad, or wild or uncomfortable. Definitely not at ease. He wasn't that sort of person and neither would he want to be.

It was when I saw *The Siesta* producer Caroline Pfeiffer for lunch at the Dome that I realised just how extensive Tycoon's operations were. His prowess had been such that he'd bought into the music business and was deep into the profits of some of its biggest stars. They wanted to make movies and Tyc made that feasible. But he was even bigger than that. He'd moved in on a major studio and had majority shares. The first thing he'd done was terminate *Quark*. I couldn't believe it. J had never mentioned it. I had noticed he was preparing something else, a political film set in Chile. But Tyc wouldn't lose money. Thousands had already been invested in *Quark* so he sold off the option and the stars for a television series. He didn't make a profit but he got the preproduction money back. He'd put quite a few projects into 'turnaround', not a popular word. Caroline had gone to him with *The Siesta* but had got Irish. She'd also got a no on finance. However, she'd get it made. It was a beautiful piece of writing, she meant the script which I hadn't read. Coppola, in spite of all the earlier excitement, wasn't interested. He'd just done *One From the Heart* and it had flopped. He was now into flops for a while so it had to be a good thing, she said. She gave me good news, bad news, so rapidly it was like taking a sitz-bath at the table. One side of my face felt hot, the other icy. I was sitting next to a particularly potent orchid. It could have been that. When I went to the lavatory I saw my face was red on one side, completely white on the other, like a harlequin. Caroline told me some of the other buying Tyc was into. Of course he was always invisible. He had several front men. They seemed to do any living he needed. I thought how right she was.

Anyway, her option money for *The Siesta* put my life into turnaround, in the good sense, and I could afford to travel as well as eat. I even paid my bills.

Caroline had not had an easy life but if it was mapped out for the average person it would sound highly glamorous.

She drove me in her dark brown square car, all shiny and new like a chocolate square, to a good place for getting a cab, the back entrance of the Beverly Wilshire. It was raining unseasonably. J said it only rained in January, not November. Because I rushed, head bent low into the cab, I didn't notice who was holding open the door. I assumed it was the hotel doorman and pulled out a buck and said have a good day. Tycoon said, 'Keep your change, lady. The pleasure's all mine.' And he let go of the door and got in beside me. 'Where are you going?'

It was going to be J's but I changed it to the Château Marmont. He asked what I was going to do there. I didn't know but at least it meant he could come with me. He gave the driver a different location. 'How about some fresh air?'

He was the only person who didn't tell me I looked ill. I knew I did and the extraordinary face-colour change at the lunch table hadn't helped. He'd seen I was in trouble. I didn't want to give him a gloomy account of my life so said I wasn't altogether sure that the air suited me, filled as it was with the toxic petrol fumes and the exhalations of gloomy trees. 'It's like trying to breathe through a wet blanket.'

He said, 'It's not a very healthy place. The Indians wouldn't settle here in the last century and that was before petrol fumes. They called this the valley of bad air. So as you're sensitive you pick that up.'

That made the place a paradox because it was most people's idea of a health resort, the sun, the oranges, the sea, the fitness cult.

We walked along the coast and I didn't speak about my loss. I told him he'd turned down *The Siesta*, or Irish had. I reminded him it was my book.

'Oh don't worry. It'll get done.'

I could have asked him then to back it. Its low budget wouldn't affect him. It would change my life.

He guessed what I was thinking because he said, 'You don't need me. Because if I do it for you, get things made, it won't have any value. You'll say it only happened because you knew the right people. And you're good, good enough to get it done on your terms yourself.'

He held my hand. I was in a new universe. Not alone, linked to someone else and through his hand energy passed into me. When he let go the good feeling lasted.

He said he was going to Paris after Christmas so I told him I often went there and how my French agent, Marcelle Simon, was getting my work attention. She was trying to get Polanski for *The Siesta*. Then I stopped talking because the ambition showed through and I knew it was wrong. I said I'd seen him in Paris at the opera. I didn't mention the very pretty girl. She was about half my age which made the memory more cutting.

'Well as you're so often in Paris I think I'll see you there.' He turned and looked at me and his eyes excited all those little responses that had been quite unused lately.

204

'I'd prefer somewhere else. Paris isn't lucky for me.'

'How about Gerona?'

'Ditto for now.'

'I hear the Jewish restoration is almost completed. They're going to have a school of cabbala there.'

'You must know people in Gerona.'

He gave a desolate laugh.

'You know more about it than I do.'

'Perhaps for me Gerona is ongoing. For you, it's over.'

He sounded sharp. I thought of Jane. So she could be ongoing. And someone had told him I was over with José. Unless the stones talked. 'Who d'you know in Gerona?'

'Oh come on, Patricia. You don't own the place. For example they do have newspapers there.'

'Or do you have a video? Let's see if the Jews do flock to the shrine. I'd sure like to see that on video.'

'It's on the way to Jerusalem. They could make it a stop-off.' He called a cab from a coffee shop and came with me up to J's. During the drive I longed for him to touch me but there was not one move I could make. Any move was the wrong move. It would be an intrusion. Sometimes I did get it right. Before I got out at Casa Valentino he stroked my hand and half a ton of strain just fell off my face. An hour in bed with him and I'd look ten years younger. There was no beauty treatment like a guy you fancied.

'For some people life is going from the dark into the light. Like in Gerona.'

'Who are these "some people"?'

'You'll find your way into the light.' He squeezed my hand. He wasn't afraid to touch me. 'Perhaps Paris then?' It wasn't an invitation, just a suggestion.

The electric gates swung shut and I didn't look back. I did feel like a Mills and Boon heroine as I returned to J.

I waited for our next spat before I mentioned *Quark*. 'How's it going?'

'Very well.'

I was surprised. I didn't think he lied. 'When do you start?'

'Oh I don't. It's being turned into a TV series.'

'But you'll still get points or a credit?'

'Not at all. I won't do television. But my new film is much more worthwile.'

I must say he took it very well. It could have changed his career, his life, made him super-rich. If he knew Robert Hartman was behind its demise he wasn't saying so. He did ask about him before I left LA. It was rather hard to talk about an Irishman when you knew he was really Italian.

'I don't think you got it quite right, Patrice. I think you found an imposter. The man at the Polo Lounge was pretending to be Robert Hartman. It's the first time I've met an imposter. Only you could find one.'

'Wait till someone comes up here pretending to be me. Then your problems really start.'

'Robert Hartman is Sicilian. He was originally a doctor. He studied at Harvard. No Columbia. He was certainly in medicine. And now he'll run Hollywood.'

'Well that's not such a bad thing. They need a good doctor up here. The ones they've got certainly don't impress me. They don't even come and visit.'

'Did you meet Robert Hartman?'

'No,' I lied. I didn't want him to feel bad, worse than he did. 'But he did want to meet me to talk about the Mills and Boon film.'

'He only wanted to meet you because your name is Chaplin.'

When I got back to London and Christmas was over, I sorted through old photographs and letters. I hated to keep old clothes, out-of-date diaries, irrelevant letters. One diary surprised me. It wasn't a diary as much as a confession of savage, sometimes unbearable pain at being separated from my lover José and later, the murderous humiliation when he'd married the young French girl. I picked up the photograph, the one I couldn't destroy. José and me in the porch of Gerona cathedral. It was taken just after I arrived. I was fifteen, sixteen. Of course it wasn't us. It was different people, a different time. This couple looked round at the camera as though it was stealing up on a precious moment of intimacy. They looked secretive. They belonged together, more married than any couple. It was really a wedding photograph.

I recognised Luis off to one side and friends from the Residencia. There were other people in the background. Amongst them I recognised Tycoon.

Chapter Thirty-two

Marcelle called me over to Paris on 4 January. Romy Schneider
wanted to film *Harriet Hunter* but we'd have to wait till the option
was up with Alain Chammas. Whatever happened I mustn't alert
him to good news. Otherwise he'd hang on to the option and ask
preposterous sums for its release. I asked Marcelle if she knew
Robert Hartman. After all, she did business with American
companies and brought plays into Paris and Europe. She'd heard of
him. In fact he'd been behind the takeover of a French publishing
firm. He'd since merged it with a Parisian theatrical agency and film
company so now had a vast entertainment complex. She wasn't sure
if the government was for or against Hartman but it was certainly
aroused. She said she hadn't met him. So I asked if he'd called her
to invite me. I was sure he was behind the invitation. But she was
a good businesswoman and knew which side her bread was buttered
on.

Paris has an effect on me. I could call it doomed. It's a spiritual
assassination with degrees of torment and suffering not normally
encountered. It also attacks my body and reverses any luck. It's there,
an enemy waiting in the air I breathe, in the beauty of the buildings,

the glamour of the cafés. As soon as I breathe in that atmosphere of the Gare du Nord Station I'm another person, a tormented soul, attracting every calamity. I cross the road to my first favourite bar, the Brasserie du Terminus, and I order up a load of good food and coffee but the yellow eyes from hell are on me and will not be appeased until I'm brought down. My friends say after twenty-four hours in Paris I'm like someone in torment. Possesed. Of course I'm not alone in this. When I read Strindberg's *Inferno* – well, it's all there. What changes? I don't know how Strindberg managed to stay. At most I've got three days, then I'm in an ambulance. On day two of the Romy Schneider visit I awoke in my pleasant hotel – money didn't make any difference – it's the same feeling on the Métro steps – and the dizzy sense of unease was in the room, in the fabrics, the smell, the air. It was also in me. And I opened the window and it was in the street and in the sky and there was no escape and my heart started its jumping and racing and my thoughts were skidding about and everything inside me said run. Then the luxury breakfast appeared and just the door knock was like thunder from hell. And I made myself eat the croissant, the fresh bread and the pale Normandy butter, drink the freshly squeezed juice, the coffee, and the unease grew until I was ready for hospital. Then my fact turned bright red and swelled up. I could feel it burning, which took me to the mirror and I looked like a scarlet demon. Was it I myself that I was so afraid of? Did I become in Paris a desperate spirit with no resting place? There was a sickening distortion in my head and I couldn't bear the next thought. I couldn't look at anything in the room. And I opened the window. I supposed I was going to jump out because I had a leg up on the ledge but the phone rang. Obedient as always to communication, I answered it, and Marcelle said, 'I hope you're looking good, darling. Did you sleep well? Today could be your lucky day so look your best.' Then she heard my voice and she told me to stay close. She was on her way.

Of course it could be the air. Something didn't suit me. Or the water. There was something about the smell of the city and its sound. It put me in touch with the most bitter suffering. Whose? For what reason? I do not remember suffering anything like it in my lifetime.

When Marcelle got to me a few 5 mg Pal Valies had tranquillised my thoughts and shut the room up. The scarlet face had gone to chilly white. She gave me the bleak look of someone who was not going to get their ten per cent.

I told her Paris was an animal that got me by the throat and it was never happy until I was on my knees in the gutter. I could arrive in the most spectacular style but sure enough it would get me in the end. I remembered the last time I thought I'd got away unscathed but it provided me with a bug on my last day, so keeping me. The hotel was full and I had to move. And I waited on the street shivering, about to throw up, waiting for a taxi which didn't come. And because I felt so ill I sank slowly to my knees in the gutter in Pigalle and I thought, 'OK. You've won.'

And another time I was coming into Paris and it was a beautiful day. I felt London-neutral and the train was empty and calm. I was enjoying myself, reading eating, forgetting where I was going. And ten minutes before the arrival in the suburbs the panic started, just an icicle in my stomach. I was determined to conquer it. And I stared out of the window and finished my sandwich and made my face up. I did everything with determination. And as I came into the Gare du Nord in my mind I saw Steve McQueen so clearly. He'd been dead a couple of years. And I heard his voice in my head. 'It's just another city.'

And I used that as a defence when everything started going wrong, as it surely did. And at the height of a particular Paris nasty I swerved into a bookshop. Not something I did as a rule. A chemist's yes. And there right in front of me was a huge photograph of Steve McQueen on the cover of his biography. And I felt that seeing him was meant. And I stayed staring and his eyes calmed me. So I was protected, but now I think that it's a place I shouldn't challenge again. I won't win. I'm sure it's a reincarnation punishment. I think I've gone to Paris. I've gone to hell.

When Steve McQueen died I suddenly said, 'Steve McQueen's dead.' It was before anything was announced on the news. I think in his passing he touched my life. I felt very drawn to him after his death which I didn't feel when he was alive. I told Marcelle some of this and she didn't like any of it. She wanted me unspooked and normal-looking. It was deal time. She poured me some mineral water and did consider getting me checked at a hospital.

'Just get me to London and I'll be all right.'

'So why do you come to Paris if it affects you like this?'

'Because each time I think it will be all right. I can't believe it myself when I've gone.'

'I think you should make a small effort. Put some powder on that face and let's go and meet the businessmen. Better take one of your books, darling. Divert attention. You're not in a very good shape. It's not the same face that I saw a year ago, not by a million miles.'

I could see my condition fascinated her. She'd have liked to have me gone over with a scanning machine at her local hospital. But I knew they wouldn't find anything. Spirits were not detectable by these means.

First I went to see James Ivory who had liked the NFFC script, *Don Salino's Wife*, even though it was twice as long as it should be. However, the problem wasn't the script but him. He thought he should steer away from its politics and Spanish background. He felt he couldn't handle either. I did some terrible pleading with him, I was so desperate to get something up on the screen. He said he'd think about it. That got me out of his door. He thought about it and two days later said no. But he was sure there was, somewhere in the world, the right director. He obviously relied on wonderful optimism.

I couldn't help passing along some of the streets I associated with José Tarres. It brought on a blistering depression. Especially the Gare Austerlitz. Marcelle was now convinced it was my immediate past with José that so disturbed me. I promised her my trouble wasn't that sort of memory. The José suffering was bad but logical. The other, beyond words. I got through the meetings with the film producers for *Harriet Hunter* and let Marcelle do most of the talking.

We had dinner at the Trocadero. She said, 'You can't go back.'

'Back?'

'To that Spaniard. I know that's been in your mind all day. Paris is near Gerona. Just one night away. It won't be any good for you. I just feel it in my bones. Your life is in another direction. I think you

211

should put on a lot of make-up and we'll go somewhere a little chic for coffee.'

The somewhere 'a little chic' was a hotel and there in the lobby was Robert Hartman.

Chapter Thirty-three

As I went with him up to his suite I said, 'It's been a funny courtship. A glimpse here, a hamburger, a couple of Cokes.'

He said, 'It's your choice.' He sounded cool. And logical. Because of course I didn't have to. But when we got into the bedroom it seemed there were some things he hotly wanted and took and I certainly wanted him. Being in bed with him was like catching fire. It was the Mills and Boon crescendo of passion – the bit the books didn't print. Just remembering that episode afterwards made my blood scald. And it certainly made me forget I was in Paris. But the physical act was something he was good at. It had nothing to do with his heart.

I sat up and he put a hand on my breast and stroked it and it was more sexual than anything I could imagine. 'On your way to Gerona are you?'

'Oh don't talk about that now.'

'You've got piano player's fingers.' He stroked them.

I didn't like that remark. Was he comparing me with his wife, remembering his wife? It put us back in everyday. I knew then he could be cruel. He got up and passed me a Coke. It was the one thing he knew about me. I drank Coke.

'You pull away fast, Patricia.'

Did I? Rather me than him. I was sure he didn't want me clinging to him, or weeping with the sweet release of having been made love to properly, of having made love with the right lover for once. And I knew he was cold and the only way I had a chance with this man was to be colder. It was Mills and Boon in a way. Want him all you like but don't let him see it.

From out of my bag I produced the Gerona photograph of José and me in the cathedral doorway. 'This was taken in 1955, '56.' I pointed to a group of sightseers. 'That's you.'

He had a variety of facial expressions that did instead of words. He picked it up and held it under the light. 'Can I have it?'

'No.'

'Can I have it copied?'

'I'd rather not.' I held my hand out. That was my past. It slid into my bag. He was part of it, just a spectator.

It was time to talk. He was quite open about it. He'd seen me in Gerona when I first arrived with Beryl and he'd never forgotten me. He'd seen me in the short Cocteau film. But what had he seen that had so hung him up? José and me together? The passion? The affinity? The remarkable atmosphere we had in those days? He'd always been an outsider. He'd seen us in the Bar Savoy, in Chez Beatrice, walking along the avenue of trees, dancing at the fiestas. What we had thrilled him. It also made him more alone and lonely. He was studying Spanish and German at the Berlitz school. He knew the Residencia Internacional group of friends only by sight. Luis was the only one who spoke to him. Luis told him my name. He watched the film being shot. It was the first film he'd seen being made and it had a big effect on him. He remembered I drank a lot of red wine. My preferring red to white was a joke with José. I didn't remember. That's why on the introduction night in Ocean Park he'd produced a bottle of Spanish red. It was an important memory to him. I supposed I did drink in those days. I remembered champagne.

'You begged money from me twice. You used to beg in the new

214

part of town so José's family wouldn't see you. I did offer you a drink and you said, I only drink red wine. Well that was no problem. There was plenty of that. But you were arrogant. And now you drink Coke.'

Then he read about my marriage to Michael Chaplin in the scandal sheets. He remembered my name. He saw it years later on Colin Diamond's Mills and Boon staff list. He went along with the film idea mostly as an excuse to meet me. So the romance company brought me romance after all.

But of course I was not the waif who sat in the doorways of Gerona cathedral and was made radiant by a charismatic Spaniard. He'd been in Gerona for eight months. He'd learned two languages and learned how to deal with loneliness. Then he went back to his university in New York and became a doctor.

'I'd love you to write that book,' he said. 'About how you met Tarres. Write it for me. Then we'll film it, recapture it all. We'll go and film it in Gerona.'

'Do you go back there?'

'No, I'd rather remember it the way it was.'

I found it hard to believe – a couple falling in love capturing the imagination of a third person. But Gerona was a strange place.

He said he had gone back in the 1950s and early 1960s. He'd taken his wife and child. But he was never more than a visitor. It was the first visit he remembered.

'As I saw you pull Tarres into your arms, I thought, this is a marvellous moment. I will never forget it. It was at a street dance in San Daniel. I saw you at most two dozen times. I've never forgotten you.'

He had the kind of wealth to made dreams come true. But he'd never tried to find me. Did he just want me, or me and José? Or was he scared of seeing me old and ordinary?

'If I hadn't been on that Mills and Boon list on my way to LA you wouldn't have seen me?'

'I doubt it.'

'And you didn't even officially invite me. I may not have arrived.'

'I was prepared for that. I didn't think about you every day of my life, Patricia.' He sat on the bed, a towel draped across his shoulders, highlighting his tan. My body was not tanned. I thought it was something that should be covered up. 'Perhaps I was waiting,' he said. 'For the right time.'

'I bet you got plenty on film.'

'In those days I hardly had the money to eat let alone buy a camera. I want you to put it all down, everything that occurs to you about 1955, 1956. And it goes on celluloid just as it was.'

As I dressed I wanted to know if it was the person I was at fifteen he wanted to sleep with or the woman of thirty-eight.

'So you wait for things.'

'Sometimes,' he said. 'If it's the best way to get them.' With one almost careless movement he pulled off my clothes and tossed them away on to a chair. Dressed happened when he wanted it.

'Are you going to check José out next?'

He didn't think so.

'You checked out J.'

'I wanted to meet him. I told you. Why don't you believe what I say? The film business means a lot to me. The way it used to be. And he symbolises that time.'

And then quite suddenly it became light and funny and we acted like a couple out of Mills and Boon. I giggled without stop before I went to sleep. I didn't realise I could have such a good time with someone.

The next day we went out of Paris into the country. Sex with him was like being on fire, it was too good because what came afterwards didn't balance it somehow. It wasn't cold but it just wasn't hot. And he made me aware I was separate not part of him. I couldn't ask questions. That was out. And I knew he didn't like gossip or too much chat. The silences were OK for him. But we just weren't harmonious for something as big as silence. It was all right when we laughed. Laughter made me safe.

I still made my mistake. It came out of curiosity. I was trying to find out if I continued in his life and if there were other women. I said, 'You could have anybody.'

'I don't. Anyway my life isn't – well, it's busy.'

'Is it sexually busy?'

'My sexual needs are my responsibility.'

I thought that meant he went with professional girls or he did it himself. But because I was in love with him, of course I had been all along but not thinking about it, I said, 'What do you want? I want to give you what you want.' I was referring as much as anything to his sexual requirements. But being in love, I wasn't at my best.

'Patricia, what I want no one can give me.'

I didn't want to hear it. I knew he meant his wife. 'What are you?' I said aggressively. 'A producer? A businessman? A gangster? What?'

'A widower.' It sounded black, cutting.

And I could see his power then. It was generated from deep sorrow and bitterness. As the sorrow didn't cease nor did the power and I could see it was the sort that could take over a studio and have J bounced.

'So now you want to keep yourself apart?' I was quite brave seeing the icy mood he was in. I longed to get back to Marcelle and her warmth and approval.

'Since my wife died, I've had women. And once or twice I even gave it a shot, living together, but I think it's better I stay alone. You see I'm too – ' He didn't know the word to do justice to all that, so chose, 'Scarred, and they're on another planet. Happy, optimistic, wholesome. I only upset them in the end. But I get by. There is not one thing in this world that I cannot use for my personal advancement.' He turned the car around towards Paris. 'I don't mean business. I mean personal evolvement.'

I got it. He meant something spiritual. He said he didn't mind that his life was unadorned. It was like taking an icy bath. He'd end up more spiritually developed than when he came in.

'What would you do with twenty-five million pounds, Patricia?'

'Worry about it.'

'Wouldn't you like houses, an art collection, cars, a business or two? Some jewellery? Power?'

'Oh please stop. You know I wouldn't.'

He dropped me at Marcelle's Paris apartment and said he'd be in touch. I thought I failed in every way except one. I hadn't said yes to twenty-five million.

I told Marcelle everything, well, nearly everything. The sex stuff

217

was vague. She said, of course he liked me. Had I no confidence? I'd just spent a whole day alone with him. He was a man who never took a day off.

His calling me Patricia, giving me back my name, disturbed me. Patricia was a serious word. I only got called that in hospital wards, the SS office. The tax people did it, so did the coroner after my Dad's death. Patrice wasn't a serious name. It belonged to dreams because it was José's invention.

Chapter Thirty-four

While I was at rehearsals of the Portuguese nun play, *From the Balcony*, at the Cottesloe Theatre, Michael Lindsay-Hogg came over from New York and offered me cash in hand to write a quick screenplay for him. As much as I needed the money I had to finish *The Rose-garden*. I worked on it every waking hour. My only release was writing. What I couldn't have in life I put into the books. I rewrote *The Rose-garden* and put more of Robert Hartman into it. It still kept getting rejected.

Michael couldn't help noticing the state of the London house. And a lump of money could improve it. Not that he was himself houseproud. Like me, he'd prefer to live on the wing, in hotels. But I still had the kids and they needed a base. I said when the novel was finished I'd do the filmscript. He said it would only take me two weeks but it had to be now. He'd even pay for me to go somewhere pleasant, like Gerona. I couldn't take two weeks away from the book. It had become a love affair. Having to go to the NT rehearsals was like taking lumps of my skin off. Each time I left the house I was convinced it would be burned to the ground. So, should the manuscript become a mound of ash or did I take it with me and have it stolen? Like a baby it needed its mother there in the house while it grew. The odd thing about the book was its effect on my health. As soon as I picked up a pen, I got ill. The virus blazed, all its symptoms full blast. I crunched down the Valies and blocked out my body and all its horrible cries.

In the meantime the NFFC, keen to see some return on their grant, wanted me to release the huge filmscript. When James Ivory turned it down, on my suggestion it had gone to Louis Malle. He liked it but wanted a different writer and I was asked to let my rights go. I said I'd think about it. Then it occurred to me that all the good stuff in the script, the ideas, for instance, that Louis Malle liked had come from my head as well as the other stuff he wanted replaced. So I hung on. Louis Malle would not rewrite the script with me. He had someone much better in mind. So he passed on the project. The NFFC were polite about my possessiveness but a coolness set in. All my projects were half born. I could never tell which ones would die. Except the radio plays and the journalism and the short stories. These had a quick turnover, an immediate response or no response.

The great thing about the Portuguese nun was I could empathise with what she suffered. At the same time I thought she was crazy to inform the recipient of her feelings. I reckoned I'd become cautious. Knowing Robert Hartman even for such a short interlude in Paris had changed me. Catch me writing to him saying what I felt. Even if I could find him.

The play, starring Morag Hood and Leigh Lawson, opened in May 1982 in the Cottesloe for a few select performances and was then broadcast in June on Radio 3 and repeated in December. By select I mean they only allowed a dozen at most. Marcelle took it for Paris and two actors from the Comédie Française were keen to play it. *The Siesta* film was looking good. They had Jessica Lange and a director attached who'd just finished making what might be a hot film, *Frances*. So some things were up and some not so up but I was out of the SS orbit. I relied mainly on my radio writing and film options to live. The NFFC film project then went to Henry Jaglom who'd made *Sitting Ducks*. It seemed an odd choice for him, his work seemed to thrive on improvisation and very low budgets. However, people didn't want to keep repeating themselves. He said yes but nothing was ever certain until it was there and then it had to prove itself. So good news for me was becoming something else. Acceptance wasn't enough. The real claw in my guts was *The Rose-garden*. I thought if it didn't get taken it would kill me off. It almost got in at Collins. They'd had it back and forth in the building three times. Someone would believe in it then a lot of ghastly marketing people would throw buckets of water over the misguided enthusiast for even suggesting it. The book wouldn't sell the requisite number. It wouldn't get into paperback. They'd never get their money back. And what sort of book was it? Literary? Mid-literary? Popular? Like its inspiration, Robert Hartman, it defied definition. Unknown to me he came to London especially to see the Portuguese play. He was staying at the Connaught and I had dinner with him. I spent an hour trying to find something to wear. I had everything but nothing looked right. I knew, I was absolutely sure, he had fantastic mistresses who made wonderful love in the afternoon. His life was mysterious and sensual and I did not belong in it. Before I went through the door of that suite I made myself promise not to be in love with him. It screwed up everything, being in love. How could you be at your best? I decided to tell him the truth. My life was not some joyous leap-frog across the Atlantic to LA. A lot of the time it was enough to stiff anyone. What got me through was the idea it would change. My god was 'change'.

So he got the Coca-Cola poured and I said the novel kept getting rejected. I couldn't understand it because I knew it was my best writing. It was unjust. I'd sent my younger kid away to boarding school but it wasn't going to take. His father was going to believe the sob stuff he pulled and let him loose. Definitely. I had a lot of grievance against Mike at that time.

Tycoon said *The Rose- garden* would be done. He was absolutely sure of that. I was going to ask him to persuade Collins to take it back for a fourth time and keep it. I was that desperate. But he had no dealings with Collins. It was all sensible, what he said, but how did it apply to my life? What was sensible about that?

'Haven't you got anyone to help you?' Seeing how curious he was about people's little secrets he'd probably had the house gone over. It would only require the grossest surveillance, like looking in through the uncurtained windows. I told him about Phil. 'But I don't sleep with him.'

'It sounds like he's a doorman in your life. He just keeps other men out.'

I didn't like that. I said I didn't live with Phil but I shared my life with him. 'Phil's all right but it's everyday stuff.'

'Why don't you go and live in Gerona as you like it so much?'

'You can get very lonely there.'

He agreed with that.

Then he threw some photographs on to the bed. José and me in the mid-1950s. José and Quico Sabater celebrating some move against Franco, plotting in the Bar Savoy, kissing Maria the maid. Me on my own in the doorway of the cathedral in the sun with a chicken on a string. I was barefoot and the sun struck just me in a shaft like a sign. Not bad for a boy who couldn't afford a camera.

He mentioned a house right at the top of the old town. I knew the one. It was surrounded by cypress trees. It stood in its own ground. It was large, old, with arches and columns, a patio, a fountain. It had been empty for years and now was overgrown. José said once it was 'the love house'. A wealthy resident of Gerona in the 1920s had bought it because his beloved wife was dying of TB. At that height the air was good and the trees gave off herbal perfume. It gave her ease, that house. The husband nursed her, adored her, and since her death it had remained empty.

'Did you think of buying it?' I asked him.

'No. I did visit the house once. It had a strong echo of that man's devotion.'

'Will you marry again, Robert?'

'A simple shake of the head for that one.

'I saw you in Paris with a very pretty girl.'

'Better than an ugly one.' He poured the coffee.

'Still, you seem to get what you want.'

'Not a chance.'

'Come on – Hollywood, Paris, the entertainment business.'

'What I want – ' he stopped. He couldn't talk about himself. And he wouldn't trust me so far. I thought it was probably, 'I want my wife back. I will never get over her.'

222

'How does J feel now he's working for television?' He sounded in control again.

'I should think he's shattered about *Quark*. Why did you do it?'

'I didn't like him. Why should I spend money on someone I don't like? On the other hand if I love someone like Scorsese or Coppola – people with talent – whatever scrapes they get into, they can always come to me. However over budget it goes I'll pay. Someone like Scorsese could have the world as far as I'm concerned. If I love someone's talent, the world.'

'What else do you love?'

'Jazz.'

'I didn't know J was working for television.'

'Nor does he. But that's where his Chilean venture will end up.'

He crouched back on the bed and he looked so beautiful and unavailable. His body, his thinking, his life, it was out of my league. He was like a superb creature who'd lost its mate and he just had to get by.

'I wish I was more successful. For your sake,' I said. 'In case you do believe in me.'

'Success!' He almost spat the word. 'Success is nothing. A kind heart is all that matters.'

When he made love to me it all changed and I didn't feel on the outside. How I wished he was mine. And I kept thinking, beyond the straight stuff, the passion, he wants something else. Maybe he didn't know. Maybe he was hiding it. Perhaps he did it with professional girls. I wanted to do it with him, all the fantasy stuff, but I didn't know him well enough to even mention it. But I could see the sense in being the one he did all that with, whatever it was. It would draw him closer to me. I'd seen him twice that year and it was now June. I couldn't ask the questions I needed to ask, like when I would see him again, could I have his phone numbers. What was our relationship, if that's what it was? I shut my mouth and left him space to throw in any ideas.

He drove me home, insisted on it. The last thing I wanted. He wasn't getting inside that house. Grim, stark, three dogs, two cats and full of Kentish Town kids. So I made him stop outside the only well-painted house in the street. I said, 'I would ask you in but it's a mess.'

'I'm sure it isn't.'

He thought I was talking about a few scatter cushions out of place.

'I'd rather you didn't come in.'

'That's all right. You're married, aren't you?' He laughed. 'To Phil.'

'Well, I'm sure you could find that out.'

He took my hand and caressed it. The first wife must have had a wonderful time with him. I was just getting good sex. Throw in the love and he'd be irresistible.

He didn't let me out of the car. Neither did he speak. He made me nervous so I didn't speak. The silence went on like something from my schooldays, when I was in disgrace. Then I remembered my writing. Thank God I had that. At least it was something I could control. I started to get out of the car. Swiftly he put his hand over mine, stopping me. 'I'm just not a very good bet for a woman. I can only really get off on pain – hurting people.' He sighed. 'So I go to girls.'

My heart was beating very fast. 'So what if I said I didn't mind? For instance you tying me up.'

'Not didn't mind. Want.'

'And whipping or whatever it is. Bondage.'

'I could teach you.' His voice softened, was now serious, desirous. We were well out of Mills and Boon land now. 'You're quite greedy sexually, aren't you? I like that.'

I didn't tell him that wasn't surprising as I hardly ever got it. 'Do you want me to do it? What they do for you?'

He laughed. 'You have to want it but not look as though you want it. It's a very precise dealing.' He got a diary from his case and picked a day and time and wrote it on a piece of paper and gave it to me. 'And you have to be professional, Patricia. There's no getting close. That's not what it's about. The downside is I don't see you very often. Also you don't mention it to anybody. And you don't sleep around. There will be an upside.' He opened the car door. 'So think about it. You can't have everything you want in life.'

'Why not?'
'Life isn't supposed to make you happy.'
'What if I can't live without it?'
'Go on a diet.'

Chapter Thirty-five

The time was ten in the evening, the day a Tuesday, the place, a modern hotel in the new part of Gerona. Of course I didn't believe it, took it to be a joke and expected a phone call to cancel the arrangement. Then a plane ticket first class to Barcelona arrived and a generous sheaf of pesetas for expenses, but then I didn't know the going rate for that kind of deal. My main worry was I wouldn't be able to do it. I'd get overcome by the falsity of the situation and start giggling. I felt OK about sex when I was actively involved with someone I liked. But this distant streamlined professional turn-on – I didn't think I'd make it work. How I longed to talk to someone just to test the reality of what I was doing. I remembered my Dad saying I'd end up on the wrong side of the white-slave traffic. Years ago he'd said that. I thought for a mad moment that Robert Hartman was going to turn me into a call girl for his friends. Then I soothed myself with the fact that I was far too old.

I took the plane to Barcelona and almost copped out when the drink trolley passed. I'd be on red wine next. I was going to play a hooker for a man I secretly was in love with. A car was waiting at the airport, a big black number, and a silent chauffeur who took it along the motorway at nearly ninety miles an hour. Professional call girls nowadays did travel. That was part of the work. A businessman in Paris, a delegation in New York. A girl was chosen for her particular twist. However, she was invariably young. Her main assets, apart form the obvious ones, were her ability to look unlike a hooker, to dress wonderfully and to keep her mouth shut.

I passed into the hotel lobby and was instructed by the driver to go straight to the lift. He told me the floor, the room. Of course I knew his game now. He was killing something off. Killing my love for him. Didn't I always spot the real stuff too late? It was as if I was about to have my appendix out and I'd suddenly realise, no, it's my left leg that's sick. But the freezing cold of the anaesthetic would already be crawling up my arm from the needle in my hand. He opened the door, shirt open. No shoes, busy on a phone. He went straight back to his conversation and I looked out of the window. I couldn't see Gerona. The hotel was on a motorway near Gerona airport.

Then he flicked his fingers. 'Come here.' I walked towards him, stopped. 'Come on. Sit on my lap. Sometimes you look like a little girl who's been caught out. Come on. I won't hurt you.' I stayed where I was. 'Come on. Let me kiss you. Little girls like that.' His voice was sexual now. 'And I'll show you something you'll really like. Come on.' He lifted up my skirt with his foot. 'Pull those off and sit on my lap.'

There was something erotic about him that spoke directly to my body. Every gesture, alluring, suggested dizzying pleasure. And in spite of the town and the fact that José was somewhere in it, I felt urgent hungry desire for this interloper. And he gestured for the skirt to be lifted higher and the lace briefs to be pulled down lower. Then they were where he wanted. I felt the sharp delight of infidelity. I belonged to Tarres, this was happening in his town. But then he'd never protected me or the gift of our quite exceptional love.

Exhausted, still breathing hard, he undid the scarves from my legs and threw me on to the bed on my back. Then he shut himself away in the bathroom. It had been a disaster, of that I was sure. I was the wrong partner for what he did. I wanted to crawl off the bed, out of the room and over to José's part of the town. There wasn't one move I could make.

He came out of the bathroom and threw me a towel. He was irritated I was still on the bed.

'I need a doctor,' I whispered, ashamed of my pain.

'Whatever for?'

'I'm in terrible pain.'

'But you like pain.'

'Oh but I don't.'

'Oh but you do, my sweet. Giving you punishment like that lets out all the pain inside you that you're not even aware of.'

'Oh I see. That was all for me. I did wonder.'

'You're choked up with unhappiness. You can't even reach it. What we did just now at least gives some form to it.'

'Well, what about you?'

'The same.'

And I could see he was in pain still. I was more concerned about myself. I tried to sit up. Nothing doing. 'I do need a doctor. My back.'

'Come on. Hookers do this twice a night.'

'They're underpaid,' I whispered.

He sat on the bed. 'Turn over.' I couldn't. My back was stuck to the sheet. He helped me turn on to my stomach and he washed off the blood. Tenderly his hands moved over my body. The caress released the tears and he held me as I sobbed. 'Let it out. Just let it all come out.'

I was the worst hooker in the world but that wasn't why I was crying. That point of the evening had been lost hours ago.

Then he did it again, straight this time. Sexually I adored him but what did he think of me? He disliked any mention of the word love. It was only permissible at the height of orgasm.

If I'd been in the old quarter and heard the clocks chiming I'd have felt terrible because I was being unfaithful, to everything I'd once loved. But this was the new part of town.

When I woke up he was dressed and ready to go. He came across to the bed and opened his slim black feline wallet and laid a dozen notes of a large denomination on the pillow. I told him to fuck off.

228

'Girls get paid. That's part of it.'

'Oh leave it out.' I swiped at the money and it fluttered to the floor. He picked it up.

'I'd rather you took it.'

'Why?'

Then I realised he was worried I'd come on for something bigger. He laid the notes neatly on the bedside table. I tore them up. 'I've been paid. Right? I won't come asking for a fucking Porsche.' I was furious. He thought it was funny. Of course he thought I was being cute so I could really dig in for something. That made me more angry. Of course I wanted money. But I didn't want to be paid off.

He had to get a plane for Barcelona at noon. If I wanted to rest the driver could return and collect me later. I could see he preferred that one. He poured me coffee, fruit juice, then left.

My plane ticket was open. I considered going over to José's part just for a look but I felt too shattered. My back hurt. I wanted to get home to safety, my dogs, my cats, my writing, a world I could predict. I found out I didn't have a choice about going to old Gerona. Mr Hartman paid for things and they had to be done his way. A different person who drove waited in the lobby. He spoke English and was prepared for any wilful move I might try.

'The airport.' And he took my bag and closed me up in a car.

I could just about see Gerona cathedral in the distance as the car whizzed through an industrial section. I tried to turn round to look but my back was rigid. I couldn't believe I was there. I couldn't believe any of it.

Chapter Thirty-six

Another person I shouldn't have let into the house found it unerringly. Colin Diamond stood on the doorstep dressed in a blanket. It was eight in the morning and he'd knocked on every door in the street. He'd described me, then said I was a famous writer whose books were being made into films. Thanks a million, Colin. I now had tax and terrible problems like VAT on my back. It took a moment to recognise him, he was so thin and brown. The blanket covered his head and hung to his shins. He looked like one or two mid-Eastern drug addicts begging in the Kentish Town Road. Their personalities were such that even the dogs wouldn't pass them. Colin accepted a cup of black coffee and talked about God. He, Colin, had had some kind of conversion and was off to the desert. He'd even changed his name. It was long and Arabic. I believed it all until he asked for a handout, which I didn't have. He wanted something substantial to get to Morocco.

'But I haven't got any money.'

'But *The Siesta* is being filmed at the end of the year. Variety's full of it. Jessica Lange – '

So when he wasn't reading the Koran he was dipping into the trades.

'If I had it I'd give it to you.'

'But you must have made something?'

'Not really. No.'

'It's not fair.'

'What?'

'Life.'

I found out everything came in its own time. It certainly wasn't my time. There was a lot of waiting to be got through.

'*Harriet Hunter* was your best book. That should have been made.'

'How's your Hollywood office?'

A wave of the hand from behind the blanket folds dismissed that. 'That's part of the bad materialistic days. I've cleansed myself from all that. I've just stepped away.'

'Leaving what?' The blanket and new religion was beginning to make sense. I said it was a shame he'd embraced an Arab religion. If it had been Jewish I knew just the place for him. And Gerona was a lot nearer.

I could see he was prepared to be flexible although he went on about the Koran and the higher states of being. It seemed, due to one or two mishaps, his de luxe LA office had sunk like a huge pleasure boat. Only the creditors remembered it. He was *persona non grata* in his NY office due to the fact that the bike boys were always at the door. I didn't think his conversion was entirely down to God. But he described the desert, its colours, its sun rise, as though he'd truly found something marvellous.

'It is the place of non-action so no reaction. You just be. The colours feed you. There's mauve-pink sky better than any acid trip. Robert Hartman first told me about the desert. He said it was a very good place to be when you wanted not to be. Have you seen him?'

I said I hadn't. I gave him what money I could. 'You know that girl in Hollywood who slept with her shrink? The one who should have been a moviestar?'

'Except she cracked up.'

'Did she go with Hartman?'

'She tried to seduce him. Then she tried to die. I told you he's not lucky. I liked her a lot. So did your friend J. So did a lot of guys. She was flavour of the month for a while.'

So I asked what had gone wrong between this exquisite girl and Robert Hartman. So Colin asked if I did see him. For real. I said no.

'I think they slept together then it got out of hand. It got into something else. She's inclined to be self-destructive. He refused to see her again and she felt rejected. At first she wanted to pay him back and she's got a husband who draws water. But she couldn't do anything because she couldn't find Hartman. I think he's into fantasy sex and that has to be done just right.'

'Does she have a name?'

'She does not. Your friend J was quite mad about her. Ask him. But she wanted Hartman and was she obsessive! If she'd just stuck to what she could have, she'd be the new Elizabeth Taylor.'

I couldn't see J being mad about anything on two legs. But there was so much I was kept out of. I said, 'I'm always on the outside.'

'At least you're in better shape than her. She may have the clothes, the parties, the men, but she's broken, a broken bird. All she does now is go to clairvoyants.' He covered himself with his blanket and looked like a beggar on smack. 'Don't forget, Patrice. I'm always your agent wherever I am.'

It was an ambiguous statement. Did it mean he wanted a cut of every buck I made? Or he'd help me in my worst moments? Letting Colin in was a bad mistake. Desperate people started coming to my house looking for him. Some wanted their money back, others were looking for packages. I think the CIA came and called him another name. I knew nothing of his whereabouts. Then, when a New York writer appeared with his manuscript for me to get published, I thought it was time to find out what I was in Colin's life.

'You're his star. He started you off. Everyone knows it. *The Siesta*. The play. The filmstar book. He's gone to find God so I think you kind of owe it to him.'

So I took the huge manuscript into my arms like an unwanted baby. I thought Americans could be unbelievably naive, except of course Colin Diamond.

I went back to Gerona because I could see the sense in getting the

Jewish story. It was getting talked about and I considered it belonged to me. I got a commission from the *Jewish Chronicle* to write it up, and one from the BBC radio to prepare a documentary. I took Chris and Tim because the place was part of their life too.

Another August and I was feeling good because *The Siesta* was due to go into preproduction in September. My agent said it was definite, absolute. Even the money was there. It would change my life because now all the Duckworth books would get noticed and at last come into paperback. Even *The Rose-garden* might get a look in.

I didn't want to stay at the Hotel Centro, too many memories, but it was cheap and in the old quarter. This time I was on a professional visit. I wanted nothing to do with José's life. Neither his love nor her hatred. I was cool, an employee of the BBC. And as I walked along the Ramblas to the hotel I felt no quickening or expectation. I used to have to see José with an urgency that made life impossible. Now I felt ordinary. I could be anywhere. The kids shook me down for extra money and went off to find a pinball machine. They were already complaining. They wanted discotheques, girls, the sea, speed, punks. They wanted a Kentish Town by water. Then Tim asked me the Spanish for brothel so I thought it was time to send them to their father.

Then I saw her by the Bar Arcada. She was pushing a pram, smiling into it, surrounded by admiring women. Her hair was short and well groomed. I'd know that sheep's nose anywhere, the harmless blue eyes. Although it was warm she was almost swallowed up in a coat of dubious fur.

I turned sharp right and stopped in a doorway, shaking. The pram had given me a turn. But if she was on the street she couldn't be in the apartment. I went boldly to the Calle Forsa, climbed to the third floor. I wanted him to know I was here and why. No fuss. I banged the knocker. I was still carrying my luggage. I heard female movements on the stone floor, a swishing sound, too quick for his mother. I realised then that a lot of young women in Gerona looked like Nina. There were two hairstyles, long and short. They went to the same three shops for their clothes. There were near versions of her nose all over the place. Her expression, soft and hard, was something she'd picked up since living there. I realised this too late.

She opened the door. We were both taken aback. I remembered all the times I'd come to this door, almost a bride. Life was out of its fucking mind! She looked pleased, not to see me, but with herself. She'd had his baby. I told her I'd come to find a friend who'd come to see José and I was about to leave for the airport in a hurry. She'd seen the bag. She shook her head about the friend. Perhaps she believed my story of departure or perhaps it was because she was now safe. She told me I could find José at the Isaac the Blind centre.

I crossed the road and went up the steep alley of steps. At least José didn't have far to go to work. All the lights, dozens of them were on. 'Smoke Gets in Your Eyes' was on the sound system and there was an atmosphere of expectation. For a moment I could have been in the 1950s. The place was empty. then I heard a cackling laugh. Old Papa Serrat gone senile? But it was a strange bird, mocking. Now I dreaded seeing José as indeed he must have dreaded seeing me. He was now indisputably married and had the baby he'd longed for. Everyone has their moment. We'd had ours. It had ended years ago. We just hadn't realised.

He came out of the bar where the same locals were tanking up for the evening. He was wearing a blue and white striped shirt and brown cords. His eyes flickered with remembered fire then became normal. I was cool and businesslike and told him about the two commissions and pointed out how it could promote the Jewish site. He saw the tape recorder with BBC on its side. It was OK with him. That night he was putting on a concert of songs. The whole town was coming. I should too. And bring the boys. And now I realised why I had them along. He had his son. I had mine. It had nothing to do with them.

He told me of the fantastic, far-reaching success of his establishment. How Jews as far away as Germany had shown up on impulse. How visitors were blown in the door and found paradise. He'd mounted exhibitions, given benefit nights for Jews from Toulouse. It all sounded OK but it was Saturday and the place was empty.

'Which nights do you have the cabbala classes?'

'They begin in the autumn. We are beginning the excavation

below the sun stone. Last week we uncovered an oven where the Jews baked the passover bread. We opened the door and there was a matzo, intact.' His eyes shone. 'If a Jew leaves bread it means he will return.'

I said I'd love to see it.

'Wouldn't I? But as the air encountered the loaf it just – ' He flicked his fingers gesturing total disappearance.

'You need a professional excavator in.'

Was that a mistake. Professional was the one thing that did not blow in that door and find paradise. He resisted any authoritative comment on his plot of history. The mention of government and local intervention made his eyes flare. In fact he wanted money from the town hall but didn't want to lose the control. Then he started wanting money from the whole world.

When I got back to the hotel the boys wanted money and a hotel by the sea.

'But this is Gerona.'

'Yeah. We've seen it.'

'But you've only been here a couple of hours.'

'So we've seen it. Two hours. That's all it takes.' It was just a pile of old stones to them.

'We've checked it out really, Mum,' said Chris. 'And the atmosphere. Well, it's heavy. It's kind of hard to get through.'

So I said they could leave the next day if they came with me to the concert. I could not say the whole town was there but the courtyard was almost full. And I reckoned at 300 pesetas a head he'd done OK. Plus drinks sales.

José made a speech in Catalan and just before the singer began a strange thing happened. I'd call it an omen. It wasn't unfamiliar to me. Four hefty guys marched across the patio and lifted the piano and carried it away. José went after them with determination. A long embarrassed pause, the worst thing for any singer. José reappeared wreathed in smiles and said the piano wasn't good enough and another better one would be brought immediately. He asked for our patience. The bar was open for drinks. Then Juan Serrat and two young boys trundled in an old upright piano. I thought it was probably the one that used to be downstairs in the

Hotel Residencia. It did not look better than the first one. The singer was from Barcelona, and sang OK, but the piano was very slightly out of tune and it set going a terrible strain of hysteria. You never knew when the wrong note would hit and you tensed up waiting. The pianist drove the song along as though trying to control a runaway horse. The singer sang an unexpectedly high note and that was war-talk for the mocking bird which then started some raucous laughter. I bent forward weeping with unexpelled laughter. Tim hopped it inside. Chris sat staring fixedly at the ground, then his shoulders started shaking. He held the programme over his face. I didn't dare look at him. They were looking, the Spanish. They didn't like our reaction. I realised how stoical they were. Good behaviour overcame anything.

Afterwards a local writer made a speech in which José Tarres was likened to a prophet. I thought profit not prophet was more suitable. Nina and José put on a good show but they were bankrupt.

The proprietor of the Hotel Centro knew all about the piano switch. 'He had a concert piano. The singer insisted on the best or she wouldn't perform. But he couldn't pay the huge fee and deposit. The piano also had to be transported. All that cost money. He ran around all day looking for money but he already owes a fortune. So he asked them to install the piano and he'd pay out of the ticket money. But he still couldn't pay because he had to pay the singer and the ticket sales weren't what he'd anticipated. He couldn't cover both. He should advertise those concerts.'

'Have there been any Jews here?'

The proprietor hadn't seen one.

When I did the interviews the next day I found everyone was enthusiastic as long as they didn't have to pay for it. The government wouldn't help because Tarres wanted it to remain a private enterprise so he got all the glory and the money.

José gave me a new identity. I was now Patrice Chaplin, daughter-in-law of Sir Charles from the BBC London. He introduced me to writers and bankers, a priest. Nina was around all the time with the baby, a large boy with a pointed hat and big brown eyes. I dreaded holding him. Everyone else got a turn. José could talk only of the Jews. He was building a museum for them, a dormitory, the synagogue would be open the following month. I did wonder if he was becoming a little obsessed. His wife did a lot of nodding, at the right times. She'd learned Catalan perfectly and joined in all conversations unless it was with me. She would not say one word to me.

After I'd met the hangers-on in the courtyard I was ignored. I began to feel upset, left out, and my professional style was on a definite decline. I started on about the glories of having *The Siesta* filmed. There was talk of it being filmed in Gerona and a location manager had already been sent.

'So Bacall will be here after all,' said José.

'No. It's with Jessica Lange.'

I said the name again, differently, but José had still never heard of it. Nina was standing close by with the child.

'You were always having such wonderful successes,' he said. 'When will they reach Gerona?' I knew that one was for her benefit but I still didn't like it.

'About the time the Jews reach Gerona,' I slapped a copy of *Variety* on to the table, but of course they didn't read English. Nina bent over the picture of Jessica Lange and didn't like her.

'What happened to Lauren Bacall?' José asked.

'She's shooting my other book, the filmstar one, in Mexico,' I said.

'Well if this new one gets here make sure they shoot the film in this courtyard. You can't get better than that.'

He was puffed with ego. His looks would go next. All that pride knocked you around as badly as drink.

The baby was staring at me. Even at fifteen months it knew. It had José's eyes. It stared at me unblinking. Nina's friends noticed and remarked on it but Nina did not give me the child to hold. Then its face crumpled.

Oh please don't cry, I begged silently. Not while you're staring my way.

But its mouth opened and it howled like a wolf.

'What now?' said Nina and they all looked at me.

'It never cries,' said a friend of hers. 'What's upset him?' And they sung little baby tunes and rocked him and shook his rattle doll

237

but he still stared my way and cried. Then José took the son he adored and the tantrum was over. José kissed him. 'My big beautiful boy.' I looked away. It had nothing to do with me.

If I could have had one hit that reached Gerona in the old days I'd have had him.

The kids went to the beach while I got everyone's dreams on tape because that's what they were. I could always recognise those. In spite of their proud air, Don Quixote and his lady wife were in trouble. They owed the banks, they owed Serrat Junior and Serrat Senior, they owed the local hoteliers. It also transpired they did not actually own the centre but only rented the various portions of land from local residents. They had not paid their rent. The restoration of the site itself had cost thousands and the installation of ordinary things like electricity put the bill up to a quarter of a million dollars. As I recorded the interviews I had to switch the tape off twice because creditors were crossing the patio wanting the meat bill paid. The electrical installator reckoned his firm would go broke if José didn't find some of the eight million pesetas due one year ago. José promised instant payment, like the following week. He was deft with the lumpen glaring unavoidable creditors like wild beasts sitting in his patio chairs. He fed them optimism, gave them huge drinks until they were so soothed they were almost snoring. The electrician was given another drink and sent on his way. When he got to the Jewish wishing-well he remembered what he'd come for. It wasn't a treble cognac and a bit of poetry from an ex- poet.

'Five days, Tarres. Then I take you to court.'

I switched the tape back on and José said the Jewish centre was an antidote to materialism. The bad old world. He'd give his life if necessary to send one chime of joy into a place of darkness. The problem was the Jews had not come. Not to settle. He still believed in the right vibration reaching them. Meanwhile the creditors were sending along something a little more practical than a vibration. He was getting writs. She dealt with them. I admired her hoity-toity manner with people she'd financially ruined. José said this came from her superb upper-class upbringing. Bills were never paid in that class. Or if they were, when the debtor chose. I could have learned something from her style myself. I thanked God with every breath she was not beautiful. Make-up could not improve her. She was considered very nice but that was not something to get hot about. But she was the goddess of the stones, his confidante, partner, surrounded by friends and people who admired her talent and the fact that she'd put it aside to help her husband's cause. So I sat off to one side. I had no place. After a while I saw the friends alternated admiring her with insulting me. When I suggested, as I had once before, informing the Jews by letter about the restoration and its intention, their reaction was such I thought I'd be burned at the stake.

'Let them come or not,' said Nina. 'Do we have to do all this and crawl after them too?'

When I heard their cabbala teacher was to be the astrologer on the local scandal rag I had to admit I was appalled. The astrologer was a minuscule balding sex maniac whose height of personal evolvement was not having two whores in bed at the same time. His predictions had about as much relevance as a fortune cookie.

Now Nina could have jumped right in and had a go. But she wanted José to have a go. She wanted to work it so José himself blew me out. So when I said in front of their groupies they were doing it all wrong, he went crazy. So what his debts could be dissolved by a Jewish grant from a foundation? So what there were schools of cabbala in New York and cabbala scholars in London? So what I knew rich Jewish people? It was not a question of money. Also it was an assault on his ego. But more than anything he did not want the Jews involved with the administration. He, José Tarres, and his wife Nina had not slaved twenty hours a day for years to hand it over to some absent foundation, because of a few debts. He, José Tarres, was the owner. It seemed the reverse of his earlier plan, to return to the Jews what was theirs. I threw that in too.

Who was I to question him? So I said it was just showtime for him and these Jews he talked about were a fantasy audience. He shouted at me and I gave as good back and she tossed her lot in and said they didn't want me. So get out. Who needed the BBC for Crissake? What had I to do with them? And then how I longed for Tycoon just to walk in with Bacall or Elizabeth Taylor or Scorsese.

And then their lawyer Manolo Mir said I knew nothing about cabbala so how dare I presume to produce a programme on the subject. And because it was hot, instead of staying and winning, I got up and ran from the place.

Chapter Thirty-seven

I did the interview with the mayor at the town hall, my voice shaking. I wouldn't cry. It was a matter of pride. I couldn't remember a time more humiliating, at least not in my adult life. Her enjoyment, her eyes, as he bruised me with insults were not tolerable. As I asked the mayor dull questions I wondered how much it cost to get someone – the term was 'whacked out'. I realised I'd flipped when I asked the mayor if there were any assassins in town. The crime problem or lack of interested him far more than Tarres's folly.

Then I went to Luis's bar. Looking at the lines of bottles glowing in the gloom cooled me down. Alcohol could enhance colour like gems did. Since hypnosis had conquered the addiction I had no interest in drink. It hadn't been the anaesthetic escape people imagined. Drink had been the umbilical cord that took me straight back to José. It put me in a brighter place near him. The cord had been cut and now I'd learned to live without that secret place.

Victor, a local journalist, joined me at the bar. He remembered when I was a kid and the local petition that had been got up to drive Beryl and me out of town. As he was on the subject of the old days

I asked if he remembered Robert Hartman, student of language at the Berlitz School. Victor remembered he was withdrawn, introverted, loved music, had qualified in medicine in the US. He came from a poor town in Sicily. He was thin and puny. Well he'd certainly improved on what he'd been dealt. 'I remember him because he used to get our photographers to take pictures for him. His eyes had fire. He'd get somewhere.'

I could see the journalist was a judge of character so I asked about Nina.

'It's a tragedy she married him. She's so talented. She won't have time to sculpt. He has her washing floors most of the time and cooking kebabs. Does he know Jews don't eat pork?'

'Will it work out?' I desperately hoped it wouldn't. I now hated them both.

'If the banks don't foreclose and the landlords don't sue for their rent and the personal creditors don't lynch him. He doesn't even own the lavatories. He owns one stone, the sun stone.'

Victor said he hoped it would work because it was a splendid site for Gerona. 'As it is he makes some money from wedding receptions. And not kosher ones. It's just a bar restaurant until the Jews come. I think it must be supported, Patricia, and you could be a great help.'

He'd given me my means of revenge. By my journalism I'd be the saviour of the Isaac the Blind centre. That would take a smirk or two off her spoilt face. I had another Coca-Cola and put off killing her.

By late afternoon José had cooled down and had spent time looking for me. I certainly wasn't talking to him but he forced me into the garden of the Hotel Centro and said I'd taken it all personally. Nina was a wonderful person, well brought up, intelligent, and she responded to and recognised well-brought up intelligent qualities in others. Well she obviously hadn't in me. I said I hated her.

He said, 'She hates you too.'

'What about you?'

'Oh come on, Patrice. We go back a long way. It's just that your way of seeing things and mine are different.'

'They weren't always.'

242

'But yes,' he said with dignity. 'We are very different people.'

He could see that one drew blood. 'Do you remember our home in Puerta de la Selva? That was a special time.'

'Do you remember it?'

'You know I never forget the past.'

'Well, I'd start. Because your present looks OK to me. You've got a baby, an establishment, a wife. You're not unhappy.'

'Of course I'm unhappy.' He spat. 'I've thrown my happiness away.'

'Don't tell me about that now.'

'You never gave us a chance, Patrice.'

I heard the trees rustling then. The way they used to in Puerta de la Selva. There was so much I didn't notice any more. He took hold of my hand. 'I'm sure you know what's between us isn't finished. And that's what makes it dangerous. Our affair isn't completed. Sometimes I think about you. Rather, you come into my mind for one day, two. It's strange because I may not have given you a thought for months. And I want to reach you but what can I offer? I am taken.'

I hadn't expected anything like that. Yet I knew it was true. If something was there it was there.

'There's a link between us,' he said.

'Maybe there is. So what! You don't have to act on it.' I turned away from him.

'I hate it when you're hard,' he said.

I could have replied, well you've played your part in that. I didn't get to be hard all by myself. I said nothing. So he suggested leaving Spain. Istanbul came into it. I didn't want to hear.

'It's over.' And I turned and walked through the hotel kitchen up to my room. I should have known if you try and get rid of someone you've got them for ever. I didn't realise he was behind me until he kicked the door open. He started making love to me before it was even shut.

I'd made sacrifices in my time, known anxiety, fear of consequences. For once, in that hotel room, I was able to be bold and clasp happiness for as long as it lasted. The magic came in after we'd made love. Harmony. I think what's what it was. I'd never experienced it like that before. I felt rich, full, alive. A tray of awards couldn't give me that. With José, I could just be. The sun coming through the shutters made a shadowed staircase on the wall of our room. The sun filtered through on to the ceiling and gave it arches and domes. I'd never noticed that before. It was as though we were in church as we lay side by side on the bed, barely touching, looking at the lovely domed ceiling. That was our wedding. Transitory, yes, just as long as the sun lasted. But weddings are inclined to be transitory. I felt I'd known him before. If there was reincarnation, we'd known each other very well.

'I often dream of Puerta de la Selva,' he siad. 'My mind like an eye searches along the beach. No, whatever I'm looking for isn't there. The eye swings in and out of the cafés, swiftly through the fish market. No, it isn't the village I'm looking for. Up the narrow steps into the fisherman's cottage. The eye stops in the living room. So what am I looking for?'

I didn't know.

'The eye's like a camera. It's a recurring dream. What do you remember?'

Memory showed the living room all yellow and warm. The shutters were open and boats lolled sun-drenched on the quiet sea below. There was a table with a red plastic cloth wet with light. José arranged a bowl of flowers he'd gathered from the beach. He was always arranging things, improving things. The feeling of the afternoon in the room reminded me of another room ten years before in Gerona. I remembered him coming in with two eggs and three pesetas worth of white beans. It had to last till the next day and the next lot of eggs and beans. He also came in with love and optimism.

He got up and put his shirt on. 'I never forget you. There's never been anyone like you.'

It was my son Christian's birthday so that night José bought a cake with candles and gave him a dinner party in one of the salons overlooking the courtyard.

The waiters sped about professionally as the patio filled up with the Gerona late-night crowd. The waiters weren't paid but lived on

244

tips and slept in a windowless room behind the lavatories. Juan Serrat sat at the till and Nina did the cooking. José blew away a lot of the profit by offering his friends, and anyone of importance, free drinks. That night it seemed to me I was sitting in an exhausting bar which was the whim of a millionaire who liked to pour drinks on a big scale against a personalised map of history. Except the millions around José were the ones he owed. Cabbala was to be found in books and special groups but when people said cabbala in Gerona they meant José and Nina.

A new group had moved in, fans of cabbala. One, a Dutch photographer, Lilly, was actually living on the premises. She had an exhibition opening in one of the salons upstairs. She told me how marvellous it was that José and Nina had created such a powerful place. She thought she'd stay on for a while and help with the endeavour. I thought her reason for staying was much more to do with José. In fact she stayed for several years but I never found out if she was sleeping with him or not. It was another of the cabbala's little mysteries. When I first saw her she was manic to the point of being in love. Her eyes searched his as ardently as Nina's had.

For Chris's birthday, the waiters served lamb, salad, wine and ice-cream. Old friends from the Residencia days came to the table. I felt so good with José. It was as though we'd never been apart. I felt so good, so did he, that we forgot completely about Nina. We had about us that immediate intimacy of two people who'd spent time making love. Our eyes met and held, our hands touched and lingered. The waiters brought the boys and José black coffee and cognac. I asked for white coffee. I was the only one who did.

Tim said, 'You really look different, Mum. Kind of – well, beautiful-like.'

I wanted to tell him I still loved José. I did see Nina once, just her eyes as she stood by the coffee machine.

José ordered more champagne and we danced on the patio. Then a waiter gave him a message and he went off to the kitchen. The boys wanted to go on the town and see the nightlife. I said this was the nightlife. When José came back his face was creased with anxiety, the result, I thought, of too much talk with creditors.

'Nina's left. Just run out. Just like that!' He stayed at the table and tried to be cheerful with Chris but things weren't quite the same. After twenty minutes he slapped a hand to his head. 'I've been so thoughtless. God knows what she'll do.'

When I left at two in the morning she still hadn't come back. He was on the phone, worried. I knew what he was thinking. She was jealous, desperate and possibly dead.

At five o'clock I shot awake. It was as though I'd been down some dark tunnel full of rotten things all jumbled together. I couldn't breathe properly. All was not well. Emotionally, I was still in the tunnel and the slime worried me. My eyes assured me the light was on and I was in, not the cleanest room in the world but it wasn't slimy. Then I became aware of the troubles in my body. The pain in my back, the dry mouth, shuddering. I had to go to the lavatory. No sooner had I got back into the bed than I'd have to creep along to the lavatory again. In the end I stayed in the lavatory. As soon as I could, I got them involved at the reception. I knew I was ill. They added, 'very'. They'd get a doctor immediately. The hotel was difficult to be ill in because there was one lavatory for each corridor and I needed to be in it without interruption. Also the rooms were not exactly Holiday Inn clean. A gypsy from Malaga did the cleaning for the lowest wages ever known. She was marvellous, full of life and music like a small dry fluttery bird. As she did the whole hotel in less than two hours a day, including washing the sheets and tablecloths, she didn't spend too long on the corners. The proprietor got her to swish things up a bit before the doctor came. She took a gander at me. I was now heading towards 'in shock'. She threw down her broom and held me in her arms. 'I will make you well. The healing from my body will cure you. You don't need a doctor. I am your doctor.' She stayed with me, one hand on my head, the other on my stomach. 'You have been poisoned,' she said. 'But I will protect you.' After a while she made me a gallon of herbal tisane.

I had toyed with the idea of making a will. I also believed this was a punishment for taking what wasn't mine. 'Poisoned.' The gypsy was adamant. When the doctor did arrive – emergencies for them meant one hour late, not two – the symptoms were on the decline. I considered the gypsy maid had saved my life.

All the doctor wanted to talk about was food and money. What did I eat the night before. What I should eat today. I nearly threw up in his lap for that one. Money he wanted now and wrote a prescription which the gypsy maid was sent off to get. He said I had a stomach poisoning.

I took the medicine, although the maid said there was no need. 'I'm better than any medicine.' She made a fresh jug of herbal remedy and put magic signs around my bed. When I pulled round enough to start thinking about things I asked her how she knew I'd been poisoned.

'Something put in the food or drink. A poison to kill rats.'

'How do you know? Do you see things?'

'I see the unseen. I am the seer of my village. *La Savia*, the one who knows.'

What helped her along were my symptoms. She'd seen that sort of chemical poisoning before. 'Inside your mouth is burnt and you have a rash.' She pointed to my neck. 'And it has a smell. But the person didn't know how much to put in otherwise you would not still be here.'

Of course I was the only one not drinking alcohol. I had the big white coffee. No one else touched them.

The proprietor made me chicken and rice and I was ready to be up and phoning José. I said I'd been ill. It was poisoning.

He saw the point in coming to the hotel for a talk.

He insisted we sit in the breakfast room so it all looked above board. He was more the everyday José. What I'd experienced during the previous day's siesta belonged to another time. His eyes were red-rimmed. He too, had had a sleepless night. My pallid face and drained looks didn't bother him, not someone who'd seen my hangovers.

'You never bring me any luck.'

'José, it was me that was poisoned.'

'Because I went to Paris with you my mother cut me out of her will. I lost my share in the Residencia. And now I will lose my child. Because Nina does not believe your story of why you are here.'

'Phone the BBC.'

'She still won't believe it. She thinks you have come here for me. The Bacall story she always said was false.'

247

It seemed incredible that with all my other professional challenges I had to prove myself to a small-town sculptress. He stood up.

'She must not be upset because then the baby's upset.'

'Why are you doing all this? This Jewish business?'

'Because, Patrice, it is my destiny.'

'A lot of men hide away from their marriage by going fishing. It would take you to dig up half a city and spend a quarter of a million dollars you don't have reviving cabbala. Just to get away from your wife! Why not carpentry? I bet she hates it. Because it takes you away from her.'

He sat down. 'You're not wrong. She wants to get me out of Gerona. She's not happy unless it's just me, her and the child on an island. I can't live like that, cut off from everybody. She wants me to see, breathe and move only for her.'

Yes, she'd had the same requirements as me but she'd got her way. Almost.

'I don't see any Jews, José.'

'They will come.'

'But how do you know?' I almost whispered. I was in awe of his unquestioning belief. He was teetering on the edge of a disaster that made Colin Diamond look like a wayward farm worker on a two-nighter in Las Vegas.

'Because it is their destiny. They are the future of Gerona. Gerona can no longer be a place of perfection if it does not fulfil its destiny. Hundreds of years ago Nachmanides and the mystics designed its future and I have the key.'

'Why you?'

'Because I was a poet. My style was a memorial to the time past. So through me perhaps is transmitted the voice of cabbala. I represent all the Jews who were expelled from this place and the ones who remained.'

I wondered, if he'd stayed with me would he have uncovered the sun stone and run round like Don Quixote tilting at banks like windmills? The mystics might have mapped out Gerona's fate. But I wasn't sure about anyone else's. It all seemed a trifle accidental. If I'd got the key out of the door in the rented house opposite his *barracca* maybe the intruder wouldn't have tried to get in. I wouldn't have caused a sensation running through the night half naked. I wouldn't have left. Perhaps he wouldn't have married her. A broken key. That's what it came down to.

He was talking about our future again. Istanbul came into it. I could see he was confused. He alternated between me and then, and her and now. But the old days were dying in him.

We sat quietly then because he didn't know what to do. It was almost like a wake, sitting there. A wake for our love that had to die before I died.

'You have to go, Patrice.' He stood up and put his hand against my hair, my cheek.

'But I'm poisoned.' I showed him the inside of my mouth, the burnt skin.

'So go.'

'I ought to go to the police.'

'And say what? You threw up on a kebab?' He started to leave.

'What about us?'

'We fucked up.'

When he'd gone the gypsy maid brought me another tisane and a bottle of mineral water. 'You've got to wash it out of your system. He's upset, your lover.' She laughed. 'He's upset because there's another man in your life.'

Chapter Thirty-eight

It really ended in Puerta de la Selva in the late 1960s. That was what José was looking for in his dreams. An ending with me. That's why the eye roamed through the village, the beach, the house. I could have told him that.

I could see myself sitting in the fisherman's cottage, wistful, experienced, in love, insecure. Music came from the café next door. The night tipped into the dawn of another day. The beginning of a fierce wind lifted the sand off the street and banged shutters. Footsteps came up the stairway from the main street, light, swift, José's. He was whistling. I sat by the gas stove like Cinderella before it all turned out right for her. 'Oh God,' he said, seeing my face.

'Where have you been?'

'A walk.'

'Four and a half hours, José?'

'There are many thing I have to do. I have nothing and when you have nothing you can end up – you just end up.'

He stepped in front of the mirror. He could see middle age lurking like an acquaintance in a doorway, uncertain whether to come in. He touched his youthful face as though saying goodbye to a dying friend.

'I don't understand you, José. You had it made with the club on the Costa Brava. What went wrong there?'

'The taxes. What else? You English have no comprehension. Here you make a buck and you give two.'

'But you got money from the Sala of Fiestas you built for the flamenco dancers on the coast?'

'They didn't pay. Gypsies.'

'What about that painter's shop? You were her partner.'

'She's hard. Mean. Jewish!'

'You never seem to involve yourself with someone who could do you some good.'

'I never meet anyone like that, *chérie*,' he said dryly.

'Honest people you don't believe. What do you believe? You were going to spend the summer with me, remember?'

'Not possible.'

'Half a day ago you said you were going to write a book here. Your life's a dance. Four steps forward, eight back. You'll never do anything.'

'Unlike some people I cannot do exactly what I want. Mostly I have to choose the least unbearable.'

'What do you think I do?' I screamed.

'You? You're always in your own skin. You have absolutely no understanding of other people. You never have gratitude for anything.'

'Thank you.'

'No,' he said lightly. 'I don't want thank you.'

'Actually, you're in one of those moods you'd be better indulging with Mama in Gerona.'

He spat on the floor.

'I expect you'll brighten up, sweetheart, when my money arrives.'

In spite of the rage there was a flash of something warm. Recognition from a time long gone perhaps. The love was still there.

And it was still there.

Of course he was bitter because he should have had money. How could I forget that so often? His uncle, his cousins, with their enviable lives and he and his mother in the Calle Forsa with newspaper not soft paper in the lavatory and tortillas twice a day, frayed cuffs and shoes with holes. That night he decided to marry Nina and he hadn't even met her, had never heard of her. He wanted what he deserved. If his youth held out, he'd get it. Of course when he got it, it wasn't what he wanted at all. The yellow brick road, the soft moneyed life.

I was sure he'd been busy during the four and a half hours he was absent from the fisherman's house. He'd been turning tricks with rich women. I did begin to wonder about this superstar of Gerona's old town, Isabella Sans-Gomez. Without ever having seen her I knew he'd screwed her. It was like a Pythagorean theorem.

When I got back to England with the BBC documentary tapes, and the *Jewish Chronicle* article, a letter from Robert Hartman was waiting for me, postmarked Saudi Arabia. He promised I would be valued and find my place. *The Rose-garden* would be published, he was sure. He'd gone into the desert and prayed for me, my health, my work. His promises were underlined. Throughout the rest of the summer I got encouraging, almost loving letters but never with a return address.

I put the BBC documentary together and it was broadcast immediately and attracted interest. José came over as a visionary restoring a vanished past which had valuable lessons for the modern age. He too was a figure from another century, giving everything up for an ideal. And his wife stood beside him dedicated, popular, exceptionally talented. I think I even threw in an 'attractive'. Her sell-out exhibitions were sacrificed in the daily toil to raise finance. Serving kebabs and drinks until long past dawn to the locals who loved anything unusual. José throwing his life away on a cause which may or may not succeed thrilled them. So what the drinks were exorbitantly priced? The guy who was turning the kebabs could be in the jail tomorrow.

In the *Jewish Chronicle* I wrote, 'The running of the bar is hard enough but there is also the arranging of concerts, exhibitions, showing visitors the excavations, keeping the enormous salons clean. Nina describes her life as exhausting. 'Each day is like three days in one. It's a sacrifice but worth it."'

It was surprising how sympathetic it came out, considering who'd written it. And as I wrote it I began to see there was a relentless masochism about the toiling, the exhaustion, the constant debts. Was he paying her back, or himself, for not doing what he should have? I must say I no longer knew what that should have been.

Dozens of people wrote to Gerona asking to help. They offered ideas, their time, even presents for the child, collections of cabbala books for the library. Then *The Listener* asked me to do a piece and that came out in America, and Jewish groups started to ask about Tarres and Gerona. Fred Zinnemann, the movie director, was very taken with the idealism and sacrifice. And Leonard Bernstein sent a telex. He wanted to meet Tarres immediately. The well-known people were drawn to this idealism that did belong to a bigger era, and I praised myself for that. My public representation of my ex-lover was a wonderful revenge because my name was on every set of lips that went there and Nina had to hear it every day.

Some things that happened around the Gerona project were coincidental. I decided I needed a rabbinic scholar to comment on cabbala for the documentary. The first person I turned to, Hyam Maccobby, writer and librarian at Leobaeck college, happened to be a world authority on Nachmanides and the Jews of Gerona. Hyam immediately became inflamed with the idea of helping José to keep the project alive and we did spend time trying to get money from Jewish foundations in this country, without success. What they gave stayed in the UK or Israel. Hyam, although deeply involved with Gerona in the medieval ages, had not been there in this one. For some reason Gerona and Spain were not popular places with Jews. Phil, who was of Ashkenazy descent, had no intention of visiting José's restoration. The Expulsion could not be forgiven. Yet these same people went quite easily to Germany. Perhaps there was a vibration, as José said. But it didn't attract them. It kept them away.

The documentary and articles were responsible for another coincidence. A group of Sephardic Jews from California on tour in Spain veered off to Gerona to see this new discovery. Among them was a leader of the community, a 92-year-old rabbi. They arrived by chance the very day José's debt had grown too huge, even for him. The local courts where he was to make many future appearances declared him bankrupt and the centre was put up for auction.

In spite of many Jews visiting and applauding José's work, no real money had been forthcoming. Juan Serrat and José were down the plug. Not only would they lose the historic site, they'd be in debt for years. José said he knew something wonderful was going to happen because the light in the courtyard turned a translucent blue and then in came the ancient rabbi. He seemed to know, in advance, José's problems. He said, 'Have faith because I have been where you are today. It took forty years to establish the first synangogue in LA. You will have the first synagogue in Gerona.' And because José was under such strain he wasn't at all sure this man was not a heavenly being. It put Nina in reach of one of her panic attacks. But then the rest of the group came past the wishing-well and surrounded the rabbi. And they put their hands in their pocket for a quick whip round so José saw they were from this earth. Among them were Zelman Goldstein, a Ladino scholar and professor of Comparative Literature in LA, and lawyer, financier Jay Stein. They saw the mayor, the banks, the minister of culture, and put up enough guarantees to stop the auction. They formed a foundation, The Friends of Gerona Jewish Quarter. Zelman spoke to the press. 'This is more than a shrine. It is a living, breathing history that is very much present. First we will pay off the bank loans then continue the excavations and follow the intention to establish a school of rabbinic study. It is one of the most important Jewish sites in the world and must be preserved. José Tarres had been right all along. He is a poet, a fighter for truth.'

Jose's new love affair was on.

The Spanish national press now filled the courtyard. Didn't José feel bitter that his own country had not given help?

'Here in Spain everything is political,' said José. 'This centre is absolutely not political. That's why they don't become involved.'

But why did he have to bear the cost absolutely alone?

Well, I could have given some answers there. José said, 'It's very difficult to resuscitate something that's been over for five hundred years.'

Well, I could agree with that. It was hard enough to resuscitate something that was over for ten.

As well as the press, helpers and hangers-on arrived in droves. Nina glowed with pride and José's destiny was fulfilled. Almost. The one sound absent from it all, which at the height of emotion was not noticed, was the chink of coins. There were plenty of banquets and press receptions and the drink flowed, but who paid for it? The arrival of the Americans excited Gerona's tradespeople and suddenly Tarres was back on credit. The travel agent, Julio Framis, decided to throw a few pesetas into the act and in return got the rights to handle the Jewish travel to and from Gerona. Julio became José's business adviser and was keen to get Isaac the Blind solvent. Also, he was not a poet so the money people felt easier with him. At one touching ceremony when Zelman Goldstein fixed the first scroll to a doorway, José was reported to have burst into tears and to have said, 'This is the moment I was born for. To give this site back to the Jews.' And José and Zelmon embraced. That was the good part.

I wasn't there but I knew José. He blamed his cousins for ripping off his inheritance. He blamed the town for not repaying him for the gift of his earlier political sacrifice. And now he was making another superlative gesture to restore the past. I knew, somewhere in his little body, he expected payment. The Jews, the town, someone would pay.

I felt because my writing had thrown light on the place and saved it, that somehow it was mine. And yet I went unmentioned. In the end I did phone José and said I'd got Leonard Bernstein interested. I knew Nina was listening in. I could hear a second phone lifted up. José didn't know who Bernstein was until I sang a chorus from *West Side Story*. José sounded breathless, as though his nerves were on edge. I told him about Fred Zinneman's interest.

'Finally they have come. I knew they would. The strain has been terrible.' He cleared his throat. 'I don't know what I would have done.'

255

I told him he sounded like someone who'd overspent on a mansion, put in too many bathrooms.

'Those sort of people shoot themselves,' he said. 'Because they are just out for themselves. I did this for history.'

There was a lot of emotion. People seemed to throw themselves on to the Gerona stones, giving up their jobs, their future. There were a lot of big words – dedication, eternal, pilgrimage. Thousands of dollars were mentioned. These would be gathered in America by Zelman Goldstein and Jay Stein. José was their superstar and his wife, the heroine who'd subdued her talent for the revival of another race. Mario Soll, a journalist from Barcelona, was so excited he gave up his job in Brussels to devote himself to the cause. I must say José had a way of stirring people up. The last one he'd stirred things for had got shot dead. I thought it lucky his present hero, Nachmanides, had died five hundred years before.

Chapter Thirty-nine

The Siesta was postponed. I couldn't believe it except I was no stranger to rejection. I knew that's what we were into, whatever my agent said. My NFFC script was now firmly with Henry Jaglom who wanted to work with me in LA trying to cut down 180 pages to 100. He said he'd shoot it in Nicaragua. I thought that was a dangerous place but he liked to think of himself as a dangerous person. I also got commissioned by BBC radio to do a documentary on 'The British in Hollywood'. I always felt safe with radio. It never let me down, I always got paid.

Before I left I heard Fred Zinnemann was in London preparing a film about the Jews of Gerona. This infuriated me to the point of madness. If anyone went near the place I was berserk. I felt it was mine. So I rang Fred Zinnemann, whom I knew slightly because we'd once almost worked together on a project, and he denied the rumour. Yes, he had read my articles and was fascinated by Tarres. But he could never do a film without at least referring to my work. So I told him I knew he had a researcher running around London talking to rabbis and scholars and getting Gerona material. He said, 'You must be careful of your material. Get it copyrighted or someone will steal it. I only mention it because it happens all the time.' So I laughed and said I thought that was exactly what he was doing. 'Anyone, should they make this film, would have to ask your permission to use your writings about this man José Tarres. Unless they went to him direct.'

'Are you going direct?' I asked, falsely calm.

He denied it. But before saying goodbye he said, 'By the way. To get to Gerona do you have to go through Madrid?'

I hoped he was joking. Of course if he'd really gone for it he'd have done it. And José would have rolled the red carpet all the way for Fred Zinnemann. So I hadn't got over the place if I had the man.

Mario Sol, the journalist, called me from Gerona. He spoke good English and worked for the BBC Overseas Service. He said Zelman Goldstein and Jay Stein were still there and wanted to use me for publicity. Mario thought I'd be a useful mouthpiece because I knew some famous people. Leonard Bernstein had been there on a visit. Who else did I know? Then Zelman Goldstein took Mario's phone and Jay picked up Nina's listening-in extension and we had a three-way conversation during which a little falling out took place. For some reason I asked who would do the food. Would it be a kosher menu?

Jay said of course everything would be kosher. But there would be no restaurant as such, not for the public. That would go. And the bar would go.

'So it won't be open to non-Jews?'

He thought not. He described a Jewish shrine in the middle of a gentile town, secret, well tended, where Jews from all over the world could come and pay homage and enrol in rabbinic classes and possibly there would be some cabbala instruction on a scholarly level.

'But it won't be of any benefit to the townspeople.' By townspeople I meant me. I couldn't bear to be left out of Gerona. It was a crazy feeling like post-natal depression or something. It was quite irrational. Except it wasn't in response to a beginning but an ending. 'And what part will Tarres take? He isn't Jewish.'

'He'll be rewarded.'

'He'll have a part in the running of it?'

There was a pause. Then Jay said, 'No. He's not Jewish. And he's not a scholar.' Jay wasn't a liar. 'Why you should worry about that I don't know. He isn't.'

Then I said I didn't think they'd get him out. After all it had been his idea and his work.

'Get him out? But it's what he wants. To return the site to the Jews.'

I realised the conversation was to test me rather than to employ me. They asked me to be careful what I printed. After all it was a delicate matter. I said I worked for a free press. It was getting a bad start. I think we were all over-emotional.

I flew directly to LA and stayed in the Château Marmont. The first thing I did was have a huge row with Henry Jaglom. Part of the trouble – he was getting a divorce from a wife he loved. Unfortunately her name was Patrice. But I just wasn't getting things right. The finality of my break-up with José had affected my sense of proportion. I was like a weathervane pointing east instead of north. Zelman Goldstein and his sister Ruby were immediately welcoming. Zelman was attractive but he was – well, he wasn't José. And he wore a yellow and white checked jacket. Clothes didn't offend me in the normal way but this didn't suit him. The checks were large and the colour made him appear liverish. He'd just got back from Gerona and felt jetlagged and, unknown to me, other negative things. He was right and not right. There was a contradiction about him. He was cold, not Tycoon-bitter but distant. He'd been in a lot of shit over a previous European project and had got ripped off. Some of Ruby's money went down with his. It would not happen again. He wanted Isaac the Blind. It was there in his eyes. He was intelligent, intuitive, knowledgeable, a scholar. He knew cabbala and could really explain it. But his eyes! I knew I should be careful of that look. He'd been decorated in the Israeli War. He was a tactician, a fighter who had to win. Even Ruby said, once he got something in his mind he never let go. Never.

Ruby came first, to check me out. She asked about my politics. Was I into the Vanessa Redgrave scene? She hoped not. Was I a fanatic? I wondered what Nina had been saying. I wasn't mad about Ruby's style. It was a little too noisy and intrusive. I said my politics were my own damn business. She said the Château Marmont was too expensive and there was something wrong with the air-conditioning. She'd get me into something better. She checked me over. I passed because I got to meet Zelman next.

He was grateful he'd found Gerona. For him it was a coming home. All he had to do was sort out the money problems and the centre of rabbinic studies would commence. He had a lot of plans. They were drawn up like a campaign and they made sense. So I wasn't Vanessa Redgrave or a fanatic. I wasn't a Jew but I wasn't trouble. So I got to meet Jay Stein and the Sephardic community.

Jay was class, he was a good man. I could see good all over him in a hundred ways and that's why he wasn't going to stay with the Gerona project. During the happy celebrations in the courtyard Jay and Zelman had discovered things were not as they seemed. José ran the show. But he did not own the site. It belonged to Juan Serrat. He'd paid all the rents. So one dreadful day Zelman and Jay did the accounts, and tried to settle the debts. Serrat was just a young quiet boy who hung around Tarres. They thought he was a waiter. He never got to say one word. But he was the unsung hero. José had not inserted one buck. It seemed everyone else in town had and they wanted their money back. Now.

The news that the Americans were paying José's bills brought Catalans from every village in the province. Wave after wave of angry people crossed the courtyard and the debt rose to a hundred million something or the other. Whatever currency, it was too much for Jay Stein and he wanted out. He had other charities to consider. Zelman wanted to continue the fight. And the day of book-keeping coincided with an important Jewish landmark.

'So we realised we were there not for ourselves but for a greater purpose, to build a new synagogue.' And Zelman had to keep Jay in because he was the direct link to serious money.

Zelman subdued the creditors with a long-term plan. Ten per cent of their bill immediately and the rest in instalments as the place began to go into profit. If anyone demanded the lot on the spot the whole programme would collapse and no one would get anything. So ten per cent or nothing. They agreed that something was better.

Then Zelman did deals with the banks and stopped any

foreclosing. He also arranged to acquire the property around Isaac the Blind which had also belonged to the Jews. Then I had to declare my interest. I think they were still cautious of me. So I played a tape of the documentary. At the end they understood I loved José and was doing it for him. That was fine. As long as they understood.

Then on to the Gerona gala dinner at the beach. I sat at the centre table between Jay and a politician, and during it they outlined what my contribution would be. I knew the entertainment world. I should pass people on to Zelman who would get their support. I should not try myself. And if anyone else like Bernstein or Zinnemann contacted me pass them on to Zelman. The same went for contributions. After all, it was for Gerona. I noticed a lot of bucks were pledged at my table and there was talk of a benefit evening in New York to which the King of Spain had been invited. Leonard Bernstein would do the music and the Prime Minister of Israel would attend. Except it was bigger than that. They were nice to me but I kept my head low and didn't talk too much. Barbra Streisand was at another table and Zelman kept telling me to talk to her. I didn't know if she was part of the Gerona group. Also I did not think she was the kind of person you just approached. The only odd note was when Ruby walked in. She was dressed as Charlie Chaplin. Seeing her sitting opposite in the black glistening bowler reminded me I was more useful as his daughter-in-law than as Tarres's lover. And at that moment I knew Tarres was in trouble. And in the side of my mind I saw the Calle Forsa and this Jewish figure walking up the hot cobbled streets. I could see only half of his face. The dark sombre eyes, white creamy skin, and the long black hair twisted into ringlets and the black hat. He'd trod that road so often. He was weary. Yet he continued. Long ago he'd overcome physical boundaries. And in times of trouble I was aware of this man, present in my mind. I accepted him as someone special who gave comfort. I did not try to give him a name. He wasn't a thought because he was of a vivid substance, more substantial than thought. and he recurred, each time the same, clearer than any thought.

Zelman drove me back to the hotel. As we left he snapped off a white flower and gave it to me. It was the same flower that José had given me years ago. Neither of us said anything. I felt full to choking with tears. It was such an odd thing for him to do.

In the car he said things were not as they seemed. Jay Stein was not impressed by deception and there seemed plenty in Isaac the Blind. 'Serrat is just the tip of the iceberg. Tarres knows nothing about Jewish history or cabbala. Historians from Barcelona university already visited the excavation and what he told them were figments of his imagination or poetry. Academically he is not correct and this had put off the universities. In academic circles the place already had a bad name. Yet he assured us no experts had ever evaluated his restoration.

'So for now I am going to appoint a new impartial director who is at least qualified in history and he will put a stop to the bad name.'

'Does he have a name?'

'He does. But only if you accept our participation. Put it this way. With us your friend Tarres will have a job. Without us he doesn't even have a building.'

'And the name?'

'Mario Sol.'

It was extraordinary the attention the Gerona affair attracted in LA. Jane Fonda wanted to know all about it and her producer came to see me for information. Jane and Barbra Streisand wanted to do a Jewish film together. Could this be it? Journalists, radio stations, TV, all wanted the story of Gerona. Ruby moved me from the unsuitable 'filmy' Château Marmont to one of 'their' hotels, the Sunset Hyatt. I got a good reduction on a very good suite.

'Don't keep everything to yourself now. Just pass it over to Zelman. He can handle people. He gave Leonard Bernstein his Ph.D.'

Ruby suspected I was holding out on some of Hollywood's élite. However, I wasn't going to just deliver everyone into Zelman's lap. But I didn't keep everything to myself. Immediately I phoned José and told him to watch out for Mario Sol.

He paused. Didn't believe it. 'Zelman is like me. We're as one.'

I could hear the other extension had been lifted up. She heard every word and did believe it. But first she told Zelman Goldstein I was an informer.

Chapter Forty

J found the 'crusade' hilarious. He loved to hear what everyone wore and what they said. The Chaplin-suit-modelling Ruby really cracked him up. But it had its serious side. 'It's tasteless, Patrice, but it's dangerous. Be careful. The Middle East didn't get into that mess just by itself. Fervent people don't like fence sitters.'

We played backgammon and went out for dinners, but we no longer went to bed. Probably he had someone else and I had no one else.

Caroline Pfeiffer and I met the screenwriter of *The Siesta*, Patricia Knopf. She was so open and balanced and dignified and warm. She said how much she cherished the book. She had just the right approach for someone who'd dealt with something valuable belonging to another person, when that other person really wanted to do it themselves. So I really liked her and because of that I didn't read *The Siesta* script. My agent had said it was fine. I explained to Patsy that if I read it and it was worse than I could do, I'd feel resentful. But if better, jealous. She was relieved we could be honest with each other. I could see both Caroline Pfeiffer and Patsy Knopf had knocked on a lot of doors in Hollywood trying to set it up and they were relieved at last a bankable director and a moviestar were on board. The director, however, was extremely difficult to locate. They said it was because he was getting *Frances* ready for release. I happened to mention it to an executive producer at EMI who'd produced *Frances*. He happened to like my writing but had never bought anything. Perhaps that's why he wanted to show how helpful he could be. So he phoned the busy director and said to make time for me and my team. He whistled up a car and within minutes we were all face to face in an office.

The director did not like me pulling rank. He didn't like having his back to the wall. He didn't say any of this – his eyes did it for him. He didn't want to discuss why he'd had to put back shooting *The Siesta*. Patsy, Caroline and others had been with this man when he was 'hot'. They'd lived with him through his excitement and possession of the project. I hadn't. I was looking at a stranger and he was cold. He did not want to do *The Siesta*. He would never do it. He was waiting for *Frances* to come out and then he'd get terrific offers. He didn't want to be saddled with a small-budget, possible art-house movie like *The Siesta* if he could make *The Godfather*. Because I was no longer modest I challenged him. Would he let the producer use his name to raise money?

'No.'

'Why not?'

'Because there are still things to do to the script. And I haven't time to do them.'

Was that Spanish for he wanted to wait for other offers? He disliked me enough to be brutal. He was also truthful. So he was off the film and no doubt Jessica Lange went too, and we were back in the street and Patsy was crying. I kept saying it's better to know. Don't hold on to false hope! Oh boy! Coming from me.

The next director they got attached was Michelangelo Antonioni and for a while that was hot. Even I felt good about it. And I happened to phone Patsy's home from London, just as MA arrived for the meeting. That was considered an omen because I was not in the habit of calling her. He was put on the phone and said, 'Hello, we are a go film.' I knew he was of a certain age and in frail health, inclined to be neurotic. I thought the humidity of Gerona, a couple of local *menu del dias* would finish him off.

I was totally absorbed by the vicissitudes of my writing career. Even in the Sunset Hyatt I was never without tension. Robert Hartman was no longer in my mind. Perhaps that's why he showed up. I was beginning to see the sense of letting go of what you loved. Let it be free. Just letting go of it, even in your mind, created a beneficial vacuum, the liberty of which I believe reached the person in question. It was then, if indeed they wanted to see you, that they felt moved to do so. If you were obsessed by them, such constant thinking drained their energy and when they thought of you they felt tired and overwhelmed. That, anyway, was what I believed. Of course if you sent someone good thoughts that could be only beneficial. But that was the reverse of obsessed.

Robert Hartman followed, in fact, after one of Ruby's visits. Her perfume was still thick in the already scented air. I was never without floral gifts, especially from people wanting to be on the BBC documentary. The English in Hollywood may be alive, well and rich, but who knew – they might one day go home and they wanted to be remembered.

The first thing Robert did was pick up Ruby's earring which she'd inadvertently dropped. He threw it out of the window. That was a surprise. I knew J was capable of crises of taste.

'You're bugged,' he said. Then he lifted up the phone and dialled some numbers. 'Bugged. Well. Well.' And he went around the room touching this and that. It was fun for him. But I was remembering the bitchiness I'd indulged in with J about the 'crusade' and I felt disloyal. Of course they now all knew of my disrespectful attitude to their clothes and some of their proposals. The only upside: J was worse than I was. I did notice that whenever he'd phoned and we'd bitched about Ruby, the manager of the Hyatt would ring immediately my receiver was replaced and ask if everything was all right and was I enjoying my stay.

Robert chucked the flowers out. No, they weren't bugged. He just didn't like their false perfume. 'They spray them before they send them to market. Their scent isn't real.'

'Not even violets?'

266

'Especially violets.'

'I can't wait till you get going on Father Christmas.'

Then when he'd finished rearranging the room he came up to me, looked at me and smiled. The minute he'd come in I was OK again. The weathervane swung round the right way. I told him about Gerona.

'Are they quarrelling?'

'Good God no. It's so friendly. It's a love affair.'

'They will,' he said. 'Wait till they all fall out. It will be like the original time. The disputes, the jockeying for power, the establishing doctrine. Don't tell me that the Jewish area was peaceful. Those ideas came out of great struggle.'

He said he'd been travelling almost without cease. Washington, the Middle East, the Far East. That hardly sounded like movie business. I asked if what he was doing was political. He paused. 'It could be.'

'Isn't it dangerous?'

'Someone has to do it. Set up a basis for dialogue or we're all down the plug.'

'In the Middle East, who is right? The Jews or the Arabs?'

'Oh, it's not Jews versus Arabs. It's Arabs versus Arabs then Jews. The whole lot.' He looked exhausted.

'Why do you do it?'

'I suppose I don't mind if I die. So I can do what other more life-loving people cannot.' His eyes were black, mournful, ageless.

He obviously wasn't in love with anyone. Love kept you wanting to live.

He made love to me and I thought about it afterwards with dizzying excitement. He could give himself to passion, make it last, enjoy it, tighten it up, draw it out. He was a fantastic lover. He took what he wanted. Took his pleasure. And for that moment you filled his mind. Afterwards I don't suppose you even entered it.

Chapter Forty-one

The Zuma beach house was all glass and the sea – blue, emerald green, and frothing – lashed against the windows and reflected in mirrors until it seemed to fill the room. Robert said, 'You won't get José. You can't break up a marriage, Patricia. The person either wants to leave his wife or he doesn't. If he does he might use you as the means of going. It's very hard breaking up even when the marriage has become lukewarm. People cling to what they know.' He looked at his nails intently. They were beautifully cared for with a dull shine. 'I'd leave him to his marriage and stay in America.'

I thought I hadn't heard right.

'You spend your life trying to get what you want. You get it. Then you find it wasn't what you wanted after all. That's my experience. You are truthful.' He did some more nail examining and I thought he might be nervous.

'Am I?'

'I'll keep you, Patricia. But the deal is you don't go with other men.'

'What? We live together?'

'That's not what I said. I give you a house or apartment, whatever you want. Here perhaps.'

'And where are you?'

'I see you when I can. We get on quite well together.'

It was the reverse of every fantasy I'd ever had about him.

'What's that exactly? Like, clock time. Every two weeks, two months?'

'Between those two. You have an allowance and you can have your children here. And you do your writing.'

It sounded deadly. It had no love in it. I could see myself shut away in this acid green room, alone. And I'd be going to the hairdresser's or exercise class every two minutes because I'd never know when he would hit town. For the first time I hated the sea because it had witnessed such a suggestion. I could feel the loneliness. I was already cold with loneliness.

'I think that arrangement would depress me. Sorry.'

We sat in silence. After a while he said, 'Well you'll have to learn to live with less. That's what I do.'

'Less? Now that would be difficult.'

His eyes were amused. Beautiful, beautiful, beautiful eyes. I didn't even want to think how much I needed him. 'Were you married in a church?' I asked.

'Of course.'

'Was it sacred? For you?'

'You've got to believe it.'

We got back into the car and turned round to the city. Was I glad to leave that house behind. It was a box of depression. I imagined living there on the allowance. Which one of the glass walls would I smash first? I imagined the hours of false patience and hairdressers.

When we got into the city the mood lifted. I had one marvellous night with him in downtown LA. All through it I heard bells ringing, music. A searing, thrilling evening. We didn't go to the highspots either. We had his idea of nightlife. Listening to jazz, drinking in one of the old bars where Raymond Chandler used to go with his friends in the 1940s. It made me feel high and light-headed, like I used to in the trad jazz clubs in Soho and on the Left Bank.

Before I got into passion, when I was new and free. Yes, that night with him was a rebirth and afterwards I wished I'd taken up the offer even if I only saw him every two months and spent the rest of the time with sexual fantasies.

At one point he said, 'You never ask me for anything, do you?'

'Does that worry you?'

'Yes. Because you're so in need.'

'I told you you could get *The Rose-garden* published.'

'I've already told you. It won't solve a thing. You can do it yourself. You're that good. It must be a timing thing.' He was obviously mystified by my continuing lack of acceptance and success. 'Don't you like money?'

'My Dad said it always came down to money. He said I was a chump because I didn't study to be a secretary and get a steady wage and save up for the future. I said money didn't matter. Unless you'd lost out. Then it was all you could have. My Dad said with that attitude I'd go far. Money made my Dad depressed. It makes people depressed.'

'It does when they haven't got it,' he said.

We took a hotel room in downtown LA. It was an erotic night. He wasn't exactly straight even when he was being straight. Something in his life had made him warped. And he was difficult. But I was completely mad about him and would have done anything to give him pleasure. I woke up at dawn and I said to myself, 'You're in love. You're happy. It doesn't get better than this.' And then José Tarres came into my head as he used to be. And I knew I had to go back to José. There wasn't any choice about that. Life without him wasn't worth having. Never had been. It was all right with Robert as long as I didn't ask real questions. My turning down his lifestyle offer didn't offend him – it was just a deal. What he did like was laughing. He had a very dry way of looking at things. And it was amazing how much we did laugh and what we found to laugh about. He became a different person then and that's when I was close to him. Nobody, absolutely no one, knew I even saw him. That was another deal which covered every contingency. I did not talk. He liked food and hotels. He loved to book a room in a seedy one and fuck all ways for hours. Or he'd suddenly crave elegance. He didn't like the Hyatt, with or without bugs, and got me to move back to the Château Marmont.

He was the financial head of many enterprises. He had a strong political motivation. Hollywood was a dream city still, but he liked to own and recycle his dreams. The business was conducted by telephone in many languages and he chose never to recount one detail to me. He was private. No one got close, unless he chose. He travelled under different names and had two passports. He had Irish do a lot of standing in. He was an outsider. He'd been on the outside when he'd first seen José and me in Gerona. Other people's ecstasy confirmed his status as outsider. Stuck some pain into it. I knew that women had made tremendous offerings of their bodies, their lives, and on several occasions that had led to fantastic sex. And for a while he wondered if he had found, at last, a partner. But he was always on the outside and these women weren't.

I did one day suggest he only loved what he couldn't have. He didn't answer. 'You can only love what you can't have, Robert.'

'Put it on my tombstone.'

'If you'll put me a fountain in Gerona when I die. Somewhere in the old sector. You choose. A beautiful fountain lit at night, changing shape and colour.'

'And called Fuente Patricia.'

'And I'll take care of the tombstone.' I asked him how he'd got to Gerona in the first place.

During his last year studying medicine he'd had a strong desire to visit the old country. During a vacation he toured Sicily but it was just another place. It meant nothing to him. He travelled in Italy and took a boat from Genoa to Barcelona. He found Gerona, quite by chance, and that place did mean something. The light, the smells, the optimism. The same qualities that had caught me, kept him there, learning languages, trying to be part of another culture. It was in Gerona he found he'd never be part of anything. Then he went home, finished his studies and got married.

Had his marriage been dull? When he talked of people not leaving when it was uninteresting to stay, was he remembering his own marriage? He said her name was Ruth. He used to be fastidious about restaurants when he crossed Europe with Ruth and the little boy. Before he'd order he'd check the kitchen.

'Didn't they mind?'

'If they did I didn't eat there.'

'How could you tell if the kitchen was unsafe?'

'I was a doctor. I knew what to look for.'

He'd spent so much effort keeping them alive and yet they were both dead.

'It was so beautiful, Gerona, but it made me feel very alone.'

Another time he told me why he'd become a doctor. Throughout his childhood his mother was an invalid, paralysed. But it hadn't made him unhappy. She'd indicated for him to approach and the love that shone from her eyes was greater than any physical embrace. He felt her love, even now. As a child he used to think up ways to free her numb limbs, the rigid mouth.

'Didn't it scare you? Seeing her so ill?'

'Not at all. She never scared me.'

He certainly wanted to stay fit. Exercise, meditation, special food, swimming. What he truly loved was to run by the seashore. Then he was free. And solitude, trains, anonymity, mystery and other people's passions. I wanted someone to be very close and I wanted passion, a marriage. I wasn't sure I'd get the two together.

J sensed I had someone else. Perhaps it was something as superficial as my appearance which unsettled him. I'd stopped dressing up when José ceased to love me, unless of course I was hunting down some career success. But I wanted to look good for Robert Hartman. He had such an inner elegance that whatever I wore always looked a mess. I just had to catch sight of myself beside him in some unexpected mirror. Who was this superannuated art student? With the hair a little too long? My shoes looked like nurse's shoes. My dress covered my body but did nothing for me. Trying to match him, which I never succeeded in doing, upgraded me in J's eyes.

His voice was tricky as he said, 'So what's your life been like?'

I'd looked into the pissholes of hell but it didn't mean I had to tell him.

'I heard some nice things about a script of yours,' he said.

272

'Nice?'

'Indeed I did.'

It turned out a friendly executive at Columbia was praising something I'd written. He had a drinking problem, we all knew that, but he didn't have to take it that far. The script was the NFFC job. It was an elephant, a bow-wow, and now Henry Jaglom wasn't going to make it throb with money. Its last rejection had killed it off. It would just gather dust, a wreck. I hated it so much, it stank of failure, I couldn't even be in the same room as it. However, a few years later I gave it a new start, a disguise. I rewrote it as a book and Duckworth published it in 1987.

'It's about Spain,' I said.

'They're all about Spain,' said J. 'Let me have a look at it. I might have some suggestions.'

I could imagine how they'd make me feel. I asked him how his own work was going.

'I'm doing the film in Chile.' He sounded bland.

'When will it come out?'

'It's for TV, not theatrical release.'

That made me thoughtful. Had Robert Hartman broken his career, not just snuffed out *Quark*? Or was I getting paranoid?

'Are you going to show me the script?'

'No. It'll get done. It's just timing.'

'You're so naive, Patrice.'

'Optimistic, darling. When I cease to be I'll stop writing.'

J saw me as I was. I saw myself as I was becoming. There was a huge discrepancy and he was on to it like a happy shark in an ocean of innocents. He saw the SS office, the dreary recurring virus, the bank manager, my limited earning, my needy growing boys. My looks would go. He saw the huge house. The huge unresolved relationship with Phil. It was too much for me and getting me nowhere. And there were too many dogs and cats. When I said I was going to write a book about my life, the idea proposed by Robert, he said I wouldn't be realistic enough. So it wouldn't work.

'You won't write about getting out of bed, emptying the ashtrays, stacking the gin bottles in the bin, looking in the mirror, seeing your hair dull and falling out and your face creased. Then you go to the door and there's a pile of bills. You'll write, 'I woke up. I was in love.'

'Whose gin bottles are these?'

'Your lover's.' He watched me, his eyes frosty. 'He may not drink, Patrice, but he drinks inside. He's no good to you.' He knew and yet he didn't know. He just sensed Tycoon's shape and menace. Later, I told Robert that my writing wasn't realistic enough for the sort of book he wanted. I didn't write about getting up in the morning and emptying the smelling ashtrays with face creased and old and hair falling out, etc.

'Who told you that?'

I admitted it was J.

'Oh, Mr J.'

'So as he's usually right I'd better start writing about the way it is, not the way I'd like it to be.'

'But you will. Your way of seeing things is different to J's . My dear Patricia, emptying the ashtrays, putting the gin bottles in the bin, the ageing face, bills on the mat, he's describing his own life.'

'Don't be silly. He's got servants and he's very together.'

'That's how he sees his life. He's finished. Don't listen to him.'

He said he was leaving the next day and wanted to know my plans. He said, 'I wonder if things are fixed.'

'I'm sure you'd know that.'

'The real things – ' and he called me by a nickname that had crept in lately.'It's funny that I saw you in that film in Gerona. Then I photographed you with José. It all looked so good. Then you turn up in the film department of a romance company. Then I own a studio. All celluloid.'

I thought for someone who was so smitten by me, when he couldn't have me, he sure didn't spend much time in my company, now he could.

He laughed. 'Come on, dope. You're not what I remember. I have to get used to it.' And he looked at me, teasing, warm and I thought we'd got very close. I almost thought he'd marry me.

He flew east or west. Wherever it was, I didn't have an address. At least I knew where I was. I'd been in LA over a month, the longest I'd been away from the kids. And Chris was now having a wobbler, everything going wrong, and Michael was considering having him to live with him and his wife in France. I thought I'd better get home. They'd been smashing kids. The bill came in with late adolescence. Also my money situation, my insecurity, it was beginning to look like one of J's mornings.

At the last minute in LA a newspaper asked me for a piece on the Gerona centre and then a Jewish filmstar wanted an outline on Tarres, so my pockets were full. Each time I went to Hollywood I came back with more than I'd gone with, even if it was just winning at poker.

Chapter Forty-two

On 4 January 1983, *The Rose-garden* was bought by Crown in New York. It was the happiest moment for me in years. I was so exultant I didn't know how to express it but I knew I had to celebrate. In the end I gathered some twigs from the garden and made a fire. Burning old wood was the real celebration. Watching the flames, letting in the new. Also I celebrated in a more usual way. I went out with friends, I even went to Paris, quite thoughtlessly, I was so excited. I tried to get Robert, got Irish. The way he copied his boss's speech was disconcerting. I left a cold message.

I was joyous for a month but the troubles were not over. Not for the book. The editor, Ros, loved it and she spent hours making suggestions, wanting more character development. So once again I had to go through the entire 300 manuscript pages and as soon as I picked up the pen the virus came back and I felt I was ill, even dying.

On the celebration trip to Paris – why I went there I don't know, except people I liked were now living there – I knew Robert Hartman was in the city. Marcelle said he was buying and selling. I suspected he was with the young very pretty girl and a stab of jealousy shot through me like lightning. Marcelle said, 'Of course he is with someone. What do you think? He needs sex. He's that sort of man.'

She knew about his background but was choosy about what she let on. 'He'd studied medicine in New York and after qualifying as a doctor worked in an upstate hospital. His ascent up the ladder was rapid, registrar, consultant, head of department. He found he had a capacity for making money, the Midas touch. He started an investment company, then got into futures, which he didn't approve of but they certainly did him no harm. He was rich by anyone's standards and he was only thirty.'

'Is he good or bad?'

'He's known some wrong company in his time and probably still does. He's eccentric about his privacy and very shy. Everything has to be on video. I told him it's so much cheaper just to go to a café and meet the person in real life. But he keeps all the videos.'

'Why is he like that?'

'He controls it that way. Owns the moment.'

It occurred to me he probably had the sex stuff we'd done, on celluloid. So I'd got on the screen after all. 'Do you like him, Marcelle?'

'Darling, he is not someone who cares if you like him. I don't like a lot of the people around him. They used to say, it's only business. Now they say, it's nothing personal.'

'So he is Organisation.'

'I am sure, darling, that he deals with them at some level. But he has his own rules.'

So I asked if I was in danger.

She laughed. 'Only of breaking your heart. He'll do that for you. But he'd never let you be vulnerable to criminals. He looks after people. Just get a good face and eat more and be in good spirits. Then he'll see you for sure. I am certain he is a man who senses things. If you're down he will not be there down with you.'

'Is that why I don't see him much?'

'He'll take for ever making up his mind about a relationship. He's very, very cautious.'

I asked about his marriage. She knew nothing about it. She did say he couldn't possibly be the same person now. He'd be unrecognisable from the man married to the pianist.

I knew she liked me and wanted to protect me but she also did business with Robert Hartman. Marcelle was trying to renegotiate *Harriet Hunter*. Since Romy Schneider's death in 1982 the project had gone into a kind of mourning. I told her she should get finance from Robert Hartman's company.

'Yes that would be smart. I am sure you want to do better with him than just collect some little preproduction money.'

'Meaning?'

'Why stop the car in the suburbs? Get to the city, the heart of the city. If you say this is it, I get out here, he won't stop you. He'll just think you're cheap. What else can you expect from a Sicilian slum boy?'

'Thank God you didn't tell me to be hard to get too.'

Marcelle took me to theatres, restaurants, the opera, the country. But it was Paris. I knew I should get out before day three began. When day four began scorch marks had appeared on my throat like tongues of flame. I hoped they were the result of an allergy to French butter. Then the unseen made itself present and all the horrors of the other world came tumbling in and I kept saying, 'But I've won! My book is accepted!' But the roses were trampled without a second glance. Before I left, the city gave me a farewell present. Two viruses at the same time and a close-up view of a fatal accident. I left the Gare du Nord as successful, as individual, as the average filing clerk. Every piece of celebration had been stripped from me. I was nothing. If I didn't like that – be a beggar! Never come to this city flaunting yourself! And the city's voice rattled amongst the noise of the wheels until I was way past the suburbs into safety.

When I got back to London Robert sent a bunch of roses and a note. 'What did you go there for?' Then he phoned and remembering Marcelle's advice I tried to be at my best. He said, 'Stop it. You don't have to act with me. Just be yourself.'

'Are you sure that's what you want?' I gave a laugh, bitter, then told him about the tongues of flame still licking up my throat. 'The doctor didn't know what it is. A contact allergy, he thought.'

278

'Put cortisone cream on. Get five per cent. Two per cent won't work. Why go to Paris?'

'I thought I'd celebrate.'

'What a strange place to do that.'

'I was on such an up. I thought this time it would be all right. It's some sinister thing.' And I tried to tell him what I believed. I was linked into some past condition and I was burned, not for what I'd done but for what I was. I'd done a lot of free thinking and automatic writing about Paris. And priests came into it. I believed something that they hated enough to kill for. It occurred to me I'd once been a Cathar, but I didn't tell him that.

'Always go near water. A river, the sea, or just wash your hands in running cold water. It's a protection.'

'So you believe it.'

'Not necessarily. But you do.'

I was always happy when he phoned. He was so good for me emotionally. The only thing wrong, I couldn't be with him. But I was learning to detach myself from what I wanted. At least that way I lived – correction, I stayed alive. Ros, the New York editor, sent another list of rewrites and the book's new name, *The Unforgotten*. Ros was devoted to the work. She became part of it. They were bringing it out the next season so she wanted everything fast. The cover was already designed. It was colourful, expensive. I assumed the book would be – well, a chosen child. It was like having Robert's baby. Duckworth were bringing it out in England finally. And a producer at Enigma, one of David Puttnam's companies, wanted to film it. I believed absolutely in that book. Yes, I'd have staked serious things on that book winning. I'd never felt that about my other books. It was the pedigree, and my other work, a bunch of ill-sorted mongrels.

The American film actor Roy Scheider, had read the Portuguese nun play and had fleetingly considered playing the soldier. Then he read the NFFC film treatment and liked it enough to attach his name. Then he read *The Unforgotten* and agreed to endorse it in America. Over there it's essential an unknown writer emerges festooned with the names of the famous saying this is worth the bucks. Buy it. The one person who hadn't read the book was

Hartman. I dreaded him being disappointed by it. And more, thinking it might be about him.

Chapter Forty-three

Gerona was now news. Zelman had promoted it worldwide and press from other countries had got the story. The BBC decided to repeat the documentary, 'Don Quixote is Not Dead' so could I go to Gerona and update it. The producer herself was very much on José's side. She'd never met him but he'd become a reality in her life. He represented bravery in the face of every obstacle. His photographs didn't do him any harm either. So, the expense clock ticking, I went back. I knew this had nothing to do with me. It wasn't personal. Just business. I took my friend James with me. That way Nina wouldn't think I was after her husband.

James had been Michael's friend too. We'd even lived together, the three of us, in a small flat in Hampstead in the early 1960s. And James had known José independently of me. When he was a travel rep he'd taken groups to José's nightclub to watch flamenco dancing. A lot more than flamenco dancing went on up there but James kept the lid on.

In those days in the 1960s he was darkly beautiful like a gazelle. He only fell in love if the guy was married, totally heterosexual and a lot of trouble. He spent a great deal of time and money on his appearance and liked a good time. A good time couldn't possibly end before dawn. He drank, he danced, he liked a laugh and I think he liked José.

In the 1980s we'd both given everything up. We were like two out-of- style cowboys when we arrived in Gerona on a cheap night flight from Gatwick. The cabbala was still open. It still did its best bar and restaurant business at night, partly because it had no competition. The rest of the town was closed after 1.00 a.m., except the brothel area. I considered myself cosmopolitan, able to work, to earn my own money. I considered myself a lot of things but in Gerona I was in José's world. And fate gave a turn of the wheel and reality was not what it seemed elsewhere. José's eyes said we knew each other. Otherwise he was gracious and charming and treated me the way he did the groupies that now surrounded him. He had more admirers than he'd had in the 1950s. He remembered James – just. I was sure a lot more would be remembered in private. He always gave a good welcome. It's what came after that wasn't as good. I spoke to Nina and introduced James. She didn't say one word. Everything in the cabbala was flourishing and they were raking in money hand over fist. Part of the attraction was the Dutch photographer Lilly's ice-creams. They were huge, multi-coloured fantasies piled with nuts, steaming with hot chocolate. They cost 700 pesetas each. She also did a nice line in cakes. She'd taken all the photographs of the restoration and they were on sale in the foyer. She said it had all been done for love. And seeing the way she looked at José I believed her.

A synagogue had been finished downstairs and there were Bibles on stands, candelabra, books of wisdom in glass cases. The Christian symbols José had put in to placate the locals were hanging and lying, obvious everywhere. The music was still from the 1950s. It seemed José was stuck there too. Only if a Jewish visitor came in did it switch to something religious.

Mario Sol sat eating a large meal. Whenever I saw him he was eating. The cabbala instructor, the local astrologer, was touching up someone's wife at the bar. Juan Serrat was trying to hold it together but the drinks showed. José showed James and me the new developments with pride. Where was all this trouble Zelman was on about? It seemed no different to me. Better.

'How's things?' I indicated Mario Sol.

'Everything is as it should be,' said José. 'It is becoming a crazy success, this place. Nina and I work twenty hours a day. Hundreds of visitors pour into the courtyard.'

'And everything is OK with Sol?'

'Why shouldn't it be?' He was angry. 'Why do you see disaster everywhere you go, Patrice?'

'Perhaps because I'm looking at it.'

'Zelman and I are on the same side. We are as one.'

Some people could shit on their doorstep and they still didn't tread in it. And he swanned off, the gracious host, showing guests his house, or at least Nachmanides' house. He was momentarily absent and José was standing in.

Mario Sol was something to be reckoned with. He held down jobs in tough places. Life was 'on change' for him. A marriage was over and the Brussels job offered no promotion. Here looked a good place for a new start. He could make a name here. He'd studied history at university, was politically informed, had been a journalist and broadcaster and had lived in Israel. He was also greedy. It wasn't just food. It was the way he looked at the stones, the arches, the patio. It was his. All he had to do was get rid of Tarres.

He didn't trust me until he heard I was recording Tarres's deeds for the BBC. He walked with James and me down to the hotel.

'This is a very delicate business and we would rather you said nothing at this time.' His voice glided across the English language with confidence. 'Zelman does not trust you and we have been told not to speak to you. But support for Tarres now would be ill timed.'

'We?'

'The Association. A group has been formed to restart Isaac the Blind.'

It included prominent politicians from Madrid, historians, a rabbi and a lot of worldwide money people. And Julio Framis, the travel agent. 'But I am the director,' said Mario.

'Where does José fit in?'

'He fits in very well if he's sensible. He can be artistic director. He will have a privileged place on the board with a monthly salary. He will have plenty of time to go back to his poems and Nina, her sculpture. That child is suffering with the long hours and strain. He is not – well, he is hyperactive.' He could have said a lot more but he liked children.

'Has José agreed to this?'

'We are about to propose it. So there is no point saying he is the owner of Isaac the Blind. He's bled the Serrat family dry. Good money after bad. They're trying to save themselves. Serrat as well as José's cousin who underwrote José's share. Which meant he paid it. But say nothing. Print nothing. You see, your lover, excuse me Patricia, your old friend is crazy.'

When we got into the hotel James surprised me. 'They won't get him out. They'll try everything but this is Spain. They don't let Americans just come in here and take over a whole chunk of the town. José may be bad but he's one of theirs. In ten years from now he'll still be selling ice-creams on the patio.'

Chapter Forty-four

I'd chosen to stay at the Hotel Peninsular because it was a new start. It wasn't, for example the Hotel Centro or the Residencia Internacional. It was absolutely free of associations. Except the owner Señor Lara and his wife remembered me from my Bohemian days. I couldn't bear to go back to a room where I'd been happy. The next morning I saw Jane on the street. As always she looked immaculate, but this time there was something wrong with her mouth. Then I saw she was drunk.

'I never see you up at the cabbala,' I said.

'It's fake. Historians have been there and they've found no evidence of any glorious Jewish past, at least not the way José recounts it. They've sifted through the excavations and when they couldn't find anything he threw them out. All the artefacts he says he's found are either locked away in the bank or have been destroyed conveniently by the contact with fresh air. He found a perfectly shaped passover bread, but woof! A lot of things disappear including Serrat's money. He did find a key. It could be the key of the main door that shut them in at night.'

José passed at that moment and invited us to a fiesta in the hills.

It was at the house of a local sculptor José had discovered when he was in charge of the art centre. I knew he wouldn't have invited me but he wanted Jane for some reason. We said we'd go.

The trip into the hills was held up by business and Jane, Juan Serrat and I hung around on the patio. The business was a couple of creditors now turned vicious, and José had to whistle up his lawyer. The creditors didn't give shit about history. They wanted a cut of the Coca- Cola and ice-cream profit, now. Nina came on to the patio wearing a new blue dress. She was surly but managed a greeting for Jane. Then José appeared, grabbed Nina's bag, took a wad of notes and slapped them into the creditors' hands. 'The money for our child's food. Go on. Take it. And sleep well at nights.'

There was a hesitation and the creditors shifted about, suddenly awkward. I didn't see the end of the transaction because the lawyer crossed to me, his eyes flaring, ready for trouble. In perfect English he spoke and made it loud so everyone could get an earful. So I was still doing stories about cabbala. Had I learned any more about the subject?

'Sure.' And I quoted Hyam Maccobby for my side of the conversation.

The lawyer disapproved. I was claiming the Hasidic Jews alone practised cabbala. Hadn't I heard of the circles of Sephardic Jews in Israel?

So I picked Hyam's brains again, in his absence, and threw in a bit of Zelman Goldstein, but the lawyer still didn't like it. 'It's incorrect.'

'How can it be? I got it from two rabbinic scholars.'

He said I was not looking at cabbala from a fundamental viewpoint.

I wasn't sure of the 'fundamental' so had no answer to that. People like me were not needed by the cabbala. He made it sound as though I was being thrown out of an exclusive club.

Jane was getting a few laughs but I was mad as hell. I explained I got my knowledge from scholars, not smalltown lawyers. He was nasty. I got nastier. But he got worse so I left the fight. Nina loved me losing. The lawyer mouthed a little joke in her ear and I realised the fight was over something nearer to home than cabbala.

Jane said, 'You allowed him to muddle you. You should have stuck to one argument.'

'But the cabbala isn't just one thing. There are all kinds of branches. I'd understood it mostly existed in New York amongst the Hasidim. I'm not a "Brain of Britain" quizz contestant but I bet he doesn't know it all.'

'Of course not,' said Jane placatingly. 'He just makes sure he knows more than the person he's speaking to.'

Serrat, José, Jane and I got into a small car for the country. James hadn't fancied the idea. I thought he had a point.

José said the lawyer had not insulted me. It was just that I was English. I refused to do one more thing for them unless he was off the payroll.

'Look,' said José. 'I'd be in jail now if it wasn't for him. He is an incredible force behind us. Once, when the electricity was cut off, he hocked his car to pay the bill.'

Nina was already at the house in the country, cooking meat and sausages, surrounded by her friends and family. I immediately searched out some tinned stuff for myself. The local astrologer was giving a lecture on cabbala. They all took it seriously. Once or twice he became totally ludicrous so I challenged him. The lawyer and Nina spat, in turn, on my views of mysticism. Then I remembered some of them had come from their financier, Zelman Goldstein.

'I'd be careful when Zelman gets here,' I said to José. 'He may not go for the local fortune teller playing teacher.'

'Zelman and I are like this.' He held two fingers close.

'Yes,' said Nina to everyone in the room. 'Zelman understands absolutely what we are trying to do. Zelman is one foreigner who is welcome.'

'A quarter of a million bucks welcome,' I said to José. 'But he'll want something in exchange. Like running the place.'

'Never!' snapped Nina. 'She doesn't understand anything. He is us. We are him. There is no division in our thinking.'

There'd be one hell of a division in their thinking when he started putting the money in and they started spending it. He was like José in one way. They both wanted the same thing. But Zelman had learned his trade. What he said had hundreds of years of experience behind it. José made impulsive poet's judgements. I challenged them about the Christian symbols. It was that kind of contest. Go for broke. 'The crucifixes and crosses are all wrong for Jews. Those symbols are not part of their religion.'

'But cabbala is one part Christian, one part Muslim and one part Jewish.'

'He's planning,' said Jane quietly, 'to go to the Arabs if the Jews don't come across with the money. He'd even find some room for the Chinese if it suited him.'

José spent a lot of time fannying around Jane. Of course he'd had every presentable woman in the town. I knew by the way he looked at them and they looked back. But he'd not had Jane.

At one point we were alone, he and I, in the kitchen. The others had gone outside to light the bonfire.

'You like her. Jane. Don't you?'

He didn't deny it. 'She is the type of woman I do like. She's soft and passive and willing. How does she get on with her husband?'

I didn't know.

'Where does she get all that money?'

I had no idea. 'Has she money?'

'Nina's cousin is the bank manager at her branch. She has regular payments.'

'He has money. Richard.'

'She! She! And she's not called by her name. Jane Graham. She's called Hartman.'

Now that did surprise me. If she was really running away she was doing it awfully slow.

Around the bonfire, the figures sitting all looked the same. I could have sat next to an enemy if I wasn't careful. Jane came and stood beside me. The fire was in full blaze and there was a bonfire doll at the top.

'It's to burn the old and let in the new,' she said. 'Just look at the doll.'

I looked. It was a doll. So what?

'It represents what's sacrificed. The old. Get it now? It's something you want to get rid of so if there is a plague it would be a plague victim. In the old days, Franco. Not this year.'

288

And I looked and then saw the long fair hair and big blue eyes and
the thin body.

Jane laughed. 'Who does that remind you of?'

'Who made it?'

'Nina of course. She even copied your clothes.' She took a new
bottle of wine and drank nearly a third in one go. The astrologer
wanted to sleep with her. He kept saying how perfectly their signs
matched. He'd never get a chance to get near her in the town
because she kept to herself. I suspected I was sitting next to a serious
drinker.

'Why d'you stay in Gerona?' I asked.

'The countryside is lovely. Good air.'

'You'd be better travelling. Or by a big town. A bit of life.'

She laughed dryly. 'It's good for my health here so I stay.'

'Robert Hartman has never mentioned you.'

'Do you still see him?'

I nodded.

'Watch his left.'

Was that Hollywood parlance? It didn't mean anything to me.

'He gives with his right but takes with his left.'

'You don't seem like you're hiding. I mean your name Hartman
at the bank for Crissake!'

She'd done a lot of drinking but she could still think. 'I didn't get
time to get divorced. A shot in the head. You can't get quicker than
that.'

'Why did he do it?'

'Ask Hartman.'

'You gave up a lot for Richard. A career, all that money, that
family.'

'Well look at you, Toots. You're in love with the second best
thing to Don Quixote and end up on the bonfire.'

Of course Robert Hartman had sent Jane to Gerona. It was one
of his places, one of the most meaningful of his life. And of course
he sent her money in her married name. Why change it? He knew
where she was and she wasn't hiding.

'Does Richard like it here?'

'Sure.'

She was still drinking. 'Nina looks drab. She looks about the same age as José's mother. She's dog rough. What she needs is a good fuck and a sit in the sun.'

Chapter Forty-five

What had started as a dream, just something in José's head, had taken over until it was bigger than him and he was trapped in the dream. He'd win or die. The following day over *café con leche* in the Ramblas it was there, the obsession, a dark light in his red-rimmed eyes. The Americans might want him out, they might have the moral right to get him out but his lawyer wasn't asleep on his feet. When he took José on he knew what he was dealing with. His skilful handling of the law wasn't quite clear to me but it meant no one could get José out. For perpetuity.

A trip to the bank had been more eloquent than a thousand of my warnings. José was now shaky because this morning the bank had confirmed that Zelman's $30,000 was sitting in a high interest account but Tarres couldn't touch it. So what if he had creditors at the door! The Americans had specifically stated no one should touch a buck. What did that mean?

I knew what it meant. They wanted Mario Sol in. Placatingly, I said, 'Perhaps Zelman wants to pay the debts personally.'

'Patrice, I have this town on my back. We're partners he and I. Let him renounce these flourishes of glory for heaven's sake!' He slumped into a depressed silence. So I asked him what he was going to do in the meantime. 'Do? What I always do? Isaac the Blind is mine!'

'But you don't own it.'

'Own? Own?' What was I talking about? You can't own something that God had given. 'Patrice, it is not a question of money. I am surprised you are so ordinary.'

'They'll get you out. I did warn you.'

He slammed the table and every eye in the café was now our way including a creditor or two.

'Nina is right. You are Zelman Goldstein's mistress.'

James got a lot of mileage laughing at that one.

'Why should I give Isaac the Blind to these robbers? They take what I have done, take it for nothing? Could you go in their house and walk out with their dining table and wife?'

'So what do you want?' I asked.

'Want?' Another clap of sound. More eyes our way. 'The proper person to run Isaac. Until then I stay. Should I give it to a fat swine like Mario Sol? Who would even look at him let alone listen? He comes from nowhere and they give him my life's work.'

I had to agree José had all the charisma in town but he looked shattered. And Nina was exhausted from endless nocturnal ice-cream sales, her eyes shadowed, face a cement colour. Mario, well slept, was in fact knowledgeable and sensible. To begin with. At least he had a correct account of history in his head. But then the daily grind at Isaac the Blind, the quarrels, the hostilities, the chaos, got to him too and he became rocky. In his case it showed itself as greed. Like the others he became obsessed. They could talk of nothing but the new Jewish age.

'They promised us co-operation. We'd work together.' José could not stop talking about the Americans. He ordered another coffee and a double gin. 'What do they do? Try and get me out and put someone loathsome in my place. And my wife is sick.'

'Sick?' said James.

'The relief when the Jews finally came! At last our ordeal was over. But then everything continued exactly the same. Her nerves –'

'I think they got a little disenchanted when they found out Serrat owned the place,' I said.

'Owned?' José couldn't sneer enough. 'What a mind you have.'

'You spent Juan Serrat's money.'

'I saved his life. I stopped him drinking, invested his money. He'd have gambled it away in two years. That family should get on their knees that I saved their son.'

'Did he want a Jewish shrine?'

'Of course he wanted it. At first it was to be a bar casino because he wanted to meet girls and he's too shy and hopeless. He's the enemy. Why did he have to open his fat mouth and tell them it was his money? Zelman was content until then.'

'Perhaps he was worried they'd think it was yours.'

'You be careful. I'll tell you something, Patrice, and remember it well. The Jewish quarter carries a curse. You are for the quarter or you are not. Those against Isaac the Blind come to a bad end.' He did some nervous throat clearing and looked round for a waiter to pay the bill. His eyes met those of several creditors. He flung his eyes back to me. I recognised the electrician. I could see he was getting edgy. What was Tarres doing in his bar publicly ordering things when he hadn't been paid?

'Does this curse affect everybody?' I tried to be conversational.

'The other night a type came from Barcelona. He was anti-Semitic. Stirred up about the Lebanon. I said this place is holy. It is not political. It has no relevance to today's affairs. He said close it. He was armed. But I'm ready for that because under the cheeseboard I keep a long knife. As he pulled the gun I got the knife. And you know me, Patrice. I always attack first. I got his arm. So he backed away, gun on the floor, and he promised he'd come back with his friends and finish! And his girlfriend, she was a whore of the worst category, shouted abuse and threats against Isaac the Blind. The next morning before sunrise she was found in the Avenue of Trees, the Dehesa, lying on the pathway, her throat cut. And he had crashed his car on the motorway to Barcelona. A month before that five right-wing Fascists from Madrid came into the courtyard and started smashing things up. So I decided to go for the biggest, the leader. And I ran to the bar to get the knife. But at that moment the sun shone directly on to the mirror in the salon and the reflection blinded him. He backed away and it happened a door to the synagogue was open. It leads directly down to the sun stone and is very dangerous. And he backed right into the hole and fell and crashed his head on the sun stone. I told the others to take him, get him to a hospital and there would be no further action. On the way to the clinic what happened? The car blew up. And bits of them were hanging from the trees.'

'Blew up? I said. He made death sound so easy.

'Obviously they had explosives. No doubt they would have blown up Isaac.'

'But why didn't you use the gun dropped by the first intruder?' said James, always practical.

José couldn't be contemptuous enough. 'I don't need a gun. I have Nachmanides, the greatest mystic ever known, here at my side. He is my guardian. Moses Ben Nachman.'

I thought there might be a little something in all that because at that moment the electrician was at the table demanding his money. His eyes said he was going to get rough. José's disinclination to pay him had meant he'd had to lay off staff. He could not meet the costs of the material he'd installed at Isaac the Blind. He'd go bankrupt.

José looked at him, his eyes full of the fire from the old days. 'Of course you will, my friend. And me with you. And d'you know why? The Jews themselves. They have $30,000 in the Banco Catalan and they will not spend one peseta. They have collected this money from people of good faith to pay us. You and me.'

'Is this true?' The electrician was appalled.

'Could I lie to you? I'm a Catalan. So go to them for your money. Better still, my friend, go to Mario Sol. He says he's the director of Isaac the Blind. Let's see how he runs things.'

José veered between the bad Jews, the Jews and the dead Jews. The Jews he'd had in mind when building the premises had not appeared. They would be a meek people in long robes who would be grateful twenty-four hours a day and listen to José, their saviour. The conflict was making Nina mad and the child, in turn, disturbed. José said they would all go howling to their graves but he would never give up what was his.

294

It was only when I came to do the tape of José for the BBC that it could be said we'd once been on the same side. He behaved impeccably during the recording. He'd had his nose in several Jewish books and talked about cabbala as though he was a 70-year-old scholar and had known it all his life. Cabbala was the antidote for the bad old world. He and his wife – she was mentioned at least five times, no doubt because he believed she was hovering in some adjoining salon – had brought wisdom back, not only for Gerona but the world. It was more sensible than that, but it was on a big scale.

He wanted it played back in case he needed something changed. He was taking it seriously because at least three cassettes had been sent to him of the earlier broadcast by Jewish communities in England. So for once I was for real. But he never thanked me, nor did she, although I was praising her life, her intelligence. She was glittering with adjectives – I even in a moment of madness, said she was likeable. She paraded around the courtyard, her nose in the air as though I was some retainer working out my notice. Her eyes were no longer blue and harmless. They were grey, gritty like the stones. And the child howled from morning to dawn, sleepless, wanting things. I never really got a clear idea what he looked like because I never saw him except when his mouth was wide open yelling. And she spoilt him and José spoilt him, and the photographer dosed him with ice-cream and he wouldn't sleep. And then one day he gave a little smile. I thought he looked like Damian from *The Omen*. James said he was very cute but hyperactive. Was he allergic to wheat? he asked Nina. Nina chose not to reply.

I rewound the cassette for José then put it on playback. There was an unexpected whirring sound. I had no answer for that. I pressed fast forward and started the tape well into the conversation. Simply whirring. No words. José started to gigle. Then I started. The whirring continued and was a comic sound. We fell about the place quite hysterical. James thought it was funny – but not that incredibly good that two adults had to laugh for six minutes. José said, 'It's the stones. They are talking. They have a most powerful influence. Mere human voice no longer matters. Not in cabbala.'

I checked and rechecked the machine and could find no fault. I had no explanation for the whirring. The next day I got Nina on tape. No whirring there. Just big boastful words. James said, 'It's obvious there is something between you and José. I didn't think so at first. The laughter convinced me. I could see it then.'

José invited us to have a cabbala lunch. James was all for it but I said we had a meeting across the river. Never would I accept anything in that place, even a bottled drink.

When Julio Framis told James and me that José was in danger I believed it. Sol said, 'Their debts are mysterious. Nearly half a million dollars. Where is it, Patricia?'

'Don't look at me. I haven't got it.'

'But you are his mistress. You must know.'

I was everybody's mistress. Except I hadn't had a fuck in two months.

James nudged me. 'Nina's got it,' he whispered. 'I'm sure she's put it away. And one of these days she's going to get herself together, her hair cut, face made up, new clothes and just get on that train for Paris. Hey ho! A fun life coming. You can't look that bad at thirty.'

'There's a discrepancy between the written accounts and what is owed,' said Sol. 'I am not saying it is deliberate. It's just the way he is.'

'What do you want me to do?' I said.

'Talk to José. Get him to see reason. You alone can do it. He's borrowed money from some wrong people. They like to be repaid. It's getting dangerous'.

When we were outside James said, 'I still can't see them getting him out. There's not one big enough to take him on.'

I felt sorry for the Jews. They'd been ripped off.

Chapter Forty-six

José followed me into the coolness and safety of Luis's Arc bar. I told him what I heard, what I knew. The lot. He swore. A couple of conservative curses then a variety of his own.

'Patrice, I have waiters, cleaners, tradesmen, phone bills, promotions. I have to pay workmen to continue excavation. I have to pay rent each month on each part of the land. I even have to pay for the lavatories. And Mario Sol sits like a stuck whale blubber eating, eating and he's never paid that much!' He gestured venomously. 'My wife pays the Jews' debts and they call her a thief. Well, we'll see about that. I will dynamite that place before I give it to them.'

I tried to quieten him by asking about Nina. How had he got her money?

'It was after the Americans came. It was the worst thing that could have happened, their coming, because then every creditor was on my back. They thought the Americans had given money and I was holding out. There were two terrible creditors.' He sighed. 'And every day I'd go to the bank. Nothing. And there it was sitting in a special investment account. So I said to Nina, You are with me or you are against me. I keep the child. So she gave me everything.

So tell Zelman that next time you get in his bed.' And then José realised we had worse things to argue about.

'Why don't you go to the town hall and get a subsidy. Or the university?'

'No, Patrice. It is my debt. I have to pay it.'

In fact he had been to both places on numerous occasions. They said other buildings had priority. They said the Jews were great but they had money. Let them pay for themselves. Also José did not want to turn his shrine into a municipal building so why should they promote private enterprise?

'I have been duped, tricked but I'll be repaid, never fear. I will turn Isaac into a brothel. Each salon will contain a girl of a different nationality. Black, Chinese, Latin American, even Jewish. I'll pay the debts.'

I'd never seen him so bitter. I'd do anything for him. But not for her.

'Well you tried, José, but the Jews didn't come.'

He looked at me with amazement. 'The Jews are here, *chérie*. We Catalans are all Jewish. Tell that to Zelman when he lifts your skirt.'

All I could see was that nowadays intellectuals grew long showy beards. 'Who's this dangerous one you've touched for money?'

He got up and called Luis. 'I can't pay.' He showed empty pockets. 'Every sou goes into the shrine. Even my son's sous.' And he did look like a genuine case of poverty. If it was an act, it was a good one.

Luis laughed. 'What's a debt when it's between friends?'

I remembered years ago Luis saying José would have to give up the revolutionary business. 'It's out of fashion in this town. They sold out Quico. He's been shot.'

'Is José in danger?'

'He's got a nose. He can smell it. He'll have to drop politics. It's money now.'

When we got outside in the burning sun I said, 'You haven't told me who the guy is? The dangerous one.'

'No I haven't. That's one piece of information Zelman Goldstein won't be getting.'

So I tried to shout at him but it was too hot. I crouched down in the shade. And I saw him walk down the Calle Forsa, and in my mind I saw the other, the Jewish scholar, walking from the other direction. And in the blur of heat the two figures met, then both were gone.

Zelman came to town. He brought a dozen celebrated supporters with him, all wanting to pay homage to their ancestors. He walked across the patio with his moneyed group and it looked good, except for his yellow and white checked coat and the merciless glare in his eyes. And José embraced him and the press took photos. José's lawyer introduced everyone, Nina, her family, her child, Juan Serrat, the Dutch photographer. Mario Sol took care of the ladies of the group. It all had a big face on. James and I were not introduced.

'You wouldn't think,' said James, 'that an hour ago José was going around like a mad beggar. I told you he's better off than you think. Look at him.' And José smiled at the ladies and kissed their hands and introduced several locals who were of direct Jewish descent. In fact the Catalans were positively running with Jewish blood. It was now fashionable to be Sephardic unless you were a creditor. Even Isabella Sans-Gomez, shut away in her elegant tower, was said to have found a few drops in her past. The welcome mat was well out and everything was decorous when the phone rang. Juan Serrat's sister said Papa Serrat had purchased a gun. Only those around the phone knew of the danger.

'He's old and might shoot one of us,' said James.

'He won't shoot anybody,' said José, loading a tray with drinks. 'I have the dirt on the Serrat family. D'you think I'm a fucking idiot? I know what I'm dealing with.'

'Which is?' I asked.

'Don't tell her,' Nina snarled in Catalan.

'Why not?' said José. 'Serrat is not an estate man in the usual sense. Serrat's property is all in one area and we all know where that is.' He took the tray into the courtyard and graciously offered the visitors a drink.

Zelman Goldstein's party sat at the tables not daring to move. The Coca-Cola bottles, the locals wandering to and from the bar, couples talking intimately in the salons, the 1950s ballads, weren't quite what they'd expected even though Zelman had done a wonderful job preparing them.

Then Zelman chose to admit he knew me. He crossed the courtyard to stand by my table and it was like an act from a play. Every eye our way. Nina nudging José fit to break a rib. Zelman got the drift of it all and turned to his group and introduced me. I was the writer whose work had brought all of us together, who'd made the Association of the Friends of Gerona possible. The guests murmured congratulations. Nina's expression was such that I formed a new resolution. Never be alone with her, even in the street.

Then we all trooped around the salons and up staircases, an exhibition, a wishing-well, glass cases of pottery, some coins. And the group admired this and that as they they could in any museum. An old man, perhaps eighty, the heat didn't bother him, said he'd read my pieces in the *Jewish Chronicle*. How come I was so involved and not a Jew? 'You fought for this place.'

'Someone has to,' I said.

I was getting a baleful look from Zelman.

'What do you think of it all?' I asked the old man.

'It's a little overdressed so I'm not impressed with the restoration. It's not anything like the orginal dwellings. But I am impressed that this is the site. Nachmanides lived here.'

I wasn't even sure of that anymore. I asked him how he knew.

'Because we've been to the cathedral and in the archives they have the records of each house. From the ninth century on the Jews lived here. I've seen the original plan. The names, dates of birth and death of the owners. It was kept up till the Expulsion. I'm impressed.'

Zelman came up alongside. 'Don't please don't tell them there's trouble.'

I shook my head, just once briefly.

'These people could resolve the financial problem. D'you understand?'

Nina was now watching.

'I have had to come here unexpectedly. And they asked to come. What could I say? We have a crisis. And now I hear Tarres is going

around saying cabbala carries a curse. What's the matter with him?'
He was jetlagged, sleepless. He'd be angry next.

'He doesn't like Mario Sol.'

'But we have to have someone we trust.'

We walked in a group, a bad atmosphere was building. Some of the visitors started singing and José was moved. I thought they were singing because they were ill at ease. As we went down the steep steps into the excavations, I helped the old man, to steady him. Nina looked at me with such hatred, apparently, that James crossed himself.

José then noticed that all the Christian symbols had been removed. In fact minutes ago Serrat and Sol had gathered them up and hid them in the attic of the Hotel Peninsular. We passed from the mortuary to the hospital to the kitchens. By the sun stone José stopped and seemed to gather strength. Then he spoke and Zelman translated for the Americans not understanding Spanish. José spoke simply, with great charm. He welcomed back the Jews to this site, which wasn't his. He wanted to give it back to whom it belonged. But the path had been harder than he'd supposed.

He was getting too much attention for Zelman's liking so he cut José short by starting some applause, then took the stage. He outlined the programme for the coming year. He was articulate, swift, clever. Even I could understand it, the mystical stuff. But I could tell the group liked José. So could Zelman. Zelman talked about Gerona as though it was a virgin territory he'd just discovered. José was quick to use that argument against him. Zelman talked down, very slightly, to his audience. José won them on charm.

Then Julio Framis had a turn. It all looked pals together until Zelman said the synagogue would not be officially open until the following spring. José assured him it was already open. The old man was perturbed. 'But that can't be correct.' And I understood there had to be a certain number of Jews present to hold a service.

José slapped the stones once and the sound stopped further argument. 'In this courtyard the angels presented Nachmanides with his vision which he put into his greatest works. We are all sharing that vision and have a right to pay our respects here, whatever our religion or practice. Here in Gerona we accept all beliefs, all religions, but only if the people come with peace in their hearts.'

Zelman told him his statements about cabbala were incorrect. Gerona style was a form he'd never come across. José replied speedily and I couldn't catch the drift. Zelman was shocked. José glared at him. 'Go on, American. Translate that if you can!'

And Zelman opened his mouth, couldn't speak. He paced about, trying to get self-control. And José attacked him, cynical, abusive. 'No my friend. You have no comprehension of this place. Go back to your textbooks. You have not eyes that can see glory.'

Zelman replied, 'I cannot even translate what you say!'

And the group looked one to the other and then it really started, the row across the stones. It was chilling and I think it must have been an echo of the past. Because the arguments were becoming big enough to fight for.

Zelman took a huge stick and I thought he was going to decapitate José. But he pointed to the markings on the sun stone and explained them historically. Historic was becoming the reverse of José Tarres. But the terrible moment passed and everyone wanted to be upstairs in the light. The woman next to me was quite shaken. 'What was all that about?'

'I don't think they see everything the same way.'

I thought the message Zelman could not translate must have been deeply offensive. But it was just a facet of cabbala. If it got like that on the intellectual stuff what happened when it got personal?

When we got upstairs the visitors' hands stayed in their pockets. The dispute across the sun stone had been disquieting. Nina by her expression showed she wanted these guests on her courtyard about as much as she wanted me. Because I'd been to America and wrote books I seemed safe, so they talked to me. Then Zelman filled a few awkward moments by playing them a part of my Gerona documentary. I was pleased, especially as the lawyer was sitting there. Throughout the broadcast Nina walked about, making noise, distracted, her mouth bitter. When it was over the ones who understood English said it was good. Nina said she found it trivial. So she did understand English. My God! What she'd overheard me saying in the past!

Julio Framis produced the banquet. It contained various items unsuitable for Orthodox Jews. The first course, the shellfish, had to go out the window. Everything in front of me went out the window. The fact I didn't eat or drink amused Nina. It was the only thing that did.

'How did Tarres get started in this?' asked a heart-surgeon's wife. She was tough, on to her third marriage, and she'd given up dreams a long time ago.

I wanted to say he hid from his failure by the obsession with the site. He's lost out so has to hide. Obsession was his choice. He could have come to Istanbul. Nina hated me because I was a friend of the Jews as well as her husband's true love.

Framis sped around with new food. Banquet size had been reduced by his various culinary mistakes to *menu del dia*. As he passed me he said, 'All this I pay too. It is on me. They don't pay. You understand, Patricia.'

He was very nice and attentive but he had an increasingly bad effect on the guests. I realised he had an upsetting appearance. He looked like Adolf Hitler. Could that be why? As the level of strain increased the more like Hitler he looked.

He made a speech about holding hands across the Atlantic. He'd just closed a deal with El Al Airlines. 'This shrine will be as well known as Disneyland.'

A tasteless comparison, no doubt, but Julio was trying to suggest the scope of the Gerona attraction. Disneyland was something he thought all Americans identified with. And it was synonomous with profit.

When the girl started singing Sephardic songs in the courtyard Zelman indicated that I should follow him inside. He shut the first salon door.

'There can't be a repeat of tonight. Not ever. What he says is fantastic even to a layman's ears. He rewrites history as he goes along. It may sound colourful but it's not true. Nachmanides, for example, was not simply a mystic. He was a scholar, versed in the law, a debater, a philospher. Tarres says the cabbala has been given to him by Nachmanides who is ever present.'

'Is that what he said downstairs?'

'No. Of course not. Downstairs he was blasphemous. All this' –
he pointed to the group in the courtyard – 'is now for nothing. They
won't give one dollar of support. And they are our honorary
members of the association.'

The old man I'd talked to was a Nobel Prize winner. It was that
sort of group. I could see they, too, were disappointed.

'There is an electrician going around to the newspapers saying
Jay Stein has bankrupted his company. Jay has washed his hands of
the whole thing. There will be no one left.'

'I'm sorry,' I said. And I meant it.

'But I will be left. I will never give up. Never.' He looked tired and
was under strain. He'd spent weeks of his life working out plans to
save the place. He thought he was José's friend. And now he was
beginning to look a little, just a little obsessed. He was becoming not
unlike his rival.

'So what will you do?'

'I am still going to buy the houses surrounding this site.'

'You can't just buy in, Zelman. This is Spain.'

'So? Mario Sol is Spanish. He does my buying. I have settled the
plans for a museum. Excavations will begin. And about Tarres. I will
offer him a very generous way out. If he stays the courts will get
him.'

There were nineteen reasons why I wouldn't help José. But the
twentieth remained. I thought I could go to Shelley Winters for
help. She'd know what to do.

But José came silently into the salon and I saw help was not the
priority. 'Discussing my future, you two? Well, I'm sure with Mrs
Chaplin's imagination and your dreams of glory, Zelman, it will be
quite interesting.' He leaned nonchalantly against the banqueting
table.

He listened to the deal. It was lengthy and thought out and
financially not bad. José's eyes didn't move as he watched the other
man. Zelman listed the moneys already paid off to creditors,
moneys earning in the bank. He listed the dinners given in LA to
collect the funds.

At the end José just shrugged. So what, Zelman had put money
in? Money could never buy Isaac the Blind.

Chapter Forty-seven

I missed the big fight. It had a wonderful effect on the town. They adored drama. And José weighed possibly ten stone and Mario fourteen, yet José had thrown him over a bridge. The police arrived and made a sort of arrest but an hour later José was free. He told the press, 'Clearing Gerona of the Americans' paid boy is like Jesus clearing the temple. How dare the Americans come here. We do not want speculation. Are we allowing them to buy up our land and houses? For nothing?'

It was time for Zelman to go home. He got his confused visitors into the hired cars straight for Barcelona, then came to the hotel to search for me.

'Do not print anything further. Broadcast nothing. Yesterday after I brought the group to Isaac the Blind I had a meeting with José, his lawyer, Serrat and José's cousin who in the past has put up money for José. I reminded them that the intention was to create a worldwide Jewish centre. I reminded them that José's intention had been to hand it over to the Jews. But I realised that personal sacrifice and personal money had gone into this intention and I wished to repay that. Serrat would receive his original investment with interest. The same went for the father and sister. José's cousin would get his, minus the interest. Nina would get back her deposit in instalments. They'd all have honoured places in the Foundation. On top, José would have a salaried job as artistic director, which is I believe his profession. Serrat said it was reasonable and signed the agreement, releasing his share to us. The cousin also signed. José held the pen, paused and said, $250,000. And then he threw the pen on to the table.'

I thought José had probably gone mad. I wasn't sure all these nights without sleep had done him any good.

I didn't have anything to say. I was on the side of the Jews because I liked them infinitely more than José and Nina.

'So his cousin signs, even Serrat signs. But he? It was all fantasy, giving the Jews what belonged to the Jews. It belongs in one of his poems. He's holding us to ransom. I have now bought Serrat's share from the local landlords so I own the courtyard, the adjoining garden and the first-floor salons. I'm leaving Mario Sol in charge. What goes with Tarres and him is now police business. Don't go around with a gloomy picture, will you? We must keep optimistic or it will be impossible to involve other helpful people.' Zelman turned round at the door. 'Let his wife pay his debts. We will not. We leave him to the mercy of his creditors.'

I still hadn't said a word. When he got to New York he was called before the Chief Rabbi who found events in Gerona distasteful. Synagogues were asked to advise their congregations to stay away from Gerona.

Zelman, however, had been touched by the stones, caught by the atmosphere. He was not going to let go. He did say, 'I'll get to the truth.'

'The truth?' asked a reporter.

'The truth about that place.'

You never found truth in Gerona. I could have told him that. Except that all was absorbed in history. In a hundred years the fighting would be forgotten. The stones would record simply that in a certain courtyard people met to revive a forgotten Jewish practice.

Serrat, the unsung hero whose money had made the whole thing possible, made a speedy exit through Isabella Sans-Gomez's garden. It was laid out in the pattern of the Tree of Life. Having seen what José could do to a big person like Sol, Serrat felt it time to run.

José and Nina now had definite identities. They'd saved Gerona from a foreign speculation. They'd been betrayed, by one of their own, Serrat, who would sell his arse if someone was hard up enough to want it. The debts were now back on José's back. He took them as if they were the suffering of the world. He genuinely suffered, scarlet eyes, shabby clothes. It didn't look like an act. Of course José wasn't the man I'd loved. He wasn't the man I'd fallen in love with when I was fifteen. Life had kidnapped that beautiful sensuous youth and put an old walrus with greying whiskers in his place. The original was gone for ever. He could only live in my mind.

Scandal didn't hurt cabbala business at all. The courtyard was crammed. José now filled the mouths of the visitors with de luxe ice-creams. At a thousand pesetas each, he filled the till. Life went on as usual at the rate of one creditor, two visitors. He had one piece of advice for the creditors. 'Don't blame me. Blame the Americans. They promised to pay. Where's the money?'

A mixture of fury and exhaustion caused Nina to be whipped off in an ambulance to the clinic and José decided it was time for revenge. He called a press conference. His own government wouldn't help with the debts and he was holding the shrine on his head like Atlas holding the world. He told a fantasy truth and people responded. It was a kind of truth of which only charismatic people were capable. In one Israeli newspaper he said he welcomed any Jew prepared to work and offered them a bed and food in return. He got dozens of letters from people eager to join his fight. They proposed to arrive in specially chartered planes with shovels to excavate the rest of the site. José asked me to translate some of the letters which were in English.

'But you're broke,' I said. 'On what are you going to feed these people?'

Nina said, 'Let them eat rats.'

James laughed darkly. It was the first time she'd spoken.

Mario Sol, forbidden to enter Isaac the Blind, had taken a flat in the old quarter and through binoculars could watch the comings and goings in the cabbala courtyard. He was still on Zelman's payroll as director of the association and as such set up meetings with influential Jewish foundations. But he had a problem. People wanted to see what they were supporting and Sol could not enter his own courtyard. The mayor finally had to become involved, the last thing he wanted. Did he support Tarres? Or Sol? He was on the fence. He told Sol he was going to shut the place down and put Tarres in prison. In the meantime scores of volunteers were about to leave from Israel and that was far more of a problem. Where did they sleep? Who paid for their food? And dig what? The street? The lavatory? So Sol had to put an announcement in the Israeli paper cancelling José's invitation. He said to me, 'It's a shame you are not married to him, Patrice. Something happens between you two even when you quarrel. He and Nina look as though they have a proper marriage but there's nothing going on. You should have been his wife because you and he are truly married.'

The mayor didn't act. He was scared Tarres would react and start blowing things up. Also José had a lot of the town behind him, and the extraordinary situation continued, as James said it would. 'Zelman will never get into Gerona. And you can't be sure how the government feels about foreign shrines. It might be a political question.'

Representatives of several Jewish communities visited Gerona trying to solve the troubles, but José was now defiant and very suspicious. He anticipated some kind of retaliation from Zelman Goldstein, in the deepest moments of the night he did, and he and Nina slept with their clothes on, bags packed, in case they had to hop it with the child across to France. But the sun brought back José's confidence and he formed a rival foundation – the Chosen Friends of Isaac the Blind, its president, Isabella Sans-Gomez. I often wondered who the mysterious dangerous creditor could be. When I wasn't in the town I actually thought it could all be sorted out. It was just like some film that had got out of hand. José had gone into it like Coppola had to *Apocalypse Now* and he went through testing difficulties, a complete absorption, and came out a different person. I sometimes believed I still had enough influence on José to change things.

Chapter Forty-eight

From the Balcony was going to be performed in the US with Joan Hackett. The plan was to start it in LA then bring it to Broadway. Antonioni was still saying he'd make *The Siesta* and for a while I believed it and went high on that one. But then I met Roy Scheider who told me MA was saying yes to everything. It was what he wasn't going to do that was significant. I did an interview on Scheider for the *Mail on Sunday*. He looked like a French intellectual in real life, nothing like the Everyman character he portrayed in movies. I felt I knew Roy. It was the way his eyes lit up. Of course he was a second José. And perhaps because of that he responded to the books I'd written about Gerona.

I never got to meet Joan Hackett although rehearsals had started in LA. But she did ask me one question via the producer. 'Was the nun suffering because she was in love with a man or was she really in love with her own suffering?' I told the producer to tell Miss Hackett the nun was in love with a fella. I thought Americans didn't see love quite the way Europeans did. But I thought Joan Hackett was a wonderful actress.

The publishing house, Crown, couldn't decide whether to launch

The Unforgotten with a party or spend the money on advertising. I said advertise. Who cared if a handful of names got together and drank goblets of champagne? I said I'd be prepared to do anything they wanted with regard to publicity. I thought I was prepared for anything. It turned out I wasn't.

Before I left New York, Roy Scheider wrote an endorsement for the jacket.

Ros still felt there was something missing in the book. The problem was solved by simply looking at Robert Hartman and Jane Hartman. All I had to do was include her and give them a relationship. I made it sexual.

Before I left, Ros admired my ring. It was thick silver with a black metal stone that looked like a television set. It was heavy, substantial, beautifully crafted by a French jeweller living in London. I'd asked him to make it for me and it coincided, although I didn't know it, with José's decision to marry Nina. I didn't know why I suddenly needed a ring. It stayed as an idea for several months because I didn't have any money. Then when I heard he was getting married I thought if I couldn't have the man, I'd give myself a ring. The woman in the train corridor on the way to Barcelona with her appetising rings had impressed me. The amber one had stayed in my mind. They stayed beautiful and didn't let you down. So the jeweller started work at a friendly price. On the day José married Nina I was walking up to Hampstead with the kids. I certainly wasn't thinking about the wedding. Then the jeweller appeared. I hadn't seen him for weeks. Collecting the ring had been a loose arrangement. When I had the money I could get it. He came towards me smiling. 'How funny I should see you, I've got something for you.' And he put his hand in his pockets and pulled out my ring. He put it on my finger about the same time José put one on Nina. I did feel odd. I said I still didn't have the money. He said, 'Any time. For some reason I just picked it up before leaving the house. I must have known I'd see you.'

Ros looked at the ring with hunger, the way I'd looked at the rings on the woman's hand on the train. I took it off and gave it to her. I said it was to thank her for all the hard work she'd done. And she wanted it more than I. At one time stones had been a big part of my life. Now it was keys.

When I got back to London, I phoned José to make sure he was all right. 'Of course with Nachmanides behind me even the banks don't say no. Nachmanides comes with me to the Palais de Justice where I give my best performances these days.' Zelman kept his plans to himself, which I considered very smart. He'd tried doing it the right way and that hadn't worked. Out of the blue José got an invitation from someone high up in the Israeli government to go to Jerusalem and discuss his problems. He would also visit Safed, home of many cabbalists in the past, and put his problem to a general council. His wife and child were invited. So were two members of the Catalan government, a priest and José's lawyer. So José locked the cabbala and set off on the twelve-day trip. He was given a good time and attention. The council liked his style and would see about getting some financial help together. He obviously didn't give them the true picture of his debts. The day before he returned to Gerona Nina had a crying attack. It coincided with Mario Sol and Juan Serrat breaking into the Isaac the Blind Centre and changing the locks.

José arrived back as they were dismantling the bar, throwing the hanging hams and bottles of alcohol into waste bags. Mario was reading the unopened correspondence which, if it had been dealt with, could have produced a lot of finance. But by then Nina and José were too fucked to open letters from strangers. The ones they knew were bad enough. Finding his key didn't fit irratated José. But nothing as mundane as a door kept him from what he wanted. He kicked it in and saw the disgraceful scene. Serrat ran for his life. Sol put up a fight. It was a short one. He was flung flat into Isabella Sans-Gomez's Tree of Life garden, half dead. Calmly José called a locksmith. The locks were again changed. He said the Israeli invitation was a trick. He would never again trust a foreigner. He remembered the bad company he owed money to. It was time to make that active.

The town was now on his side. As he walked down the streets the locals leaned over the balconies rattling keys. They lit candles in his honour. Zelman retaliated and, using Sol as his front man, bought up every stone as far as the bar. The bar was José's. All he had was a licence to trade but it could not be revoked. The lawyer had done a good job.

The battle hit the papers. Those with something to lose like Framis and the academics wanted to keep American good will. Tarres was crazy and would lose a fabulous chance to bring back real history. The creditors started to howl. Zelman said let José pay his own debts. José was selling ice-creams hand over fist but never enough to keep even with the bills and the interest rate on his bank loans. José got the front page in every local newspaper. He promised to sacrifice himself to save his town. If the bad Americans got in, he'd dynamite the shrine, with them in it, blow it up and throw himself on the fire. That sold a lot of papers.

I phoned Zelman in LA and asked what was going to happen.

'He said some terrible things but I'll ignore that. I thought the legal process in Spain would get him. But he walks around as free as air. But don't worry, Patrice. I can take care of myself. We'll put our own person in.'

He continued buying the land around José, pinning him in, as once the Spaniards had pinned in the Jews. He bought, and he paid for what he bought. He was a right person. But he didn't allow for one thing. You couldn't buy Gerona. Doing good deeds like financing the cabbala didn't mean they were on your side. They'd give you banquets and press shows but look in their eyes. They'd kiss you, then spit. And why? You weren't one of them.

Colin showed up with his blanket from the desert. I told him about the callers who'd come to my door. He reckoned it wasn't the right time quite yet to return to New York. I told him to go to Gerona. That was such a mess. No one could find anyone there.

'I heard about that place on my way back from Morocco. It doesn't sound that lucky. I don't think it's a good thing to get into.'

And if Colin said that it was as sure a stamp of failure as you could get.

Chapter Forty-nine

The Unforgotten came out in America early in 1984 and was quickly forgotten. The reviews in the trades were so bad, it was like spraying insecticide over the roses and killing them. I knew then how I would die. I'd go to a railway bridge and throw myself in front of a fast train. I'd never realised before that's how I'd do it. The reviews nearly killed off Ros too. She went into a depression and eventually left the publishing house. Let's say the book wasn't lucky. And that was the one thing I wasn't prepared for. I would never have believed it. Duckworth were bringing the book out in England so I wanted to keep the American dissatisfaction quiet. Luckily it was the trade papers, not the press in general that slammed it. It wasn't exactly a wild seller and at the end of the day it was remaindered in piles in New York bookshops.

Roy Scheider was angry because only his name was used as an endorsement. It looked kind of lonely stuck up there in the rather large *New York Times* ad. For a long time he and I didn't speak.

The first thing I did was crawl back to Tycoon. I was ready for the once every three months or whatever it was in the glass house on Zuma beach. The trouble was I still had to be at home in London.

The boys still needed attention. They were now both on drugs, as were half the area, and it was costly. Both the drugs and the treatment. I still didn't make enough money to pay for everything. Somedays the wolf wasn't at the door. It was in the house. Tycoon knew I was in trouble before I even opened my mouth. He said the Americans would never go for a book like *The Unforgotten*. It showed someone at a disadvantage – well, being in love was a disadvantage. Americans only liked books about winners. They have to exercise their way out of everything. Exercise your way out of cancer, divorce, bereavement. 'Now if you could have written a book about exercising yourself out of being in love, fine.' He held me, folded me against him like a distressed child. At least it showed me one thing. He hadn't pushed it into the publishing house himself. Sometimes I had wondered if he was behind it. My depression was so bad I didn't want to be alone. It was a gnawing black soreness but I could never cry. I was too bitter for tears, as it could be too cold for snow.

Then the producer who'd wanted to film it for Enigma, put in her share of bad news. Puttnam, just back from shooting *The Killing Fields*, said it wasn't right for him. I wondered how much rejection my body could actually bear. It was becoming like a miniature Isaac the Blind, my life. But at least José had Nina. But when the book came out in England, three months later, it got some good reviews and sold OK. I photocopied them immediately and sent them to Roy Scheider with a caustic note. The book had its private fans and it did get me work. I got offered scripts about supernatural love stories. Nothing that came after hurt with the scalding pain of *The Rose-garden*. And none of the success I got later meant that much. I think I put everything in that one book and when it went down, so did I. But I had to go on living, so started writing the book Robert Hartman wanted to film, *Albany Park*, published by Heinemann. Antonioni was off *The Siesta* but Mary Lambert was on. And now it went ahead. The time of false hope was over.

When I went to Robert Hartman for help he was very busy and once the initial comforting was over he expected me to leave. As I felt so terrible I asked to stay. He made it hard for me.

'When I offer you something you don't want it.' He meant the glass house deal. 'You're a very fussy waif, I'll tell you that.'

Being around him was the only bearable thing and I told him that. I was so distressed I didn't know what to do.

'Go on writing. What else?'

I tried to be more explicit about my state of mind. He was irritated. 'What do you want, Patricia? A miracle. You've got both your legs. Your sanity. Your health – well, within reason. Children. Isn't that a miracle? I've learned to be grateful.' His eyes were cold. He was remembering his wife. She didn't gripe about a work failure. Only that her body was falling apart and she'd have to leave the man she loved. So I kept my mouth shut. But I never got over that book. *The Rose-garden* was Tycoon and all the other stories, José. It wasn't just a bit of writing.

We flew from New York to LA. A car waited by the VIP lounge and sped to Ocean Park. He was super rich yet he had few possessions. Clothes in every city, books, a record collection. He never took more than hand luggage on a journey.

Dinner was a healthy affair and afterwards he listened to opera. He wasn't in the mood to have sex and we slept in different rooms. He wasn't inhospitable. It was just I was there in need and it didn't coincide with one of those days off when he could see me. It wasn't in the deal.

But he gave up his morning run to walk with me along the coast. 'You realise in the consumer world how much there is, the variety of waste. In a prisoner of war camp the smallest things are valuable. You deal in very, very small things. You still need to find the smallest thing just to make a key.'

'A key?' I didn't know what he meant.

He kicked at the sodden garbage at the water's edge.

'I expect you're upset about Gerona too. I expect you thought success was the key. To get you back in or close the door for good.'

I almost mentioned Jane Hartman. I knew she'd told him everything. I just knew it. And I thought how beautiful she was. How lucky to be so beautiful. And the rest of us had to crawl by with a bit of a facepack and some Royal Jelly and eyemasks and the right haircut.

'Why don't you go back there?' he said. 'And get your spirits up.'

'Are you kidding? It's like a mine field. No one trusts me.' I tried to describe Nina's hate but couldn't do justice to it.

'It must upset you, surely, that he doesn't trust you . Never mind her. Do you still sleep with him?'

'He sleeps with the fantasy of a million applauding Jews or $250,000.'

'Well, I'll give you a lift up. How about you buying the centre?'

I supposed it was some kind of joke. Not funny.

'Everyone else is trying to buy it. There's a travel agent here doing busy with a local guy in Gerona – ' he said.

'That would be Julio Framis.'

'He wants the land. Land is always valuable. And d'you know what? He wants to put Disneyland in there. He's got the concession.'

For the first time in a week I laughed. 'Not by the cathedral surely. Let's hope they keep it way off up by the Pyranees.'

'I'll buy you in.'

I didn't know what to say. 'I thought Zelman was busy buying everything.'

'My dear Patricia, how the hell is he going to give cabbala classes when his rival is running a busy bar? I will buy Zelman out and buy Tarres out and you have it. You're the one, perhaps the only person Tarres will not blow up.'

We walked back to Ocean Park and I thought what an evaluation of love – not being blown up. I imagined the look on Nina's face. Not bad. And José. Perplexed to begin with. And then I thought about their friends, and the town.

'And you put the money in yourself,' said Robert.

I could. But I'd get nothing back except contempt. For a poor person I was saying no an awful lot to a rich guy.

When he was absent Irish took over. It was quite disconcerting the following morning to hear Irish calling up to me, 'Come and get your breakfast, honey. It's a quarter to six. Don't be long. Eggs over easy.'

Then he'd do the ten-mile run and the work-out and the phone calls.Then he'd do the meetings in the kitchen, for the real partners.

Others got one of the many office suites. Irish kept telling me to have a lovely day. That's one thing Robert didn't waste time with.

I thought Irish was not a nice guy. He had some terrible people around him, not criminal but sycophantic. He got off on being Robert Hartman's shadow. I caught sight of a mistress trying to shake him down. She dressed very correct, almost too conservative, but when the clothes were off she was bad. I saw it all from my upstairs room. She wanted money to open a nursery school. She had a list of her backers who'd come in if Hartman did. I thought the nursery school had to be Spanish for brothel. So did Irish. They romped around naked on the wall to wall penthouse carpet, then he said no.

So she told him how wonderful he was, what a wonderful guy he was, how he made her feel good, how just seeing him made her day. She finished up with, 'You're just a little itsy-bitsy mouse. And I'd like to put you in my pocket and stroke you all day.'

And he gave a little boyish laugh. He was very pleased. The answer was still no on the nursery business.

American women went to amazing lengths of dishonesty building up the man they were with. What was incredible – the man, although not stupid, seemed to believe it.

Irish took me out for a drive. 'Come along, Baby Blue.' That was Robert's nickname for me. 'We'll go and sample a little God-given sunshine and maybe some real hot Mexican food.'

I said I wanted to go out alone. I had friends.

'You're Mr Hartman's friend and he looks after those. It's nothing personal.'

So I insisted I go out. I wanted to visit J.

'Now you don't want to get me into any trouble. If anything happened to you – well, you're special to him. And he's back tonight.'

I paced the penthouse, did my exercises, read a book. It all felt wrong. Then Robert came in from some plane journey and it was all worth it – maybe. He fell back gracefully on to the sofa and put his slim business case beside him. He stared at the pale carpet unseeing. I said, 'Would you like a drink?'

Then he pulled his thoughts back from wherever they were and said, 'Yes, that would be nice.'

'Does Irish have to be around me all the time?'

'Irish?' He was amused. 'He's my stand-in. Well, it is the town for stand-ins.'

'As long as he's not a stand-in in the bed.'

'If I ask you to sleep with someone, Patricia, you would do it.'

'I would? Why?'

'Because you belong to me.'

Chapter Fifty

I kept expecting to hear José had been killed. Someone would have exterminated him against the much admired eighth century wall with a kebab skewer. James called that wishful thinking. I was furious because José kept me out of everything. Nina was his confidante.

One of the hardest things – to know you don't mean as much as you did to someone you love. What was between you has changed without your agreement or participation. What was I to do? Sob in the street? Beg him to come back? Kill myself? I chose bitter arrogance. I cared even less than he did. James said, 'It's amazing you got over Tarres.'

I did expect a violent outcome. None came. Was José in prison? Had he violated Mario Sol? Or had some Jewish authority shut the place down? Even Hyam Macobby, a patient man, was getting fed up with all the squabbling and no progress. Being sensible Hyam simply went off and wrote his play about Nachmanides which was later filmed and then staged on Broadway. The further you were from Gerona, the better you did on Gerona.

James was sure it was all going on the same, except the ice-creams would be bigger.

'But what about this man José took money from? The dangerous one.'

'I don't believe it. He'd have paid his debts if he had.' He paused. 'They're not as poor as they make out. She's got money. She's hidden it. And one of these days she'll get the train for Paris and start a new life and enjoy herself.'

So on impulse I said we should go to Gerona, just for a look. There was no reason for our going, except curiosity. It was April 1984.

José was still behind the till. And the place was full. The people went there to see what a survivor looked like. How could a guy owe millions and stand behind a till, make money for himself, run around free and, what's more, blame it on an absent race. It was worth the price of the drinks to catch that floorshow. The courtyard was crowded with visitors taking photographs. To go down into the synagogue now cost money. And the Dutch photographer charged an entrance fee to see her exhibition on the second floor. The Christian symbols were now back on the walls. Retrieving them from the attic of the Hotel Peninsular had been an ugly scene. Mario Sol and Serrat had fought with José amongst the crucifixes. José was defiant about the cabbala. It was a three-part business. I suspected the man he'd borrowed from secretly was either Christian or Arab.

Isaac the Blind now attracted everyone with a gimmick. All the flakes came to Gerona. There were mystics, film makers, fortune tellers, people who specialised in numbers. One or two hung around José writing books recording his sayings. And others just hung around.

José's eyes were permanently veined and he could talk of nothing but debts and grievances. He looked unkempt. Nina too looked finished. James said to watch it. 'It's a guise. Going around like beggars. Brought to their knees by the Americans.' Mario was living at Juan Serrat's flat, collecting money for the restoration of the Jewish quarter of Gerona. José might have collected some too but he never opened his letters. Most people outside of Gerona did not realise there was more than one association and sent their cheques to a general address. The journalist Victor was now against José and foresaw the scandal destroying the town. He published his opinions in the major national papers but under a different name. José saw through that.

I realised José had gone slightly mad. I thought it would be put right with a quiet life and a lot of sleep. But he was now so bitter and suspicious it had affected his thinking. His hair was white and receding, his face pink from rising blood pressure and his eyelashes had dropped out. I dreaded seeing one more change.

In fact he had gone a touch insane more than once in public and two shrinks were whisked in to deal with him. He didn't let them put him away, neither did he pay them. He made them the head of his association alongside Isabella Sans-Gomez.

Nina was still young. She'd lost her looks, her talent, her youth, her health, her money and finally her nerve. Her body was so large I thought another child was on its way. It was water retention. The veins in her legs were so bad she had to wear white thick stockings in all weathers. Her hair, too, was greying. Her face was grey. I think I did her good. She remembered she hated me and it gave her a reason to be alive.

I spotted Zelman's 'man' immediately. He was the cook. He'd come from Chile because he'd heard about the centre and said he would give his life to save it from – whatever the enemy was. He wasn't going to kill José. He was simply going to stop José killing Zelman. However, José won him over. After all he was there and Zelman was thousands of miles away.

When Mario Sol arrived with a delegation of 'important' people to show them his land – after all, he'd bought the courtyard, the gardens, everything except the bar, the sun stone and the lavatories – the cook did nothing. José shot out of the kitchen and got Sol by the throat. 'Back off. This is holy territory. Not some two-bit playground for failed academics.'

Sol grappled with José's fingers and got himself free. 'Cross me, Tarres, and you'll pay.'

'Really,' said José sarcastically. 'Cross me and you'll never stop paying. You just see what I can do.' And his voice was centuries old, full of the venom of the dark ages. It wasn't a modern voice at all. Then José, waving the knife for cutting ham – he still served an international cuisine – got the group out and down the steps of the eighth-century street. He was a fighter, he was obsessed. No one cared that much about the Jewish stones or how much they'd donated, to go up against that.

'And give me my money, Sol! All that you collect in my name. Give it, you shitbag, or I'll be coming for you!'

And the cook stood shaking in the doorway, his job as Zelman's man a thing of the past. But he was so impressed he was almost in love with José.

As the whole place was in an uproar my news that Zelman's man was in town didn't even register in José's mind. I said it could be the cook.

José sighed exasperated. 'He's anybody's. Right now he's mine.'

And the drink sales shot up in the courtyard. Nothing was better for business.

It surely had its dark side, the Jewish centre, and it attracted darkness. People fell out who normally would not have spoken. And it became even more complicated because so many extra deals were hanging on the back of the cabbala promotion. Framis's Disneyland investment, his Sephardic tours, his kosher dinners and the journalists, waited for the famous to arrive, and the mayor was negotiating good relations with Zelman by arranging a university exchange scheme, and a French film director wanted to get cabbala on celluloid. But his star, José, never looked the same two days running. Yet he was behind the till and cabbala was local slang for a posh bar restaurant.

José distrusted me. Because Nina had stuck her money into the creditors' gap she had more say. It was expedient for José to see things her way. I wasn't wanted or valued. But José and I were familiars. If it swung too far one way something happened so it swung the other and a new balance was made. Then he valued me if only because of the past. And he believed we had some mystical connection. I always felt terrible in Paris. So did he. We both felt the same sort of terrible. The atmosphere was a real presence during the 1970 visits – something to be watched. It was as though we'd just left there, the place we were about to enter. If other lives did come into it we'd been there a minute ago. It was familiar and the depression it gave made no sense.

What brought the balance back this time was a visiting fortune teller. Well, I took him to be another mystic flake thinking Gerona was going to give him the answers. He didn't do cards or palms, he just held José's hand for a moment to get 'the vibration' and started speaking. He said José had lived in Gerona before and he had a debt to pay to the Jews. And he'd had a wife, a foreigner. So José thought he meant Nina. Had he made the same mistake twice? But the fortune teller turned and looked right at me and beckoned me over. So José and I had lived in Gerona, man and wife, and José had betrayed the Jews.

'I can see fire and a burning of buildings,' he said.

That put it in the 1300s during the fires of Gerona. I'd heard about that from Hyam Maccobby.

José closed his eyes and said he could see clearly the fires, could smell the burning. I saw nothing. José was deeply impressed with the idea that he and I had been attached and had a debt to pay. It made sense of all his suffering. It also gave me a proper position in his life. So I asked the fortune teller exactly what I had done against the Jews. He said I hadn't done anything. That was my burden. Together we'd fled. Watching the fires from the top of the city I'd felt great compassion and had said to José, 'One day we will return and put this right.'

'And I bet I know where we fled,' I said. 'Paris.'

José was very moved and would not speak. Then he asked the fortune teller to stay and eat but he was going on to Seville. As he left he looked at me with his glittering green eyes and he paused, and I knew he had something to say. And I was glad he didn't say it. He walked with dignity across the marble patio and through the dark archway. I remembered Robert Hartman saying, 'You'll go from the dark into the light. Like in Gerona.' I'd said, 'Somedays I feel very far from the light.' I felt very far from any light in that cabbala courtyard.

Although I thought the fortune teller had picked up more on the present condition than the past, José now looked at me with something bordering on respect, so I kept quiet. Yes, I was the person he'd known for twenty-five years or seven hundred years, depending how you viewed it. Then quite sensibly he said, 'What d'you think we should do?'

'Do?'

'You're in it too. How can we be freed from this past debt?'

So I thought about it and said we should sort it out in our present relationships with others. That was the key. He didn't like that one. I sighed and said, 'If we have done something terrible to others in the past we'll have to wait for the right time to make amends. For now it's just the ones that are here. We must not betray the Jews again.'

And he laughed mercilessly. 'Oh I love it, Patrice. So now I should have that blubber of fat Professor Sol sitting in my place. Is that what you mean? And then we'd have Professor Zelman pointing out the mysteries of the sun stone with a long stick, getting a little glory, which he can't seem to do with his work. He doesn't mean a thing where he comes from. He'd shave his balls in public if it would get people asking his name. He's out for power. I like the straight shits better. Failures, Patrice. All of them. And yet you want them here. If I didn't know that that psychic came from the house of Isabella Sans-Gomez I would have to wonder if you'd sent him. It's ironic that what he advises fits in so well with the Jews' wishes.'

'I didn't bring the Jews, José.'

'Oh but you did, *ma chérie*.'

And he got up, full of icy malice, and went swiftly to the bar. I thought he'd gone to strangle a creditor, they occasionally showed up in pairs. He came back to the table with a pile of newspaper cuttings and dropped them in my lap. He watched my eyes.

'You brought them.'

I looked down at my articles from various papers. 'I spent hours working on your behalf.' My voice shook. I was almost crying.

'You got paid for it, *ma chérie*.'

'Very little.'

'Better than my wife and I. We get nothing.'

'But I did it all for you. My very first article brought the moviestars. The cultural minister in Israel. Leonard Bernstein –'

'And Zelman Goldstein. Thank you!' He spat. 'You should have kept out of it. Your writing those articles brought those Americans and disaster.'

'I've done the best PR job ever known on your wife. Beautiful, talented, and you're not even grateful.'

No, they certainly weren't grateful. And I thought James had a point. Since his travel agency job had gone bust he went bust with it and did nothing. Doing nothing was suddenly most attractive. Some days I longed for the desert where there were no actions and no results of action.

Nina, upstairs, hearing his voice raised against me rushed down to join us. She had moved so fast it was like a mystical apparition. She looked like a big bad dusty mouse, her eyes gleamed. The child hung around behind her skirt. The child hated me from its first moment. He watched me with malice from behind doors, under chairs. If bad things happened to Patrice he laughed. I suppose he got that habit from her. If ever I was misguided enough to speak to the child, it would bustle away putting as much rudeness into the movement as possible.

I fought back. I told José if Zelman had not arrived he'd have lost it all anyway. 'The auction. Remember? They saved you that day.'

'Go back to them!' she said. 'If they're so wonderful go *chez* Zelman. We have no need of you here.'

I kept my eyes on José. 'Your ripping off Serrat was to blame.'

'Well you would say that. The mistress of Zelman Goldstein. Yes, we know. Nina knows. She's right.'

And in spite of the hostility, there was something alive for me in his eyes. She saw it.

'But you're in it too. Our debt,' he said. 'I'm surprised you're so naive.'

'Naive how?' Nina asked him. 'Do you forget what she is?' And I heard the jealousy then. It lashed swiftly in and out of the words. But how in control she was. How different to me.

'Yes, Nina sensed all along you were the enemy. You carry vengeance. You, Patrice, are our true executioner!'

And I walked out and the child roared with laughter and the laughing bird mocked. And I turned down towards the Calle Forsa.

326

'You are our true executioner!' I couldn't believe this was the man who'd dominated my life, for all my life.

For a moment I leaned near the flower pots waiting for all the emotions to subside. Nina with her ugliness and her greed – she'd spoiled our love.

Jane Hartman was coming out of the grocer's at the bottom of the Calle Forsa. She was always recognisable far off because of her clothes. Today she looked lovely and frail like the heroine from *The Great Gatsby*.

'Isn't it wonderful,' she said. 'Where else could you get such scandal? Let's have a drink. But where? Up at the cabbala? It sounds like some British comedy. That's what it should be. The fact is there's nowhere else to go.'

And I could see Gerona had shrunk into social lethargy. Things only happened around Tarres.

We drank at an artists' bar by the river. I tried to appear normal. I felt as though I'd been assaulted. I could not believe the unhappiness I'd just passed through could be followed by something as mundane as a Coca-Cola by the river.

'I read your book by the way. Friends of Richard sent it from the States. Did you know Robert Hartman planted a rose-garden for his wife? Did he tell you?'

'No.'

She said I was looking a little less than my best so tried to cheer me up by local gossip. The town was now in two groups. Sol's lot and José's supporters. José had one on Sol because he was from Gerona. But Sol had got foreign money people and José had debts. The politicans and academics were with Sol. 'Tarres tried to get me to go in with him. As a partner. I'd be vice- president of the – I can't remember the name of his group. It's just one word different from Mario Sol's. He's persuasive, very. I can see what you see in him.'

'Saw.'

'She's still crazy about him. Nina. He turns her on so much she reaches a frenzy and tears her skin and claws him. Sometimes her whole body is a mass of scratches.'

I had an unwelcome stab of jealousy then. I'd rather not have heard that one. 'How do you know? D'you sleep with them?'

'I know because they have sex on that sunstone when they think everyone's gone. Apparently it gives her energy and the sex is fierce. The waiters hide and watch. Well, they have to do something. They don't get paid. And I know the waiters. Let's hope they don't tell the Americans.'

People still said 'the Americans'. But it was now just one, Zelman, and in fact he was Polish by birth, and a few absent, well-meaning Americans who'd paid money to try and save José's dreams.

Chapter Fifty-one

José came to me in the hotel and lay beside me on the bed, in my arms, and said it wasn't me he was angry with. He'd been up, he'd been down. He'd been at the point of fulfilment, so near his aim. He'd suffered to the point of near breakdown. His wife's mental health was ruined. She no longer sculpted. She worked like a slave to try and pay the debts.

They always said they worked themselves to death but every time I'd been in there she was either sitting at the bar smoking her lungs out and reading a newspaper or having a frock fitted. And he spent most of his time standing on the patio complaining bitterly. He occasionally turned a kebab. They looked to me as though they were dying of boredom as much as anything else.

In some ways setting up Isaac the Blind resembled setting up *The Siesta* film. The near hits, the big names, the harrowing collapses, the American money, the Jewish producers, the dreams and the persistence. And of course it was also about Gerona.

I suggested his best way out was to make it up with Zelman.

'I can see you spend time in Hollywood. When everything is disastrous it is not the time for Hollywood.'

'You were keen on him once. And he's the only Jew you've got.'

'Be very careful what you say, Patrice.'

'You don't like Sol so get someone else. At least speak to Zelman. He's probably feeling as bad as you.'

His present mood was far from reassuring. He had the most sudden mood changes that belonged to a lunatic.

'Be very careful, Patrice. The curse isn't fussy. So what! You loved Gerona once.'

'Does this curse affect everybody?'

'If you don't know about it, it doesn't have an effect. Visitors come and go and the good Jews know they've found something wonderful. The moment they enter the courtyard, if they are truly Jewish they sense their past. And they cry and they sob. Men, women. But cross me and you cross the Jewish quarter and then you pay!'

I asked how he planned to pay his debts.

'I have someone, don't worry. It would give the Jews such a surprise.'

'Not someone we know?' I was thinking of a particular volatile Arab political figure.

'Now it's the time to go because if I am more than thirty minutes absent some disaster will happen. As long as I'm there it is protected.'

When he'd gone Señor Lara said, 'The Jews go into the courtyard and cry and sob when they see what's on their plate. Even I'd cry. One thing about that cook. He really can't cook.'

Señora Lara said, 'Of course now he has to be the perfect husband.'

Nina's father had finally stepped in. She'd got too ill. Too distressed, and the child was suffering. In return for José taking more care the father put in a real dollop of money and Nina was going to buy the big house at the top of Gerona, the one surrounded by cypress trees. The house had been mentioned last by Robert Hartman. But after persuasion from José, Nina saw the wisdom of staying in the cabbala. After all, what better house could she have than the one where Nachmanides was born? He shook the money loose and it got rid of the most ferocious creditors. In return he made her a gift of himself. He would be utterly faithful, he would look after her all the days of her life.

'They were like two newly weds, except some days she looked old enough to be his mother,' said Señora Lara. 'He would walk most correctly by her side, his arm around her waist.'

'Will it last?' I asked.

'Sure. As long as the money does.'

But I felt José had changed. She'd stayed beside him through the bad times. They often made a stronger link than the good.

I did try and straighten out the mess. I really did give it my best. As it happened I was innocent. I wasn't Zelman's mistress. I did want the best for José Tarres. I couldn't bear to see him looking so ill. The more I did the worse it got. Zelman didn't trust me and Nina hated me. It was like some huge illness – the cabbala and all the players were different symptoms. And I wished it could all be covered over with earth and put to rest.

So before I left I tried to straighten out my relationship with José. I arranged to see him in Luis's bar. Luis polished the glasses and waited for night. Daylight never did suit him. He had a house in the country, another by the sea, a shop in Figueras, the next town going north, and a month each year he stayed in the Waldorf Hotel, New York. He had everything, wife, children, except he wasn't in love. He never went near Isaac the Blind outfit but he got all the gossip.

'That lawyer's the real hero. He's got José such a deal. Who would think of renting the bar to yourself? Vendor, buyer. A good catch. José can be as crazy as he likes and they'll forgive him because he does what the Catalan bourgeoisie cannot. Through him they live their dreams. But he's lost us a valuable piece of history. That site, properly run, could have enhanced the town. Because of Tarres we've lost an enormous amount of visitors and trade. And we're in recession. You can see that. The Residencia Internacional is still closed.'

'Why don't you talk to him, Luis?'

'Everyone talks to him and he agrees with everything but then he goes home and she says something else. It's a shame for all of us you did not marry him.'

José came in exhausted and flopped on to the bench and said the sky was on his side. 'It's turned blue. A brilliant strange blue. Go and look. It's the colour of the Jews of Gerona. Even nature is on my side.' Luis poured him a large gin. 'And Nina is having a dress made. And d'you know what. It's exactly the same colour as the sky.'

'Perhaps you should call it Nachmanides blue,' I said.

He sighed. 'The signs are everywhere. It cannot go on.'

'Well, that's just what I was saying to Luis. D'you want me to write another article and state your case?'

'I don't think you can understand it well enough, Patrice.'

I didn't like his tone.

'We don't need the newspapers.'

'Well, I'm sure the sky will take care of everything then.'

'My son is right. He said, Isaac does not belong to you or the Americans but God.'

Luis was pretending his best not to listen but he couldn't help laughing.

'We are not grateful to you, Patrice, you are right about that. Because what is your reason? For what you have done?'

'Reason?' Well I had to get one up on Nina but I wasn't going to tell him that. I wanted to do better on the cabbala business than they did. Why? Because the town knew I'd been his mistress and each time I came back, they sensed, even if I did not, that I'd come to get him. And they found it amusing. My only answer was to do better than they did. It was the only revenge. 'We go back a long way,' I said. 'Friends are rare. You could at least care about that.'

'I care no more about myself, my mother or my wife. My baby, yes. I adore my baby.'

'At the end of the day you'll still need friends.'

'But you brought ill luck. You brought Zelman Goldstein.'

'I told you right at the start, get the Jews involved. Include them. And let them start paying. Go to the universities. But no, you wanted to do it all yourself. You wanted the glory. That's why you fucked up. You wouldn't share.'

'I wanted to save my town.'

'You did all that because your father was a drunk and you were ashamed. So you had to shine. And you had Mama on your back too,

332

saying be great for me. Forget the two quacks. I can tell you what's wrong because I can remember.'

He took my hand then. 'So what should I do?'

'Decide what you want and get it.'

He no longer knew. He kept getting muddled. The Jews had had a bad time and that he identified with and yet he blamed them.

'Maybe I can't have what I want.' His eyes were glowing and a bit more normal.

'You should have asked for money at the beginning. You didn't ask them for what you wanted. And that's cost your happiness.'

A moustache now almost covered what had been his fabulous mouth. Was nothing going to be left?

'My happiness went a long time ago, Patrice.' He looked at me sardonically. 'In its place I'm going to bring back the glory of Gerona even if it costs me my life.'

'How can you do something when it's already been done? The great mystics have come and gone and left a record. You can't get better than that. It's rather arrogant, José, to suppose you could get better. Who have you in mind? The local horoscope guy?'

'We're both in it together, my sweet. Remember that. When I'm free so are you.'

We did try and sleep together once but it was over. There were little touches from the past, like the key getting stuck in the hotel room door. I couldn't open it. José couldn't believe it. Then he tried but it still wasn't moving so we started laughing. So he kicked it in. He'd had lots of practice.

The minute he'd had sex he talked about the Jews. Before he had sex he was already talking about them. I had to agree he was obsessed. Having sex with me was perhaps the only relief he got from the subject. I got nothing from it.

I said I would not come back to Gerona but if he got into real shit he should call me and I would always help. And I mentioned Robert but of course he'd not heard of him so wasn't impressed.

He said a hit man had had a drink at the bar the previous night. 'Everyone knew what kind he was. He asked me to have a drink

333

with him. He said there might be someone you want taken out. It'll cost you $10,000. How did he know I was in trouble?'

'José, everyone knows you're in trouble.'

'He said he'd call back.'

So I asked what nationality he was. I just wanted to be sure. It was only a feeling.

'Spanish, Madrid. Why would he ask me that?'

I had no answer. Isaac attracted the odd, the broke, the hopeful. Why not assassins?

He couldn't get the guy out of his mind. So I suggested we spend the day together outside of Gerona. At the sea for instance. Was that a mistake. So I was getting him away and then what? He didn't trust me even for something as simple as a day at the sea. He would not be persuaded from the Calle Forsa.

'Even a priest and the mayor couldn't do it, Patrice. And they got me as far as Israel.'

On hearing this I hated him, for all the waste, the lost dreams, the missed opportunities. Happiness was such a rare commodity.

He washed his face and asked for my comb and put back on his beggar's outfit. Then he said. 'It won't work.' For once he was talking about me. 'Your being with another man.'

'Why won't it?'

'Because you cannot turn your back on Gerona anymore than I can. What's he like this man?'

'Rather quiet.'

'So what does he do?'

And to tease him I described Zelman Goldstein and his sister Ruby. He stopped listening to all that and said, 'Is he Mediterranean?'

'So many questions suddenly, José.'

He knew my love had been withdrawn. I hadn't realised that would matter to him.

'He's not Mediterranean,' I lied. And José seemed relieved.

'Well, at least you won't have with him what you did with me.'

I walked with him as far as the Calle Forsa and we said a formal goodbye. We might even have shaken hands. The fire of love was out. We looked at each other over a cold grate. It was unendurable. Much worse than dying. I'd have preferred to be dead.

Isaac the Blind was José Tarres. It was his dreams, his Hollywood, his chance to make something of himself. To leave would be a death and he'd take his tormenters with him. He had luck. He turned the cook round but the cook was with him, miles and miles away from Zelman's influence. José even became beneficent to his enemies. They were just misguided victims of American speculation. When they'd mended their ways they could return. It was still a cafeteria, a restaurant, a Catalan promotion. It was never certain of anything except chaos. He made 143 appearances at the Palais de Justice but Nachmanides was with him so he always got off. I thought that might have something to do with the lawyer also being with him.

And Zelman, the other side of the ocean, waited. He too, had been betrayed. And José would say, 'Yes, we are beggars, Nina and I, thrown from our home. We are the original Jews.' His ego bloated, like a drinker's liver, he sold his form of cabbala – ice-cream and the photographer's cakes.

On Palm Sunday I went to say goodbye. And I saw them, José and Nina, eating at one of the tables in the courtyard. The one under the grapevine in the sun – eating a huge breakfast. They were ordinary and greedy. And children passed through from the town carrying palms. And in the sunlight I saw – I suppose it was an imprint from the earlier time when the courtyard was filled. The Jews in the Middle Ages, suffering. I heard the screams. I heard in every part of my being their horror. And amongst it I saw Nina and José, like two filthy concierges coining money from the Jews' pain. And in that moment I hated them. I never visited that place again.

At the train station I saw a familiar figure in a blanket. Colin Diamond was in town. José's troubles were just beginning.

Chapter Fifty-two

Sometimes I saw New York as the reflection of another planet, a bad one that had drawn near Manhattan Island, and all the skyscrapers and towers sprang up under its influence like mushrooms. New York didn't belong to this world at all. It was an outpost for this malevolent planet and an exit from ours. You didn't have to see it this way. Like going into Isaac the Blind you could see just a pile of stones and a nice light. There were bits of Gerona that belonged even here. The atmosphere at St Patrick's was so much like Gerona's old city. Except for the smell. That was missing. And through a side door of St Patrick's I looked from the darkness into the sun. And the trees were noisy in the autumn breeze, their leaves on the turn, and amongst them I saw the word LOVE. It wasn't in church writing. I thought it must be a hallucinatory message from Gerona. It was in fact LOVES, a popular diner. So I crossed the street and went inside. It was clean, sparkling and light with an up atmosphere. I took Robert there and he was always glad if I found something he didn't know about.

Really I was living with him, but we didn't call it that. I'd sort of slid into his life, it was not a spoken commitment and I still had to go to and from London because of the boys and the pets. One day Robert said, 'If you are going to do this – be with me – you'll have to give up the ecstasy.'

Well, I hadn't found too much of that in the last years. He said if I hankered after the past, thinking I could get it back, he'd know and it wouldn't work for us. I promised him that all that was over. Then I walked straight into St Patrick's cathedral and it was like a body blow straight from Gerona. Forget me? Fuck you!

Robert took me to the house where he'd lived with his wife Ruth and brought up Jamie. It was in Connecticut, large, dour and full of ghosts and gloom. The dead wife's aunt and uncle had stayed on to look after the property. At one point they lifted the lid of the grand piano to show him how immaculate the keys were, like good teeth. Robert said sharply, 'Close it.'

On the drive back to New York he said nothing and nothing was what he wanted to hear. We planned to spend the following spring in Italy together. We'd maybe go to Sicily. He knew what I'd like and showing me would make it all fresh for him again.

If I was going to be with Robert I would have to leave Phil. Something would have to be said, even goodbye. Leaving Phil should cause no pain. That was the thing about the relationship. We had never unpacked our cases emotionally speaking. But it was the things that we'd been through, the everyday stuff, the problems, horror stories, small triumphs that would make it hard to part. But I kept that to myself. I kept rather a lot to myself.

One evening in New York I ran into Ellen Burstyn who'd taken over the Actors' Studio. She knew about the nun play with Joan Hackett. I asked her how it was all going on and she replied, with her lovely smile, 'If you need to talk to Joan, talk to me or someone at the studio.'

What was she saying? Had I offended Joan Hackett? Was the play not going on after all? When I heard the producer was up from LA, staying at the Helmsley, I went to see him. He said the play wasn't opening. 'Joan died on us.'

I thought it was American for she'd given up on the play. So I said get someone else. 'There's hundreds and thousands of actresses out there.'

337

'You English are tough. I see what they mean about the stiff upper lip.'

I'd had my share of rejection in my life. And he expected me to cry all over him? Then he said Joan had died in hospital of terminal cancer. She'd got sick suddenly and people had been keeping it quiet. She died in fact the day before. As a gesture, although I didn't realise it at the time, I didn't have the play offered to any other actresses. It seemed the right way to pay respects.

I told Robert the actresses attracted to my work died around me like flies. 'Sign with me and you get a quick death.' Two performers in my radio plays had also recently died. He said it was a coincidence and he was intolerant of those. He had to get the next plane to LA. A lot of our life was spent in airports. I hated them. He took them as they came. I got jetlag, his body moulded itself to any situation. He never carped on about his health or mood. I sometimes wondered if he was really there. It was like he was listening to a different voice in another room. But then he'd tune in to me and say something normal.

By now some people thought I might be sleeping with him. He was sexually attractive to a lot of women, their fix, their fantasy. One young film actress asked me what it ws like to sleep with Mr Fix. It was all subjective, that kind of thing. He could be fair with me and fabulous with someone else or lousy with everybody. How could I answer? But I always denied knowing him personally. It was just business. And he would say, 'My private life is my own.'

He said he was glad I hadn't gone for the 'kept' deal. He enjoyed the everyday arrangement and said he felt easy with me and was getting to like it. But I knew he needed to be on his own. He was just beginning to see that. I doubted whether he could have lived with anyone. And at the same time there was a possessiveness about him which was out of place and crude. He'd want Irish or one of his assistants to drive me and pick me up and he liked to know where I was. I didn't think it belonged to me at all. He'd just never got over his wife.

And one day when the plane was going through what they call CAT and I thought my last minute was up, even the hostesses had vanished, he held my hand. He was the only calm thing around, apart from the pilot. He said, 'It's OK. It's only the sky. It's not the plane. It's when the plane does this we're in trouble.'

And when we finally got on the ground I said, 'I bet you were scared.'

'If you're waiting only to die what is there to be scared of?' And we were shut away into yet another limousine and I'd rarely felt so depressed.

'Is that what you want then?'

So he laughed, a small bitter laugh. His laughter – something he kept to himself, not to be shared. 'Of course. But you're so life-loving you don't notice.'

That made me rather quiet. I thought perhaps I should have another little trip to London. I might feel a lot less life loving there. And less hurt.

He held my hand beautifully. His hands were so soothing, they were almost healing. 'When I die will I find my wife again?' he said quietly. 'What do you think?'

'How do I know?' And I felt choked with tears. A live rival was bad enough.

'I think you're a bit psychic.'

And I thought it was so like Mills and Boon romance. Which was which?

'You'd do well in Hollywood with all that,' he said. 'They'd pay *d*'argent fou for a spread of cards.' And he told me that one of the leading hostesses was crazy about clairvoyance. She spent hours every week going for readings. She could talk about nothing else. 'Her staff only keep their jobs if they pretend to be clairvoyant. I went there and the cleaning woman was sitting, broom in hand, in a trance supposedly. Telling her what she wanted to hear.'

'Which is?'

'That she'd get a particular man she was infatuated with. I could have told her the answer and saved her thousands of dollars.'

I could guess who the man was and what the answer was. He had a cruelty. He liked women to love him then he could hurt them because his wife had been taken away from him.

'Does she go to a shrink? Was she broken as an actress?'

'Is that clairvoyance or hearsay?'

339

I knew he was talking about the girl everyone else fancied, the one who'd made love with her shrink.

I sort of navigated myself past all the points of pain because I ostensibly loved someone else. I had a certain independence. I got on with my writing and stood on my own feet, not his, at the bank.

He encouraged me to have dinner with J. I played it down, said I found J difficult to be with, far too challenging.

'Don't be too hard on him. He got your writing going. Stirred you up, made you go for it. He wasn't so bad for you.'

Robert didn't have a social life. It was business or it was home life. I saw the bit that went on in the house and it was hard to believe he did deals on a world scale, negotiated political changes, helped build empires, decided fashion, helped make stars, and possibly killed people. At home he drank tea, watched television and said yes, he liked 'Hill Street Blues'. He didn't exactly wear slippers but he was quiet. Of course it was only a matter of time before I would self-destruct. Home life was too much like childhood with Mum in Albany Park. As soon as the curtains swished shut for the evening a horrible depression set in. Robert said it was cosy. I took a Valium and agreed. But he didn't miss much. He knew about the pills and where I hid them. One evening he said, 'Just take the pill. You don't have to crunch it away like some mouse in the corner.'

'I thought you only liked healthy people.'

'No, Patricia. You're muddling me with your other lover. J.' And he took my hands and pulled me up on to his lap and held me. 'You don't have to be anything. Just be yourself. Please.'

I never told anyone how I lived. I just said I was away working on some script. I suited him because I hadn't had a rosy life so couldn't complain about things like absence, and the absence of wedding ceremonies. I certainly wasn't born with a silver spoon in my mouth. I expected dead bodies, not roses. Sometimes when he was going away on his own I said life with him didn't suit me and he'd reply, 'I told you at the beginning it wouldn't.'

And then he'd laugh and get hold of me. 'I want to fill you up. I want to make you peaceful.'

340

Chapter Fifty-three

The Siesta was finally scheduled to be shot in Madrid by Mary Lambert. Sometimes I thought it must be the unluckiest film ever made. The money dropped out just before shooting began and the new money dropped out every day shooting went on. It was a nightmare of tension and uncertainty for Mary and her team. Eventually it starred Ellen Barkin, Martin Sheen, Jodie Foster, Gabriel Byrne, Julian Sands, Grace Jones, Isabella Rossellini, Alexei Sayle, with music by Miles Davis. Its struggles into the world were not dissimilar to those in Gerona. José and I couldn't be together but at least we could have coincidences. When it was finally made I wondered if I was now free. Was its creation my debt? I never found that answer.

In the early spring of 1985 I ran into Ruby, Zelman's sister, in a New York street. She asked me to write something that would get that shit José Tarres out of there. They'd tried everything. He seemed to think cabbala was a commodity he owned.

'Our community in LA stands to lose money and we had started to buy the empty houses around Tarres. But we can't put one foot on to our property without a scandal.' José accused them of land speculation, somehow he'd got the Disneyland story. Did the Spanish want one of their oldest cities turned into a home for Mickey Mouse? It seemed to me as though Julio Framis had gone back to Tarres. Perhaps he saw more profit there than with the absent supporters.

'We've got courses on cabbala slotted. People have booked. We can't do anything all the time that man is in the place. Can't you take him off to Israel? We'll give you two an apartment and he could study cabbala for a year.'

I loved that. We were well past the stage of taking each other anywhere.

When I told Robert about the cabbala crash course he was amused. 'A year studying cabbala? It's like a first-year medical student performing a heart transplant. He'd have to learn Hebrew. Just for a start. I'd keep out of it.'

Something about his tone said I should ask why.

'Because it can't go on. It's a boil about to burst. You can't save him.'

'Save' was a big word for Tycoon.

So I called Zelman Goldstein and said I'd do what I could. I was on the side of the Jewish programme and I thought the community should have the shrine. Cautiously I asked what he planned to do.

'Well, I'm not abandoning houses which I've bought because one man is two- faced. I will not see all our endeavours come to nothing. He's made us a laughing stock. José Tarres is an embarrassment to the Jewish people. If I do lose, so does José, because to get my money back – guess what moves in? Disneyland.'

Then Ruby got on the phone and said if I loved Tarres I'd better do something because the revenge would not come from the Jews. 'He owes money to some wrong people. He's made a mistake. These kind of people are not like us. They want to see their money flourish. But, it's disappeared into the huge mysterious black hole known as the cabbala. Those people have sent someone into Gerona who will take care of the problem. We do nothing. Our hands are clean.'

This of course was meant to activate me and it did. Ruby was inexact in the description of the 'someone'. She let drop he was of

Sicilian origin. He was just on business. I took it to be extermination business and took the next flight to Gerona.

He was still all over the town and the locals might or might not like him but you'd never get them telling a stranger, or siding with one against his misdeeds. The town may even hate him but it wasn't going to let an outsider see. And I wasn't one of them, never had been. I stayed in the Hotel Peninsular and even Señor Lara and his wife were quiet. 'It goes on, Patricia. It goes on the same.'

I had no desire ever to go into the cabbala courtyard again so I rang José and asked him to meet me. He sounded nervous. 'Don't say anything. Understand?' It was a voice of trouble. 'Do you remember where we first met? Be there.'

So I went to the Hotel Residencia Internacional where I'd first met him when I was fifteen, on the steps leading to the bar. The doors on both streets were locked so I waited in the alley between the streets, full of rubbish and starving cats. He looked not unlike he did in the political activist days. At least he wasn't depressed. He knew he was fighting for his life.

'I think you should just get out,' I said.

'I think so.' He didn't ask how I knew.

'I think it's a trained guy, a professional, so I wouldn't bother with the ham knife. Do you know who it is?'

He shook his head.

'Any strangers around?'

He described Colin Diamond. 'But he seems positive. He's got a lot of energy. He's helping me run the bar.'

Colin Diamond running the cabbala. Why not? He'd done everything else.

'Who did you borrow from?'

'Well, I'm in a heap of shit, Patrice, because it's the Mafia.'

'How did you find the Mafia? How do you know what they look like?'

'They came to me. One day this slim, intelligent Mediterranean type, of very good class, walked on to the patio. He was like me. I understood him immediately. We had a complete understanding. And we had some wine, being Mediterranean, and he sensed I had

343

troubles. He understood totally what I was going through. And then we went to the Barrio Chino together and looked at some girls. And he spoke Spanish perfectly. We were like – ' He lifted up two fingers, the ones he'd used for him and Zelman. 'Before he left he said I should be in a position of strength. Then I could negotiate. He said, "If you want money. I am behind you." I didn't do anything but – and I can't remember clearly when it was – around the time Mario Sol changed the locks, he phoned me. We did a deal.'

'A deal.'

'He put through the bank immediately a sum of money.'

'How much?'

'More than I asked, Patrice. And the deal was I repay him a part in three months, the rest in another three or we'd be on interest at thirty percent. It was high but I was sure the Americans would help. I spent a lot of the money getting the synagogue ready. The set of lamps and the fifteenth-century chairs and those ancient manuscripts – '

'And the Mafia had obviously known you'd go on a spending spree, José, and you'd never meet that interest.'

'He encouraged me in some ways to do just that. He said, get a good front against your enemies – ' He did a lot of sighing.

'I knew he was Mafia when this other type came in and offered his services. Was there anyone I wanted taken care of? I told you about it. I knew it was the Italian he meant. For $10,000 he'd take him off my back. Then the Italian called in the loan. If I can't pay he takes everything. Or I die.'

'Give it to him.'

'Patrice, I don't even own the place for Crissake! I'm sure I told him that.'

'Well, you didn't tell the Jews. Does he have a name, this Italian?'

'Baby Blue.'

Robert's nickname for me.

'I've been set up,' said José.

'So have I.'

'You remember our plan, Patrice, to go to Istanbul. I think now is a very good time for me.'

I waited for him in Figeuras because that was one move Robert Hartman wouldn't guess. The next town north. Robert would go for the airport or the frontier or Barcelona harbour. I waited for José to get Nina and the child off to the country. I had *The Siesta* money. I had big book money in America. I had enough for Istanbul, for ever. I could have more or less anything I wanted these days. There would be no more money shit. It was like having a sick organ removed. Since the operation, doctor, I've never felt better. It cut no ice with José. But he needed an exit. It was all about taking what wasn't yours, the trouble we were in. He took the Jewish quarter. I'd take him.

Robert Hartman walked into the Figeuras Hotel, quite effortlessly, and paid my bill. Then he drove me, as some kind of punishment, to Paris.

Chapter Fifty-four

Robert Hartman said, 'Of course I wanted Gerona. Sometimes you're not smart.'

'But how did you know where I was?'

That was so naive he couldn't be bothered to answer.

'So will you get it?'

'I've got it.'

'But the Jews own – '

'Nothing. They've sold to me. How could they do anything? It's mine.'

And I thought there was a little flicker of triumph.

'All I had to do was give him a real creditor. He spends more than some women – your lover.'

'So what are you going to do? I mean with the Jewish site.'

'Turn it into a motion picture palace. Because that's where my movie dreams began. A glittering 1930s style building with an organist and curtains that change colour. And a tea room with a palm court orchestra and dancing. Right there on the site where I'd first seen a movie being shot. Remember? You should. You were in it.'

'And Jane Hartman as the usherette.'

That amused him. 'Oh Jane, Jane. What a mess she is.'

And he was going to tell me as much about her as he did about his dead wife and dead son.

'Is she in danger from you too?'

'That's an old- fashioned way of putting it.'

'So she's your mistress?'

'Patricia, she was married to my son.' He was very hostile. 'She chose to go off with someone else.'

'Is that why he died?'

'He died because he saw no point in staying alive.'

'So why send her money?'

'Oh, the money comes from Jamie. A punishment to her for being unfaithful. The one condition, she stays in one place. And my choice was Gerona. The money's from his trust.'

'Well, I don't think it does her any good.'

'No I'm sure it does not. You can feel lonely there. Great loneliness. I know. So will she.'

Just like that, he fixed up a life. I wondered what he was like with death.

'But you like her?'

'She could have had a career. A sub Angie Dickinson. She's sexually attractively available. But she blew it.'

'I think she was your mistress and your son found out.'

'Don't challenge me! Ever!' His tone was deadly.

'Is he alive? Tarres?'

'I hope so because he has to sign over his bar licence to my lawyers. I didn't sleep with Jane. Sex isn't my scene. I loved my son. And it's none of your goddam business.'

'So what happens to me?'

'You?' He was taken aback.

'Well, I haven't given you the sort of experience you like.'

'I can make good use of every kind of experience.'

He was now descending into one hell of a lousy mood. But I was already getting a wave or two of horror from the Eiffel Tower so had my own problems.

So the businessman had a dream of Gerona. José had a dream. So did the Jews. Nina had a dream of life with José. I didn't have any dream.

A frequent visitor, at least in my mind, was the Jewish scholar walking up the Calle Forsa. The heat was intense but he remained cool. For what reason did he return to my mind? It certainly wasn't imagination because the figure was always stronger than any thought and, unlike thought, it could be recalled effortlessly without change.

I was beyond speaking to Robert Hartman, I was so angry. I asked to return home. 'Where's that?' he said. I thought staying quiet was the best solution. That way José stayed safe. Robert was out at meetings in Paris throughout the day and at night he watched television. On the third night he sat at the edge of my bed.

'Are you going to let me?' He meant have sex.

'I'd rather not, if you don't mind.' I couldn't sound scathing enough. 'At least there's nothing in my life you can rip off.'

So he ripped my nightdress. Then he got hold of my chin and turned my head slowly and we were into some violence. 'Come on, Baby Blue. You got to me. You made out to me. You must have known enough bad things about me to stay away.' He smiled most attractively. 'But you're the same naughty girl you've always been aren't you?'

The way he said it made my heart leap as though touched by a tongue of flame. I wanted him then, ached for him to be on top of me. I looked away and remembered he was another one who kept me out of things.

'I find your attitude to places and people uncompromising. I don't like it.'

'I don't compromise,' he agreed. 'It takes courage to be yourself as obviously as I am myself. But I've had to have pretty strong muscles to live the way I do. I saved your town. On your next visit you could have been screwing Mickey Mouse.'

He was hurting my chin and I asked him to let go.

'Your face is all hot. What about the rest of you?'

He put his hand down the sheet. I made a show of resisting but the hand ended up between my legs. 'You want fucking.' He whispered other things he'd do. I tried to shut him up. 'Don't you like dirty talk? That does surprise me. Knowing you.' Then he pulled the sheet savagely and I almost fell on the floor. 'On your knees, Baby Blue,' he said coldly. 'Like you do in church. And do it.'

I adored him sexually but what kind of man was he? I didn't think he was good. Dangerous perhaps. The good stuff he kept to himself.

When I got up off my knees I said I wouldn't see him again. I took the first plane to London. But when ever I thought about him, my heart, it gave an awful lurch of being in love.

Chapter Fifty-five

Chris was doing a painting and decorating job. Tim was starting drama school. And Phil had a mistress who rang a dozen times a day. She sounded perfunctory, like a gym mistress. Phil tried to say she wasn't his mistress.

I decided to buy a new house near Hampstead Heath. So Phil said he'd come along too and buy half. So we still hadn't entirely split up although I half planned to go with Robert Hartman to Sicily. He rang me in London and said why be upset about a movie house in the Calle Forsa. The local people were dying for entertainment. And José's live show was going to be closed anyway. He said we got on well together and he didn't want it to end.

'I promise you I'll take care of you.'

No one had ever said that.

'Do you believe me? I'll fill you up with peace.'

I didn't think he'd marry me but I didn't think too much about the things I couldn't have. I said to Phil he should consider carefully about moving to Hampstead. 'Put it this way. If I got an offer to go off I'd go. I'd leave you. Just like that. So don't lose the mistress.'

He said he knew that but he loved me.

I'd been in London a few weeks when Marcelle rang me. She said, 'Your lover is dead.'

For a moment I thought she meant José.

'Oh – my lover.' And then I realised.

'Shot here in Paris. Four bullets in the back of the head. It looks like a Mafia killing.'

Paris was never lucky for me.

The house was empty and I went outside and sat on the kerb. I said aloud that I wasn't here in this world for myself but for others. That way it made sense. I was always alone during the bad times. When Chris was very ill with a bust appendix they said, 'You may lose your boy.' And I went outside of the hospital and sat on the kerb. There was no one to call, not with that sort of news. And now there was no one to call, not with that news.

Marcelle phoned again because she didn't know when they'd have the funeral or where. Should I be there? It was all hushed up.

'Who did it?'

'He was political. He was into a lot of things. They are not sure at all it was the Mafia. It was just made to look like that. Apparently he had agreed to a film being made showing the Mafia in a bad light. So they could have got him. Other papers say it is the right wing. He was in the death business.'

'Don't tell me he makes snuff movies – '

'His wife, his son, now him. What was he?'

I remembered him saying, 'A widower.'

'Will they get who did it?'

'I am sure, darling. I am absolutely sure.'

So I asked how it had happened.

'He was getting into his car. He saw them coming apparently but he couldn't get the key into the lock in time. He died from four shots. There may have been five.'

And I thought. The key. What is the key? And I remembered José and his curse. How those against Isaac died. He made death sound so easy. And now the Tycoon was turning Isaac the Blind into a movie palace. It was irrational but I blamed it, the curse, for Robert's death.

*

351

J was no different when I was successful. Whatever I did, he could do it better. And I got a few very good years. He managed to put them down but it had become a kind of game between us. I realised he was upset I was getting so much work, making so much money, when he took me to our favourite Indian restaurant in LA. He wouldn't even let me have the menu. He ordered for me.

'She'll have her usual, a vegetable curry, and I'll have chicken pilau.'

There was nothing usual about a vegetable curry for me. I called the waiter back and changed it to prawn curry. The waiter put popadums on our plates. J kept getting his stuck on his elbow and when he gestured, while talking, it sailed off his elbow across the room to the floor. So they'd bring him another one. And that got stuck too. He didn't know where the hell he was at the table because I'd just told him how much I was getting on my latest film deal. Once again the popadum flew across the room like a flying saucer and the waiter trod on it. Another waiter replaced it. Finally J put his elbow down in a cross thrust and shattered the popadum on the plate. The waiter took it away and gave up on the popadums.

When the prawn dish arrived for me, the waiter, sensing J was in a bad mood, tried to placate him. After all, from J came the tip. He spooned a large pile of prawns on to J's plate, for him to try.

J waved his fork frantically like something from Alice in Wonderland, the remains of a popadum still stuck to his sleeve. 'Get it off! Off! I hate prawns. The vermin of the sea. Give them to her.'

So the waiter scooped the mixture up but J smacked a hand on his arm. 'Leave it, leave it I say.'

The waiter asked if he wanted a clean plate. J couldn't hear. He'd gone deaf but wouldn't admit it. So the waiter lifted the plate and J said, 'They try and poison me. Now I'm not allowed to eat. Why are you so difficult, Patrice? I don't have trouble here normally.'

The tantrum subsided so I said, just to be playful, 'I'm with the Lantz office.' They were the top agents he vowed I'd never get to even see.

He had no popadums left to destroy so the napkins started getting a bad time.

Apart from the deafness he looked more or less the same. He

hated my success. To be modest, I said, 'Well I've got one foot in the water perhaps, J?'

'One toe more like it. How's your bank manager these days?'

'In a state of shock.' And we both laughed.

'Well, it's better than the old days. How you lived in that house with the wind coming in I'll never know.' And he lifted his whiskey glass to himself for having survived there one night.

Later, when I was really rich, how I valued those years of poverty! How proud I felt that I'd experienced and come through them. It gave me a self-respect no amount of acclaim could have done.

Chapter Fifty-six

They never did find out who'd shot Robert Hartman, or it was expedient for someone to keep it quiet. Marcelle always said it was political. Whenever I thought about him I saw a rose-garden. My book *The Unforgotten* was dedicated to him. And whatever success I had didn't mean anything compared to that book.

When I thought of his dying, all that came into my mind was a night in Barcelona after I'd left Michael. It was one of the worst nights in a life not exactly empty of worst nights. I'd brought the children – still babies – out to live with José in Puerta de la Selva and he'd realised he was getting old and there was no money. So we'd quarrelled and I left the fisherman's house and took the boys to the airport. They were both in napkins and I had no money for clean ones. And I couldn't get a plane to London because they wouldn't take my cheque – previous ones had bounced – so back into Barcelona, into the worst hotel in town. I went to a friend of Michael's who'd known us when we were married, a theatre designer, wealthy, gay, and I asked him for a loan. I needed a couple of hundred pounds. He made me stand at the very edge of his luxurious property as though I was a leper and then he gave me the equivalent of ten pounds.

'But that isn't enough!'

'Then go to the Consul. How can you be in this position? You are Mrs Chaplin. You belong to a famous family.' I was thwarting him of the chic image I'd played before with Michael. Had he spent all that time sucking up to a waif?

I spent most of the money on drink. It really killed despair. The kids, although young, knew plenty was wrong. I went up to two English diners in a bar and said I was dying. They ignored me. I went down to six and a half stone before I got back to London. I truly could say I was experienced in despair. That's all I could think of concerning Robert Hartman's death. The keys in the car door and straight into Barcelona.

Sometimes I think fate is just a luxury for the rich and fit. When you stop worrying about where your next meal is coming from you start wanting it good and fate comes into it all of a sudden.

Immediately she knew of his death, Jane Hartman left Gerona and took a flat in Rome. She and Richard broke up and a year later she looked me up in Hollywood. She'd run out of money. Now Robert was dead so was the allowance. She was doing some spectacular drinking and I put her in a detox clinic, but she only stayed three days. She'd lost her looks. Age had just descended and taken over her face.

'I don't know whether I'm dead or alive.'

She had a new friend. He'd dyed his hair gold with green streaks and grown a moustache and wore shades. He was still Colin Diamond.

'A funny thing happened to me in Santa Barbara the other night. It was all planetary, of course. The new moon was in Taurus. I was passing a house and music was playing, one of my favourite numbers, so I stopped to listen and a man leaned out and said come in. It was now the new moon in the tenth degree of Taurus in conjunction to my Mercury. I went in. It was a party. A murder happened and I felt guilty. It was my fault I'd activated vibrations. Today I'm safe because it's retrograde.'

I said I was glad to hear that.

'But I've got to look after her. She's got to work."

'Work?'

'She's a moviestar, I'm her agent. She's OK now because Saturn has passed through her Scorpio.'

I remembered Robert saying when you don't know what you're doing, you end up in all kinds of trouble.

'I think I should change my name,' he said.

'How about Angel?'

I challenged Jane about Tycoon. What was he like?

'Not unlike what you wrote in *The Rose-garden*. You were lucky. He was so possessive of that wife. She couldn't draw breath that he didn't know about. At first she did concerts and it was OK but when she was asked to play abroad he wouldn't allow it. She wasn't allowed out of his sight. She stopped playing. Something died in that lady long before she died.'

'Why was he so insecure?'

She paused then, had another drink. That helped her think. 'I think he liked people to be there, not moving.'

'His mother was paralysed.'

'Maybe that's it. He had all the charm in the world but he didn't really get on with people. That wife didn't want to live in the end. She smoked, Jamie said, three packs a day. And then when Jamie blew his brains out, that was too much.'

Colin tried to stop her pouring another gin. She wouldn't be stopped.

'Why did he?'

She put her hands over her mouth. I thought she was going to throw up. Colin got her some water. 'Disillusion,' she said.

'What about?'

'What he came from, of course. I don't know about Robert, but his father was in the Mafia and his cousins and it was kept from Jamie. He was a very good person. An idealist. Sort of optimistic. Beautiful really.'

'Was that enough reason to kill yourself?'

'He did it to get back at his father. Rotten blood. He couldn't bear it. And he knew how much his mother had suffered. The wonderful idolised father wasn't what he seemed.'

356

'It had nothing to do with you?'

She shook her head. 'I was just house decoration. You never get near those people. It was their dirt they were dying about, not mine.'

'You didn't sleep with Robert?'

She shook her head. But I still felt she had. Perhaps because I had resolved my book that way. Richard was just a decoy. When she passed out I asked Colin if he knew.

'It makes more sense. To kill yourself because your father's having your wife. You walk in and see it. Despising your blood? Well it doesn't work me up.'

Some things in life always remain unknowable.

I thought by being successful I'd find out who I really was. Success was the one thing I hadn't had. Maybe I'd find out I was just lonely and should never have left José. It was when I was working on a film in Italy, at the end of the 1980s, that I realised that I had enough money to retire. The word must have got around because quite soon after Irish paid me a visit. Now that was a surprise because I'd forgotten that he'd even existed.

'How you doing? How's the good things in life?'

I said they were OK, for someone from a London suburb.

He threw a handful of documents on to the table. 'Now you're what I call rich.' He rubbed his hands and did a tap dance. I didn't want to look at the documents. 'He said only to give it to you when you'd done it yourself.'

Then I looked at just one or two of the papers and I saw I was rich. It wasn't a pleasing feeling. It was like eating too much sugar. I went outside to get some air. Florence in August? No air.

'Who killed him?'

'You're a funny little lady. He makes you Queen of the May and you're not even pleased about it.'

'Was it political?'

'Did you love him?'

'I didn't dare.' And I laughed. 'Because he didn't love me.'

'Honey, he was closer to you than anyone.'

'Tell me, who did it?'

'He was into politics. He was doing a deal for the French government. It wouldn't mean anything to you if I told you.'

And I knew he didn't know. 'Was he involved with the Mafia?'

'His family may have been at one time. His father, sure. Their paths crossed. I'm not saying he was Mr Right Guy. He knew some wrong guys but he knew how to play 'em.'

So in the early 1990s, I decided, I will do what I want. Live the way I choose. I will simply go back to Gerona and buy the house at the top of the city surrounded by cypress trees. But it always comes down to Gerona in the end. And from the windows overlooking the old part I will see down on to the cabbala courtyard and it will be all run down and overgrown and decaying. And sometimes I will see José and Nina grubbing about, stacking up stones, scrabbling in the earth like two moles. And he'll have become like her, they'll have dragged each other down. They'll have become old and stained. I will not want to see him or have anything to do with him. I will still see them as two dirty concierges against the background of the suffering of the Jews.

I saw it all. I saw him in the street, his hair snow white, eyes red-rimmed like a spiteful rabbit. In my time I'd tried everything to get over this man. He finally had made the change. He'd got old.

I wasn't a recluse but I liked to be alone. I felt I'd done enough living to live off for the rest of my life. One day, the mysterious one, Isabella Sans-Gomez, paid me a visit. She was so unlike anything I expected. She had grey woolly hair, big brown eyes, a soft mouth. She looked like a sheep. And she told me no one owned the cabbala, it was all falling into decay. José and Nina still stayed on trying to restore whatever it was that had been the idea. Isabella was a perfectionist and had the money to do something about perfection. From her beautiful house sixteen years ago she'd looked out on to the cathedral. From her east windows, down on to the river. From her other windows, off to the mountains. But her south windows! It almost gave her a nervous breakdown.

'You mean the Isaac the Blind Centre? It seemed to give a lot of people those.'

'No, no! Before.'

'But surely with the cafeteria business and music up till four in the morning?'

She described that as a lullaby compared with what went on

before. So I said she'd been very helpful to José in those years. Why was she never in the Isaac the Blind building? I never once saw her. And she spoke honestly, one householder to another. I mean we both had property to protect and knew the downside of the dreary view. She wasn't at all interested in Jewish resurgence. She simply could not stand the squalor of the sight, covered from all eyes except hers. 'It was filthy and they used to fight, the gypsies and the tramps. And they were drunk and they'd look up at my windows and shout curses. And they' – she used a word for shit – 'everywhere.' But what really drove her crazy wasn't the brawls and the harmonicas but the sound of digging. Every night at two or three a man would come and dig and dig for the treasure of the Jews. And the noise of the shovel in the earth ruined her nerves. And she took sleeping pills and put in ear plugs and one day God answered her prayer. José Tarres married. He was now a respectable man but he was bored. How he wanted to get out of that domestic life! He was never cut out for that. So Isabella suggested he acquire the site below and turn it into something pretty. A garden perhaps? And she'd given some money and got the street opened. And he involved Juan Serrat and they decided to open a bar casino. And they got rid of the stench. On hot nights it had been unbearable. And José threw out the rough trade. 'It was funny, but those gypsies and whores weren't scared.'

'Scared?'

'Well, it carries a curse.'

So she was the key, this woman who wanted it pretty when she looked out of her windows. Her selfish wishes had inflamed José and brought him Zelman. She'd have had Disneyland in next. I considered her selfishness had brought disease into my beloved city.

'No, I didn't mind José's night life. It was a concert after what I'd been through. But now the area is falling apart again. It will become a health hazard.' And she looked at me with her soft eyes that hid hard thoughts. I think she was going to suggest I helped out. But I didn't like her. And I remembered the image of the scholar who used to come so regularly into my mind. I never saw him any more.

Another time the mayor came up to welcome me to Gerona. He'd sent his own people to fix my garden. I said I'd quite like a fountain in the old part. I'd pay for it. After all you never knew when you were going to snuff it. And he looked over my balcony and saw José clearing rubble. 'He never gives up. They wanted this house, you know. For years.'

I knew. I couldn't bear her getting the house with the cypress trees. At one time I wanted to kill her. But age did it for me, age – the worst murder. She wasn't the girl who'd bought José.

James visited several times and tried to get me to live according to my means. That made me laugh. I'd heard that all my life. And he'd peer down through the medieval buildings on to the cabbala courtyard and see the white-haired bent man in the same red jersey burning rubbish. And then he saw Nina. 'I don't believe it. They've got money, they must have.' He looked again through the binoculars. 'What did they do with that money?' I had no idea. 'Look, she put in an offer for this house, so she must have it. She's hidden it. Definitely, it's down there. Under the sun stone.' And he pointed angrily.

James had changed, as we all had. He walked like a figure out of Proust, arched back, hand flapping, hair coiffed, he celebrated the artificial.

He tried to get me to go with him to Barcelona but I was quite content, or perhaps it was peaceful, in the house alone. I thought a lot about Tycoon. He never said he loved me. J almost said it. Phil did love me but didn't say it. José, well that was another story. He had, and the memory didn't go. It was like our names had been written for all time on the blackboard and however much he rubbed at them they would not go away. José – Patrice. What date? 1955 or 1397? The important thing was I had to love myself.

Full of life. It used to seem such an asset. Now I saw life was the enemy. There was me and there was life. I saw it as something to be avoided. There was a better state. Peace. Be full of peace not life. That's what Tycoon wanted for me.

Sometimes, hidden behind the cypress trees, I'd stand and watch them below, José and Nina, still grubbing about, old and dirty. And I went back into the house and looked at the jewellery and cool vases. And I realised only the eternal mattered. Only that which did not change. Gems, creations. And at night I heard digging, the shovel chinking against stone, loosening earth, and a dog barked.

And I laughed. I was sure it was James digging for the treasure of Tarres.

So I perceived that only the permanent was beautiful. Amber rings did not get old. But sometimes the wind howled bringing back the passion, the glory of those first years in Gerona when I met José Tarres on the hotel stairs.